LIBERATORS OVER THE ATLANTIC

LIBERATORS OVER THE ATLANTIC

JACK COLMAN AND RICHARD COLMAN

FONTHILL

Fonthill Media Language Policy

Fonthill Media publishes in the international English language market. One language edition is published worldwide. As there are minor differences in spelling and presentation, especially with regard to American English and British English, a policy is necessary to define which form of English to use. The Fonthill Policy is to use the form of English native to the author. Jack and Richard Colman were born and educated in the United Kingdom; therefore, British English has been adopted in this publication.

Fonthill Media Limited
Fonthill Media LLC
www.fonthillmedia.com
office@fonthillmedia.com

First published in the United Kingdom and the United States of America 2017

British Library Cataloguing in Publication Data:
A catalogue record for this book is available from the British Library

Copyright © Jack Colman and Richard Colman 2017

ISBN 978-1-78155-650-4

The right of Jack Colman and Richard Colman to be identified as the author of this work has been asserted by him in accordance with the Copyright, Designs and Patents Act 1988.

All rights reserved. No part of this publication may be reproduced, stored in a retrieval system or transmitted in any form or by any means, electronic, mechanical, photocopying, recording or otherwise, without prior permission in writing from Fonthill Media Limited

Typeset in 10.5pt on 13pt Sabon
Printed and bound by CPI Group (UK) Ltd, Croydon, CR0 4YY

In writing these pages, it has been a personal pleasure to remember the splendid chaps I was privileged to meet, particularly those who were prepared to fly with me, and to two 'old men' who gave me a lot of good advice.

In particular, however, I wish to dedicate these pages to a group of men, with whom it was an honour to cooperate, but none of whom I knew personally. These are the crews of the Merchant Ships and Escorts of the North Atlantic and Arctic convoys. They suffered hardships and heavy losses but, if they had not won the Battle of the Atlantic, we could not have carried on the war.

I had more than my share of luck—hundreds of thousands of other folks, in the Forces and Civilians, ran out of theirs.

CONTENTS

Introduction   9

1. I Join the 'Shortsnorters'   11
2. Prelude to War   27
3. Accepted at Last   33
4. A Slight Hiccup   37
5. Off to Canada   43
6. Canadian Hospitality   48
7. Airborne at Last   52
8. Wings Parade at Brantford   59
9. Across the Frozen Water   68
10. Christmas Wonderland   74
11. Slush, Mud, and Prangs   82
12. York, after the 'Baedeker' Raid   94
13. A Testing Time   99
14. Trans-Atlantic Captain/Navigator   105
15. O. P.'s Little Black Book   116
16. The Battle of the Atlantic   124
17. The Liberator Squadron   127
18. A Quiet Wedding   134
19. To Reykjavík   138
20. 'Lows' over Iceland   150
21. Atrocious Weather   163
22. Introduction to the Arctic   176
23. Ginger Finds us a U-Boat   191
24. The Critical Stage   203

25	The Big Battle of the Atlantic	216
26	Diverted to Gander	225
27	The New Wingco	234
28	Icelandic Safari	247
29	Quiet Time	254
30	Wolfpacks Return	265
31	The Hunting Horn is Silent	277
32	Away From It All With Peggy	280

Epilogue 282
Appendix: List of Significant Events 285

Introduction

Sometime in the early eighties, shortly after retiring, my father wrote a record of his war years as a pilot in the RAF. At the time, I was not aware of him writing these memories of his circumstances and experiences, which he would have considered to have been normal for many at that time. Once completed, in the foreword, he suggested that the record was there and that I, my brother, or our children might find them interesting at some time in the future—how I wish I had absorbed these pages more into my consciousness while he was still alive.

My generation of baby-boomers must live with the question of how would we have coped with what fate asked of our parents.

Jack was a quiet man, possibly shy, and so his account is not one of self-aggrandisement boasting exaggerated bravery, or smugness at mastering the necessary skills of flying and navigation. It is an account of a young man learning about the adult world and falling in love and marrying while he could, a man who wanted to fly from the age of ten, who enjoyed and was fascinated by the mechanical and technical skills of flying and navigation, skills which he was conscientious in acquiring; he was aware that life might be short.

His stories are told dryly and without exaggeration, with a cool head necessary for survival when the rash ill-judged decision could be fatal. In writing this account, he relied heavily on his hand-written notebooks, flying log book (now lodged with the RAF), maps, and photographs, and I sensed that he relived the moments and experiences of those times over again as he wrote about them. It must have given him much pleasure to do so which is perhaps the greatest justification and benefit of his work. The RAF and young pilots of today have appreciated this record of life and flying in those more mechanical times and a complete, unbound, hand-typed copy of his memoirs is lodged in his old Squadron's archives.

Originally entitled 'My Friends the Stars' (for reasons apparent in the story), this abridged version is to appeal to the wider audience and covers the period to late 1943, including selection, training in Canada, and spells with Ferry and Costal Command flying Hudsons and Liberators over the North Atlantic. His time flying Beaufighters and Mosquitos mainly in the Far East is another story. Aside from this introduction, the epilogue, endmatter, and the background historical information regarding the Battle of the Atlantic, this book is entirely the work of my father, Jack Colman.

Richard Colman
May 2017

1

I Join the 'Shortsnorters'

Having previously only been on Training Units we were rather taken aback by our reception at Dorval (Montreal). We were shown into an office with 'Trans-Atlantic Ferry Command' painted on the door, where we were collectively greeted as gentlemen and offered cold drinks. After introductions, we were told that they would send a coach to pick us up at 10 a.m. the day after tomorrow. A call was made to Montreal's most prestigious hotel, The Mount Royal, to reserve accommodation for us until then.

When the time came, we were duly bussed back to Dorval where we and the rest of the aircrews were given a talk on the history of trans-Atlantic flight. The crossing by Alcock and Brown, who crashed in a bog in Ireland after sixteen hours in June 1919 was the year I was born. Then, there were a few crossings by folks, such as Lindbergh, but the first 'service' flight was not until 1939—only three years ago. The latter was known as the 'British North Atlantic Mail Service'; the only way they could make it was by mounting a four-engined floatplane on top of the four-engined flying boat, the floatplane starting up its engines and separated from the flying boat, part of the way across. In November 1940, it was decided to try to fly Hudsons from Newfoundland to the UK as they were losing too many sending them by sea with the boats being sunk.

At least some of the time, perhaps most of the time, you will be in cloud and you can't keep formation in thick cloud so you will go singly. Nobody will tell you when to go. When you get an aircraft you will decide when the conditions are right. The aircraft will be your responsibility and it is better to get it to the UK next month than put it in the drink tomorrow.

You will go from here to Gander in Newfoundland and wait there for suitable conditions. You will hand the aircraft over to the RAF at Prestwick. We suggest you fly Gander–Prestwick direct. It's about 2,000 miles but as you work in nautical miles it doesn't sound so far. You may wonder why we do not go via Iceland—the reason is that the weather can be very unpredictable in Iceland—there is only one airfield you could use and if you found you could not get in there you would be up the proverbial creek. It may be a week or more before we can allocate you an aircraft, in the meantime I will arrange for Captain Thompson to fly with each of the Captains on the usual Single Engine, Instruments and Beam Flying Test—that will take about four hours and for Mr Conduit to give each Captain some time in our rather unusual twin-engined Link, on approaches into the UK and SBA (Standard Beam) approaches on one engine. Tomorrow I have arranged for you all to spend the day with the Engineering Officer who will explain and demonstrate the fuel system, particularly the use of the overload cabin and bomb bay tanks, it is important that all the crew understand these, and to give the Captains their engine data tables, charts and graphs.

After a break for lunch, an operations controller had a chat with us. He pointed out that on take-off at Gander we would be overloaded: 21,000 lb instead of the normal maximum of 18,500 lb. Although we would want to fly as high as possible to take advantage of the westerly winds, which usually increase with height, we would use too much fuel if we tried to struggle up too soon. We should study the fuel consumption, in conjunction with the Met forecast, before making our flight plan and always make sure we were maintaining a 'tail-up' attitude, as, if we were 'mushing' along with the tail down at an altitude we could not maintain, we would just be wasting valuable fuel. He pointed out that, at this time of the year, there was only about five hours of darkness when flying west to east, and most crews prefer to fly overnight in the hope of being able to get some Astro fixes as there is nothing else available in the middle of the Atlantic, so he suggested we should time take-off to get the darkness where we thought it would be most useful. He gave us airfield charts for Gander, Prestwick and other possible alternative air-fields, along with a selection of charts and Astro tables. We then took the coach back to the hotel.

We had a lot to talk about in the hotel that night but Tug [Jack's navigator] did not seem to have much to say; he seemed to take the view that flying 2,000 miles across the Atlantic was no more than another exercise after which, somebody would criticise his log. Peter and I decided we would phone the Pearsons in Toronto to let them know that we would soon be on our way: home by air. Mr Pearson immediately said that they would drive over for the weekend and that he would book a table at the Normandy Roof (the nightspot at the top of the Mount Royal Hotel) for Saturday evening.

We duly had our night at the Normandy Roof. The Pearsons seemed really delighted to see us, so much so that it was rather embarrassing. Mr Pearson kept saying how proud he was of us and that he knew when he first met us twelve months ago that we would 'make it' and how he wished he had a son of his own. The drinks were flowing after the meal, the music was good, then they had to spoil it by getting the bandleader to dedicate the next tune to two English boys who have been in Canada for twelve months training as pilots and were now going to fly their own aircraft home. The ruddy spotlight swung onto our table, folks started shouting and clapping, and Mr Pearson pushed us to our feet; there were shouts of 'speech'. Peter, with his public school education, evidently brought this nonsense to a conclusion by saying something like 'we would like to thank our good friends in Canada for the hospitality and the Royal Canadian Air Force for their excellent training. We hope the people back home would be looking after your boys over there'. The Pearsons spent the night at the Mount Royal, returning to Toronto on Sunday evening.

The day with the Engineering staff was very interesting when explaining the linkage of the fuel tanks. We also discussed how we should take-off on main wing tanks, then go over to the cabin tank when at a safe height because the main tank's must be shut off before the big red cock on the cabin tank is opened, otherwise there may be an airlock. When the cabin tank is down to about a quarter full, we go back on main tanks, making sure the red cock is fully off before opening the main tanks. Then by using a big hand pump, the fuel from the bomb bay tank has to be pumped up into the cabin tank, after which we were to go back on cabin tank until empty, then finally back on two main wing tanks. The opening and shutting of the cock on the cabin tank and the pumping has to be done by the navigator or WOP (wireless operator) so everybody has to know what they are doing, otherwise there could be an airlock; as you cannot afford to leave a drop in the cabin tank, the only way to know that it is empty is to wait for the red fuel pressure warning lights to come on and have someone standing by to turn off the red cock as soon as you shout at them, then get a signal back that it is off before turning on the main tanks, hoping, in the meantime, that you do not lose too much height and that the engines pick up. It was suggested that we should check over this routine on the way to Gander.

The next week saw us complete our flying checks and Link exercises but my wireless operator went sick with an upset tummy and was taken to hospital. I was given another W/op, so Tug and I had to go to Dorval a couple of times with him to make sure he understood the fuel system and had all the gen on the radio side. We came to the conclusion that he was pretty 'green'—only just out of radio school.

It was now just a matter of waiting. We rang the airport at 10 a.m. each morning to see if they had any news, having a chat with some of the other ferry crews in the hotel trying to pick up tips from them. They all seemed old men to us (although probably only in their forties) with lots of flying hours and some with pre-war civil flying experience but, they seemed quite happy to talk to us youngsters with just under 400 hours total flying time. We were a bit surprised to learn that the Hudsons were packed with as much freight as possible, up to the maximum gross weight of 21,000 lb—all things that were urgently required in the UK but most of it was loaded at Gander.

Three days passed with no joy, then I learned that my aircraft had arrived and will be ready to go in a couple of days, so Tug and I with 'Moe' (the new WOP) went to have a look at her. There she was: FH451 not yet in her RAF colours. I was pleased to see that she had no gun turret; this would be fitted in the UK. I also noticed that she had smooth tyres, which may be because they had encountered trouble with the tread coming off the other sort, like had happened to me at Dartmouth. Finally, I noticed that the loop aerial was bigger but not enclosed in a Perspex pear-shaped fairing. Fitters were installing the overload tanks. Inside, everything seemed to be in the same place but we had to explain a few things to Moe.

The next day, it was a matter of a compass swing after some boxes of freight had been put aboard, then a short air test and back to the office to sign lots of papers. Signing for receipt of the aircraft from the US government under the terms of Lend-Lease (I did not dare ask how much it was worth), lots of ships papers and forms and the Loading Manifest. This is when I learned that the boxes contained flame floats, flares, and pyros; when I told Tug, he dryly remarked, 'well if we prang, at least it will be bloody spectacular'. I realised why it said 'to be kept dry' on the boxes. We plan to go to Gander in the morning. Cyril is ready too; Peter and St John are still waiting but one of the other lads went yesterday.

The flight towards Newfoundland was most pleasant. We had some fuel in all tanks so that we could check the transfer routine but we did not have a full load so flew at 19,000 feet, above the top of the civil airways, just following the radio ranges. Tug had nothing to do, except deal with the fuel cock and admire the view, but his nose started to bleed and he looked a sight with blood oozing out from his oxygen mask. On starting a let-down over the Gulf of St Lawrence, the coast of Newfoundland was clear and bathed in sunshine but way ahead, it looked very murky: not cloud, just murk. We called Gander to advise we are approaching at 5,000 feet, flying 085 magnetic on the south-west leg of range, give them our ETA (estimated time of arrival) and request landing instructions. We were given the altimeter setting, told not to come below 2,500 feet until within 25 miles of the airfield, the runway was 090 (which is anything but due east with 30 degrees of variation), the surface wind was less than 5 knots, but visibility varied between 200 yards and 1,000 yards. As there was no mention of cloud base, this could only be one thing: one of Newfoundland's notorious summer fogs. There is no SBA (standard beam approach) here so we told Control that we would maintain 5,000 feet till over the Range station, then let that down to 2,500 on the north-east leg, return to station, out on south-west leg for four minutes, and return on south-west leg, hoping to see the airfield on our starboard from 750 feet. We could not see a bloody thing so, on with the power, we climbed back up to 5,000 feet and headed back to Harmon Field, the American airbase at Stephenville, on the west side of the island. The book laid down all sorts of identification procedures before entering within 20 miles; we appeared to do these okay as we were readily given permission to land. Almost before we had stopped the engines, a big, burly top sergeant with his stripes upside down rolls up in a Jeep. He tells us there was no point in thinking of going on to Gander tonight if they were having one of their fogs as that was why they had built their airfield on this side of the island. He found us some very cosy rooms for the night.

The next morning, we learned that Gander is okay. We took on some fuel, which we signed for under Lend-Lease, and flew visual all the way, landing after one hour and fifteen minutes. We found that Cyril got in last night, but two hours after we tried. We were shown our rooms; Tug and Moe shared one room and I went in with an old Czech who had been flying with Czech airlines before the war. He had an unpronounceable name so he was known as 'Old Zig'. Fate must have decreed that I was to move in with Zig; were it not for him, I am sure I would not be here today.

The routine at Gander was to call at the Met Office about 9 a.m. local time and have a chat with the Met Officer to see whether a crossing was 'on the cards' for that night. Sometimes, he would immediately say there was no chance as we needed a fairly strong westerly most of the way, so we would retire to our rooms for the rest of the day as there was nothing else to do in Gander, other than have a stroll over to the tarmac and look over your aircraft. If there seemed to be a chance of getting away, we would go back to the Met about noon, they would give you a folder containing a weather chart and several 'forecast sheets' dividing the crossing into ten zones. Tug and I would then study it and work out a flight plan based on ten rhumb lines to approximate the Great Circle, after which we would decide whether or not to go, but before announcing our decision, I would compare notes with Zig. If he said 'no', I said 'no'—after all, he had done this trip many times and I had not done it at all. This routine went on for over a week. The odd Hudson had come in and gone off during this time, but there were now twelve Hudsons waiting to get away, including Peter, Cyril, and St John. One of the other lads who went to Dorval with us had gone on the day after he arrived and we later learned that nothing more was seen of him.

During those waiting days at Gander, I learned so much from Zig—particularly about flying in bad weather—that I began to wonder whether I really knew anything at all. We would spend hours stretched out on our beds talking. He would tell me of his experiences with Czech Airlines and of his Atlantic trips; weather and fuel consumption were usually the main topics. Zig pointed out that forecasts for the Atlantic were always very dodgy as the forecasters had very little to go on and you must always expect icing at some stage of the trip. He asked me what I had been taught about dealing with carburettor icing. I confidently informed him that when the outside temperature dropped to plus two in cloud, I would put the carburettor pre-heat on as the air would cool down two degrees as it passed the butterfly and ice would start building up. 'That's fine', replied Zig, 'but, when would you knock the pre-heat out?'

'When the temperature rose back above plus two', I replied.

'Okay but I didn't mean that' said Zig, 'I mean when it keeps getting colder'. Then Zig went on to explain that the pre-heat merely increased the incoming air by about 12 degrees, so at minus 12 degrees, the air was merely being warmed to zero or thereabouts, the very worst temperature you could have as the ice crystals would be damp and build up around the butterfly in a matter of seconds. So, he went on to explain that at minus 10 degrees, he always knocked the pre-heat out and let the air go through cold because at that temperature, the ice crystals would be dry and pass by the butterfly without sticking. It made good sense, but nobody had told us before by how much the pre-heat raised the temperature. I told

Peter, Cyril, and St John about my chats with Zig and they joined us in our room for many an hour of absorbing conversation. He seemed to like talking to us. He never talked down to us or shot any lines; he was a real gentleman and just seemed to want to help us by giving us the benefit of his considerable experience.

On one trip to the aircraft, we found that it had now been loaded with the rest of the freight; in fact, there was hardly room to get in and there was a bloody great inflatable rubber dinghy rolled up and lashed to the side near the door. The role was about 5 feet high and about 3 feet in diameter. Tug and I agreed that if we ditched, there would be no chance of getting this bloody great thing through the door as the tail would be stuck up in the air, even if we managed to get back that far before she slid under. We agreed that we would pitch it out before we took off and save the not inconsiderable weight, but we would not do it yet or they may stick on more freight to take its place. We also decided that with all this freight on board, we had better do another compass swing as only one degree out could make a lot of difference over 2,000 miles. Finally, that day, we checked over the loading manifest to see what we were carrying and how heavy it was as well as obtain a provisional clearance from Customs so that when we were ready to go, we would only need it re-stamping. I learned from Zig that he always chucked the big dinghy out just before take-off; he reckoned that all that weight so far back adversely affected consumption because it moved the centre of gravity too far back.

We had two more days of hanging about, then it was 3 June, the morning met forecast seemed favourable. At noon, wind seemed okay, westerly most of the way and up to 40 or 50 knots above 15,000 feet, a lot of cloud but not till about two hours out, and with tops at 12,000 feet, we thought we should be able to be above that by dark and see the stars, minus 12 degrees at 10,000 feet and minus 25 at 20,000 feet. The degree of confidence was shown as uncertain for the later zones. Tug already had a note from me setting out the height I hoped to fly for each zone based on the reducing aircraft weight and the indicated airspeed this would produce. He got to work on the flight plan, which came out at ten and a half hours, which seemed okay. I had a word with Zig; his navigator got almost the same so, it looks as if tonight would be the night. I gave Peter, Cyril, and St John the nod: 'now, what time shall we go?'

Tug and I had already decided to aim to be at 18 degrees west at first light, as after this, there will be no Astro but we should be getting near enough to start picking up some radio beacons. First light set at 18 degrees west would be about 5.30 a.m., so that made take-off 9.30 p.m., which gave us two hours daylight, six hours dark, and two and a half hours daylight, arriving at Prestwick at 8 a.m. We did not have long to go.

We got our stuff together, had a meal, picked up some rations, got the customs clearance re-stamped, filed the flight plan, and went to the aircraft. There were twelve of us going that night, spread over about three hours. Zig and St John were going before me, Peter and Cyril shortly afterwards. Half an hour before take-off, I ran up the engines then we had the tanks topped up to the brim and it was soon time to taxi out across the massive grey concrete area in front of the Tower, on which you could easily lose your way, down to the end of the very wide, 4,800-foot-long runway. After the usual cockpit checks, we were cleared to go, conscious that many eyes would be on you to see whether you 'made it'.

Mindful of all that fuel and all those 'fireworks' we had on board, and the wind sock only showing a slight breeze down the runway, I was sweating under my Irvin Jacket on this warm, sunny June evening, as I opened up the throttles on the brakes. Then, she did not seem to want to move and very, very slowly, we gathered speed. Boost was okay. Revs were okay, though I wished could get the ruddy tail up. I had the stick right forward but we were still pointing up in the air instead of level (thank goodness, we slung that dinghy while they were topping us up). With half the runway gone and the tail just coming up, now we were right but I still wanted another 10 knots. The markings at the end of the runway were just coming into sight as the airspeed needle told me she should lift off; I eased the stick back and she held it, quick up with the undercarriage, and I kept her down, straight and level till we got enough airspeed. She gently climbed to 500 feet and I started reducing flap. Then, we performed a gentle turn onto course and a slow climb to 2,000 feet, where I told Tug we would level out for a while; we told the Tower, 'All is well with FH451. Thank you and goodnight'.

After two hours, we were at 5,000 feet and were on the cabin tank. It was getting dark, and we reckoned we were 312 nautical miles out and the sky ahead looked very black. Soon, bloody great snowflakes were speeding at us. I put the landing lights on but the eerie sight of this white wall rushing to meet us made me turn them off right away. I had carburettor pre-heat on and kept shining the Aldis lamp along the leading edge of the wings to see if we were picking up any ice, but the light did not penetrate far through the snow. Tug seemed completely unperturbed; he even gave me a course alteration—how the hell he got it in these conditions I will never know, but I knew Tug well enough to know he would be right. We decided to get up a bit to see if we could get out of this muck. As we slowly ascended, we got into cloud and started icing up like hell; I was constantly watching the leading edges of the wings with the Aldis lamp and cracking the ice off with the pulsating rubber de-icing 'boots'; you must not leave the 'boots' 'on' all the time though, otherwise the ice would build up over them and they would just be pulsating away in an empty space under the ice and doing no good at all. Every so often, the engine would start vibrating as ice piled up on the propeller tips, so it needed some squirts of alcohol onto the slinger ring round the prop so that it would run down the blade and hopefully get the ice off; the released lump of ice then sometimes would clout against the sides of the aircraft, which was not very nice. Tug was busy eating sandwiches with his feet up, just as if we were sitting in the front of the fire at home, while I was trying to keep on course, watch the wings, keep the props free, and keep a spare eye on the outside temperature. We were at 8,000 feet now. We agreed it was time to bring the fuel up from the bomb bay tank so had to go through the performance of closing and opening cocks to go on main tanks while Tug got pumping. I could not see Moe from my seat but got the impression from Tug that he was not looking very well. Judging by the airspeed we were getting from the boost and rev settings, I reckoned we could try for a bit more height. We managed to slowly make 10,000 feet. On the way, the outside temperature dropped to minus 10 degrees so I thought, 'what would Zig do now?' Straight away, I knocked the pre-heat unit out. We were still in cloud and picking up ice on the wings, but not so much on the props; I had a feeling the ice was getting less severe or we were merely getting more used to it. We now had the inconvenience of being on oxygen.

Four hours on, we had made 13,000 feet, outside temperature minus 18, still in cloud but icing now only moderate compared with what it was earlier; thank goodness, we did not seem to be picking up much on the props now, otherwise we would be running out of alcohol and I did not like that vibration one little bit. Back on the cabin tank, this time, we would run it dry, reckoning this would be in about another hour and then we would have six hours left in the main tank.

I got Tug to come up and watch 'George', the autopilot, while I went for a pee. I realised how damn cold it was when I took off my leather, wool, and silk gloves and touched a piece of bare metal. I talked to Moe to see if he was okay as he had not had much to say over the intercom; he was all huddled up, not looking as if he was enjoying himself at all. He said he had not been able to pick up anything from anywhere for over two hours. I told him not to worry, as when we got nearer the UK and out of this cloud, he would be able to let the trailing aerial out as we may have lost our fixed aerials in the icing. He told me that he let the trailing aerial out when he could not get anything on the fixed ones. 'Christ,' I thought, 'that will have gone too. So we've no bloody aerials'. I had overlooked that Moe was straight out of Radio School; he had not been to an OTU (Operational Training Unit) or flown as a crew, otherwise he would have learned not to let the trailing aerial out without first checking with the pilot. Anyway, there was no point in telling him off as we should still have the loop on which to pick up beacons and ranges. I checked the cabin tank with the dip stick. In the light of a torch, it was difficult to be sure of the reading but at least the bottom few inches looked wet.

Back in my seat, I told Tug that it looked as if we had lost the fixed and trailing aerials, to which he replied, 'Good job we didn't know earlier, or you may have decided to go back, but we are past the point of no return now and I'm looking forward to a Scottish pint tonight'.

Tug gave me a change of course for the next rhumb line leg and I asked him to be getting himself plugged in by the cock on the cabin tank and stop there, ready to turn it off when I gave the word. It should last another half an hour, but I did not want to take any chances. With one eye glued on the fuel warning lights, it was about forty-five minutes before they began to flicker. I shouted 'Cock off, Tug', over the intercom; he answered with a dry 'okay Cock' and I looked round to see him at work. Both red lights were steady and bright; the engines seemed to be going quiet, so I put the nose down to maintain speed. Then, I heard 'okay, cock closed', so opened the main tanks; the red lights went out, the engines picked up, and I breathed again. The whole job only took seconds, but it seemed more like minutes; we had only lost 300 feet. I climbed back, re-trimmed, and re-engaged 'George'. Tug sat beside me and we decided it was time for sandwiches and coffee. The coffee was almost cold and it was a damn handicap wearing an oxygen mask while eating sandwiches. Tug said 'we only have 1,000 miles to go.'

We could go a bit higher now. At nearly 14,000 feet, I noticed that little clumps of cloud seemed to be flashing past, caught in the glow escaping through the Perspex nose (the glow from the light over Tug's navigation table). Then, there were stars—hundreds of stars and a peculiar yellow glow in the sky on our port side, away to the north. We were out the top of the cloud. I told Tug it was time he started doing some work and getting some Astro shots. What a relief to see those friendly stars—the Great Bear high above us, pointing the way to the faint pole star, Regulus low on the horizon, and all our old friends. I told Tug I would keep her steady and level so as not to affect his bubble while he took some shots. After a while, he gave me a 6-degree alteration to starboard 'to be going on with', but said he would try another three shots. After a while, he told me that his two fixes tied up very well and that we had gone about 40 miles too far north but our ground speed had been a bit better than expected so we were okay; if I altered another 2 degrees to starboard, this would put us back on track at the end of the next zone. He would get another couple of fixes in an hour from which he would get a check on the wind. We expected about another couple of hours darkness yet. I busied myself with my weight, engine, and fuel charts and decided we were doing okay, even though I had to use higher revs and boost than I intended early on due to the icing.

I thought it was getting nearer the time Tug ought to be taking some more Astro shots so I called him on the intercom to tell him we were now comfortably settled at 16,000 feet but I got no reply. I leaned over to look into the nose up where Tug had his head on the table; all I could see was the light shining on the back of his helmet. I thought, 'Christ, he has passed out', so called him louder and started screwing up bits of paper and throwing them down at him. Slowly, he moved when over the intercom comes, 'What's up? I'm having a kip'. He got his shots and seemed quite happy. Only a slight alteration in course was necessary; he gave me the ETA for Lough Erne beacon and for Prestwick.

I reckoned we may soon be getting within range of the powerful Lough Erne radio beacon, so tuned to 263 kC and leaned back to reach the handle on the roof behind my seat to rotate the loop but found the handle just turned around easily as if it was not connected to anything. I asked Moe if he had used the loop; he told me he tried it out taking some back bearings on the Gander range early on and it was okay. Then he tried again later but found it would not rotate so he used a bit of force and then found it spun round easily as if something had snapped. That was when we were picking up all that ice, so that was charming. The loop must have frozen and with trying to force it, he had buggered up the rotating mechanism. I turned the volume fully and could hear crackles so at least it seemed as if the aerial connection was okay so, with a bit of luck, we would be able to pick up beacons and ranges—as long as it was not stuck with the minimal signal area dead ahead—but it would be no use for direction finding. If only we had had one of the small loops in the Perspex fairing like the Hudsons at OTU, this could not have happened. Poor young Moe, we would have been better off without him; at least I could not think of any more damage he could do but, to be on the safe side, I told him not to touch anything else. I told Tug that not only were we unable to transmit for DF bearings or receive any weather reports, but now we could not take any radial bearings ourselves; all we could hope for was that we could pick up the radio range well enough on the loop when we got much nearer. As it would be getting light soon, I suggested we get some good Astro fixes while we could; I thought, 'Wish we had set off an hour earlier to be nearer UK before we lose the stars'. Tug did not seem to be worried. That funny glow on the Northern horizon seemed to be slowly moving round towards our port bow.

About eight hours out, we had some 550 miles to go. There was a faint pink glow down on the horizon ahead and slightly to port. Then, as if an increasing number of concealed lights had been switched on, both ahead and several thousand feet below, we saw a vast pink fluffy eiderdown. The pale pink edge rushed towards us, followed by a progressive shading through bright red to deep crimson as though the whole billowing eiderdown was about to catch fire. The sun was shining up at us from under the cloud, so it could not be very thick. Then, in a matter of moments, a small crimson arc appeared above the horizon and rapidly climbed into view; it was a great big glowing sun. The eiderdown was no longer red but a brilliant white, so bright that we reached for our sunglasses. We had all watched this never-to-be-forgotten sight in amazed silence; even Moe, who had left his seat to look out the front, looked to be smiling over his oxygen mask. Yet now, bathed in the bright light of dawn, for the first time, I felt so very alone, alone in this huge sky with no friendly stars to look down and guide us on our way. It was now going to be up to Tug's homing instinct, plus a bit of inspired guesswork and the hope that I could pick up a range well enough to ride in on it, or there was the chance that the clouds would clear and we would be able to map-read our way in.

Tug had a look out of the side windows and confirmed that there was no sign of the fixed aerials that ran to the tail fins. Through the cabin roof, he was able to see the top of the loop and confirmed that it was at an angle of about 40 degrees. We were comfortably holding 23,000 feet now, which should have given us a good ground speed. The layer of cloud seemed to be breaking up. Soon, quite large gaps appeared to reveal the sea below. As the gaps got bigger, the blue surface of the sea was mottled with shadows from the clouds. Then, the last remnants of cloud disappeared. The sea looked ever such a long way below—no chance of taking drifts from this height—in fact, we could not even judge whether the surface was rough or smooth. Somehow, I expected to see some ships.

There was not a lot I could do at this stage, except watch the compass and airspeed. I found myself thinking about salmon. I thought about what a marvellous fish the salmon is; it leaves the river, maybe in Scotland, swims hundreds, maybe thousands of miles out to sea to Iceland, Greenland, perhaps even Canada or Newfoundland, then swims back to find the very same spot in the same river—how does it do it? I was going back to the same river I left twelve months ago: the Clyde. At that moment, Tug climbed up from the nose with blood round his oxygen mask; his nose had been bleeding again and I thought, 'He looks like a bloody salmon that's been hooked'. I asked him where he sailed from when he left the UK. 'The Clyde', he replied 'Why?'

'It doesn't matter,' I answered, but thought, 'That's good.'

Nearly nine hours gone now. I found I could faintly hear 'UU7' using the loop aerial, so turned to port and then to starboard, to see if it affected the strength of the signal. At one point, it did get significantly louder, so I knew the gyro heading at this point and told Tug. I did not want to do too much turning off course as this could waste precious minutes. After a while, Tug said that the bearing looked quite good. He showed me his working out, convergency angles and all, but it could not tell us how far we were away.

It was 6.30 a.m. local time, so if the UK was on Double British Summer Time, it would be 8.30 a.m. at home. I wondered what Peggy was doing, just finishing her breakfast and getting ready to leave with Uncle Tommy for the office. Little did she know that all night I had been on my way home, getting nearer by about three miles every minute. I would give her a ring at the office—bet she will be surprised. I wondered how soon I would be able to get home and wished Father would be there; he would love to hear about this trip.

At 6.45 a.m., after nine hours and fifteen minutes, we were forty minutes off Tug's ETA for crossing the Irish coast, forty-two minutes off ETA Lough Erne beacon, and one hour twenty minutes off ETA Prestwick. I reduced boost and revs to lose height from 23,000 feet at 250 feet a minute, which gave us very good consumption and brought us to 3,000 feet over Prestwick. After fifteen minutes or so, I realised that a layer of low cloud had formed and the sea was no longer visible. 'Shit,' I thought, 'this could make life bloody difficult.' This was because with not being able to home in on Lough Erne beacon, we were hoping to map read our way into Donegal Bay, to follow the short approved 'corridor' over a narrow bit of the Irish Free State to the beacon position at the west end of Lough Erne, and then alter course for Prestwick up the south-west leg of the Prestwick Range. For a moment, I considered losing height quickly, to get under the cloud base before we made the coast, but I quickly kicked that idea into touch.

At 13,000 feet, Tug said we should be crossing the Irish coast. We were a few thousand feet above the top of the cloud, which looked pretty continuous. Tug said, 'it's always raining in Ireland'. I have been trying to pick up Prestwick Range, only getting a lot of crackles. We altered course to port, to make good a track (we hope) of 076 degrees magnetic, which should coincide with the south-west leg of the range. Soon, we were in the cloud; it seemed to be very dark. I told myself that I would not come below 5,000 feet if we were still in cloud until I had established some position on the range, as the highest mountain in the UK (Ben Nevis) was not all that far from where we are heading. It was 4,406 feet and my altimeter setting was possibly all to cock. Then, faintly, through the crackles, I heard '.–.–'. Yes, those were 'A's. 'Okay come on, let's be having a call-sign.' Then, it comes 'AR'—that's Prestwick all right, still lots of crackles and very weak, but no doubt about it, it is Prestwick Range and we are in the 'A' sector.

I told Tug that I was turning 45 degrees to starboard to find the beam. As I turned, the signal got even weaker. I thought, 'let's hope we haven't passed by Prestwick and got in the opposite 'A' sector, meaning that we are going further away. No, we can't be that far, or we would have seen land before the cloud cover came over, unless we passed north of Ireland altogether, but, in that case, if we have gone too far, we would be in the 'N' sector, so we must be okay.'

I contemplated a while and decided the signal had got weaker due to the angle of the loop, so decided to turn another 15 degrees to starboard, so that, altogether I had turned 60 degrees off the original course. Maybe it was my imagination, but the signal did seem a bit louder. After a few minutes, I lost the 'A's but could not be sure whether there was a steady note, due to the crackling in the background, when I heard 'AR'; as we were crossing the beam, almost immediately, I heard 'N's. Turning steeply 90 degrees to port, the signal became so loud that it almost blew my ears out; as soon as the 'N's faded away, we made another steep turn to starboard onto 076. I told Tug that we were in the beam, but we could not be far away as it did not take us long to fly through it and that I was now going to try to sort the drift out. Down to 5,000 feet, as I knew where we were, it was okay to keep coming down.

Instead of being in featureless cloud, lumps of cloud were now whipping past. We were coming out of it and then we could see not land but more sea—a hazy grey sea. I was just telling Tug that we were still over the bloody sea when, presto, I see a big lump of rock, sticking up out of the sea like a floating bread loaf, almost dead ahead. In seconds, I recognised it as Ailsa Craig, almost the last thing I saw as I left on the Windsor Castle, twelve months ago, and which I had sailed around with Mother and Father when we were on holiday at Rothesay when I was twelve. Out to starboard, through the haze, we could see the Ayrshire coast, and then, on the port bow, the tip of Arran. Tug said, 'Are you okay now, then?' Then, he started chucking his papers in his nav. bag. Moe stood behind me; I looked around at him and say, 'Only 35 miles to go and you will be down in Scotland'. I did not think he expected ever to see land again.

We tried to call Prestwick on the R/T but with no joy; at least we hoped that the IFF (Identification Friend or Foe) was working so that the radar on the ground would know we were friendly. Tug was sitting by me now as we flew over the airfield. The countryside looked just like a picture of Toytown in a children's book—tiny little fields of different shades of green and yellow, divided by neat little hedges, toy cars on the roads, little clumps of trees and a few brown and white cows in a small field—so very different from Canada. I noted the landing tee, indicating the runway in use and asked Tug to signal the Tower with the Aldis lamp. While I circled, he flashed 'No radio'. We got a green light from the Tower, so commenced a circuit. On the final approach, I realised we were coming in a bit high, the altimeter was quite a lot out, so we came in rather steeply. At about 700 feet, Tug tapped me on the shoulder and pointing to the undercarriage lever, said, 'aren't you going to use that?'

We had taken ten hours thirty minutes exactly and had a good half hour of fuel left. I congratulated Tug on his night's work and almost before the props had come to rest, a tractor, drawing a couple of trailers and carrying four huge, tough looking women in blue boiler suits, pulled up alongside. One of the women was soon on board demanding the freight manifest as they wanted to get that freight unloaded. I did not argue and gave her one copy of the manifest.

By now, a corporal had arrived in a 15-cwt truck to take us and our personal kit to 'book in'. We had a look around the aircraft before leaving and sure enough, it was stripped of all aerials and there were some sizeable dents in the fuselage where the ice had come off the props. First to customs, then to the control tower, where we learned that we were only the second Hudson to arrive, then onto the Ferry Command Office where we met Zig. He beamed when he saw us and said, 'I told you the Met. was mostly guesswork. That icing could not have been in a worse place—before we had used enough fuel to climb out of it'. I told him that it was only thanks to him that we got through it and then told him about losing all aerials and what had happened to the loop. He had lost his fixed aerials too, but was okay with the trailing aerial and loop. Zig asked if I had a dollar bill; he wrote on it 'SHORTSNORKER—3/4th June 1942' and handed it back to me saying, 'you are now a member of the Shortsnorkers Club.'

While we were in the office, handing over the ship's papers and other documents, we saw another Hudson coming in. It turned out to be St John. He had taken nearly eleven hours and was almost out of fuel. While enjoying a bacon and egg breakfast, we were wondering about Peter and Cyril, as they ought to have been here by now. Later in the day, we learned that Cyril had landed in Northern Ireland and that Peter was still at Gander. We then tried to get some sleep but although our eyes were sore, we could not wind down and get off to sleep properly. I had phoned Peggy at her office to let her know that I was back in the UK and asked her to let my mother know. Tug and I got up about 6 p.m. and decided to get some transport into Ayr to find a pub.

The next day, we learned that Peter had arrived and that the night we came over, all but one crew had been accounted for, some had landed elsewhere, and some had returned to Gander. I now set about trying to get some compassionate leave, which seemed to create some problems to Ferry Command. However, after three days, Peter and St John, with their crews, were posted to Coastal Command Wellington Squadron at Chivenor in Devon and I was granted seven days leave. Tug also got seven days leave, so that was good; it looked as if we would be staying together. Moe went off to an OTU to complete his training.

2

Prelude to War

My journey to becoming a RAF pilot began thirteen years earlier. The pilot shouted 'Contact', the fitter heaved on the propeller blade, a choking cloud of black exhaust gas drifted over the open cockpit, and the engine roared into life. In a few moments, we were trundling along the grass, turned, and the roar of the engine increased. For a while, we were bouncing across the field, then the ride became very smooth; we were airborne. There was no need to climb as we had taken off from the top of Racecourse Hill at Scarborough. The ground just fell away and as I craned over the side as far as my safety belt would allow, I could see that we were over the sea, going around Castle Hill, a fascinating view of the harbour, then round Oliver's Mount and, in spite of the streaks of black oil that were now making it difficult to see through the goggles with which I had been provided, I could see we were heading back to the racecourse.

The year was 1929. I was on holiday with Mother and Father. We had heard that there was someone on Racecourse Hill giving aeroplane rides at five shillings a time and Father said that I could have a flight for my tenth birthday. Father was rather keen to have a ride too. As we arrived, the aeroplane was just coming into land as we drove over to it in our little Austin 7 tourer to the wooden hut near where the aeroplane had stopped. It was a single-engined biplane, which carried the pilot and two passengers, one behind the other, in open cockpits. Father and I went together, with Father in the back cockpit so that he could see if I fell out. Then, I got a second flight as Mother wanted to go too, so I flew with her. As I climbed out, I told Father that I was going to fly myself someday.

During the following summer, we often saw the airship R100, which was built at Howden slowly cruising around York. Each time, it brought a tingle of excitement as did the view from the top of Sutton Bank where I would stand looking down over the flat countryside below and imagine flying over it. Then, in October 1930, there was the bad news that the R101—the somewhat larger sister ship of the R100 and built at Cardington—had crashed on the Beauvais Ridge in Northern France on the first leg of a flight to India, with the loss of forty-eight lives. After this, the R100 was scrapped and airships were given up.

In 1935, the year had come for me to leave school; I would be sixteen in September. I fancied being an engineer working somehow with my hands. I had won a 'foundation scholarship' at Archbishops Holgate's grammar school, which took me up to the age of sixteen but going on to university was out of the question unless you were extremely bright or your parents had a lot of money and had been to university themselves. The last thing I wanted to do was office work but with unemployment at about 2 million, my mother, father, and headmaster considered that the 'plumb' jobs for Grammar School boys were to be found in banking or insurance. In June, the headmaster arranged for me to have an interview with the Yorkshire Insurance Company in York and they offered me a job subject to my matriculation results being satisfactory. The results came out in September; they were quite good—in fact, I had two distinctions. So, on 15 September, my sixteenth birthday, I became an insurance clerk.

As soon as I started work, it was impressed on me that I must obtain my insurance examinations so I enrolled for a correspondence course with the Metropolitan College, which was to govern my social life from September to May for the next four years. I studied every Monday, Tuesday, Wednesday, and Thursday evening but tried to be finished by 10.30 p.m. so that I could listen to the late-night dance music on the wireless—Ambrose, Harry Roy, Jack Jackson, Roy Fox, and other great bands from the London hotels. Maybe, there was a bit of studying on a Sunday as the exams got nearer but Fridays and Saturdays were strictly 'no study' days.

Saturdays were kept for rugby. We usually worked on a Saturday morning but had the privilege of being allowed to wear a sports jacket, grey flannels, a pullover, and cap instead of the usual dark suit and trilby. If we were playing 'away', which was usually in the Leeds area, we met outside the railway station and travelled in private cars or occasionally in a coach, in which case the team secretary made sure to collect the match fee plus your share of the costs of the coach on the way out, to make sure we did not spend it on 'refreshment'. For some reason, we always seemed to break down on the way back, just near a pub in Tadcaster and just get it going again in time to be at the Davey Hall in Blake Street by

10 p.m. The club ran a dance every Saturday night in the Davey Hall and all the teams met up there. Anyone with a girlfriend arranged her to meet him there inside; it only cost her one shilling and sixpence to get in. Some matches were played on a rather undulating pitch behind the 'Woodman'. We changed in the outbuilding behind the pub and, after the game, bathed in several big zinc tubs, which the landlady, Mrs Fenner, had filled with lukewarm water. While we were all having a scrub, Mrs Fenner would come around with a big tray loaded with pints of shandy, often to the surprise of the visitors.

By 1937, things were happening in the world. Hitler had established himself as dictator in Germany, repudiated the Locarno Treaty, and remilitarised the Rhineland; we saw frightening scenes on Pathe News of mass gatherings in Germany. Italy had occupied Addis Ababa and civil war had broken out in Spain. The only 'bright spot' in a negative sort of way was that unemployment, based on the number of people in the country insured against unemployment, had fallen from 22.1 per cent to 10.9 per cent over the last five years, but this was mainly due to our re-armament programme. My father had been a tank driver who was captured by the Germans in August 1918, was released one year before I was born; he was certain that we were in for another war with 'Jerry' and most of the people I knew seemed to share his opinion.

I was now eighteen, had passed my driving test, and taken dancing lessons at Miss Cowper's Dancing Academy in Stonegate as we all felt that peace was not going to last forever so set out to enjoy ourselves. Most Friday nights during the winter, there would be a dance at the Assembly Rooms or the De Grey Rooms until 2 a.m. run by some club, society, or charity; tickets were three shillings and sixpence, or five shillings if a buffet were included. We all wore Burton's dinner jackets, starched wing collars, patent pointed shoes, a red carnation, not to forget the white artificial silk scarf. Most of the girls wore long back-less evening gowns, some were rather low at the front as well and those in our crowd all seemed to like to dance nice and close so it was all very pleasant as we tried to show off our prowess at the quickstep, foxtrot, and tango. The music was either by Bert Keech (a very big chap who played the piano) and his quartet or by the Rialtonians. They were a big band of thirty or more, very smart in their cut-away scarlet jackets, the saxophones, trumpets, and trombones standing up in turn and usually a singer sitting at the side to come on and do the vocal as they belted out 'Anything Goes', 'These Foolish Things', and other tunes from the Fred Astaire and Ginger Rogers musicals. There was always the inevitable 'Palais Glide' and in 1938, 'The Lambeth Walk'.

The girls I took to dances always seemed to live at the extreme other end of town. Sometimes, Father would allow me to take the car—a new Vauxhall 10—but Mother would not let him get to sleep until she heard me come back so it was not fair to over-do it; I only asked if I could have the car on 'special occasions'. It was usually a case of getting a lift with someone who was going to near where the girl lived and then walking back home. If the night was fine, the walk was quite nice with a friendly chat on the way; there was often a bobby on the beat, who often came some way with you for someone to talk to.

Several of the lads at the office were joining the Territorial Army, namely the Yorkshire Hussars. I would have liked to learn to ride a horse but I was more eager to learn to fly so I wrote to the Air Ministry to enquire about joining the Auxiliary Air Force. They told me to write to the commanding officer of the Auxiliary Air Force Squadron at Yeadon requesting an interview. Father lent me the car so that I could go to Yeadon one Sunday morning and I parked it between a big open Bentley with a strap across the bonnet and a SS sports car. I went into the offices and was shortly shown in to see the adjutant. 'I assume your university does not have an air squadron? Have you done any flying as a pilot? Have you had any officer training?'

I pointed out that I was not concerned about being an officer, all I wanted to do was to join the Air Force and learn to fly but it very quickly became obvious that there was no place for me in the Auxiliary Air Force without having already learned to fly, preferably with a university air squadron. This made clear, the interview then became less formal, so I asked if I could have a look at some of the aeroplanes before I left; he agreed and then suggested that I should write to the Air Ministry again about the Volunteer Reserve as they had just started to open RAFVR Flying Schools in several parts of the country where they would train people who had no previous flying experiences. He thought a school may be opening somewhere near Hull fairly soon. The interview over, he called a fitter and asked him to let me have a look at the aeroplanes.

As I drove home, I was not too despondent as I realised that I would be a bit 'out of my depth' with some of the people I had seen around and would not be able to keep up with them socially, although they all seemed very friendly. The thought of these RAFVR Flying Schools gave me encouragement.

I duly wrote to the Air Ministry again. They sent me some long forms for completion and promised to contact me within the next few months as they were arranging to open a RAFVR Flying School at Brough, near

Hull, in the spring of 1938. Spring came but I heard nothing, then about mid-summer, some more forms were sent for completion and eventually, I was called over to Brough for an interview. This seemed to go very well; then, there was a medical by the MO. Outside, there were some Tiger Moths flying around and a couple of Hawker Hart trainers on the ground. I was told that if accepted, I would be expected to attend on Saturdays and Sundays and do at least two weeks of 'camp' during the year but that I would have to come back in another few weeks to sit some written examinations. The examinations seemed reasonable enough and by the end of the year, I received a letter to say that I had been put on the list for acceptance in due course, but that it may be several months before I could commence training. This was great news and I felt as if I was already 'in'. However, the months came and went and there was still no letter from the Air Ministry.

The Navy had already been mobilised, and as 1939 wore on, Hitler annexed Bohemia and Moravia, Italy seized Albania, the Spanish Civil War ended, and Britain introduced conscription. Hitler denounced the Anglo-German Naval Agreement and also the Polish Non-Aggression Treaty. Prime Minister Chamberlain re-affirmed our pledge to defend Poland so we were getting in a tight corner and the Territorial lads were away on their summer camp, but still the RAF did not seem to need me. So, in August, I took my week's annual holiday and went to the Cumberland at Scarborough with my pal, Billy Fearn and there, it happened. A friend of Billy's called Heather was also at Scarborough for the week with a cousin called Peggy. One day, we met there quite by chance, at the South Bay swimming pool. Now, Peggy was a bit different from the other girls I had met; not only was she wearing a two-piece swimsuit, which was a bit daring in those days, but she worked in London as a secretary and she seemed to know a thing or two. She was interesting to talk to, a much better swimmer than I was, good fun, and, although she was born in Scarborough, with working in London, she had much more experience of life than a mere Yorkshire lad. She was almost a year younger too but, although we all met once more, she was going back to London at the end of the week so it looked as if that would be the end of that. However, at least Hitler was about to do one good thing and bring us together again.

We had no sooner returned from our holiday when things really started to happen. Men of twenty and twenty-one had already been called-up in April, but I was not going to be twenty until September. Anderson shelters were being delivered for people to erect in their gardens, a trial blackout had been carried out, the Woman's Auxiliary Air Force was set up, air-raid precautions were being put into effect with trenches being dug in the parks, sandbags were filled, identity cards issued, and gas masks fitted.

On 1 September, Germany invaded Poland as anticipated and evacuation schemes were put into effect to get children out of the cities and into the country. Mother thought we ought to get her mother and sister from where they lived in North London and bring them to York, which should be safer. So, on the evening of 2 September, Father and I set off for London in our Vauxhall 10 and what a bloody journey that was. The blackout had just come into force so we had to have an arrangement on each headlamp, which just let the light come through three narrow slits; the metal had been cut to make the slit being bent forward to stop any light going upwards. The sidelights were reduced by masking down to no more than an inch in diameter and a piece of tissue paper put over the hole to reduce the light even more and as time went on the tissue paper became brown with the heat. Rear lights had to have smaller bulbs, but there were no such things as stoplights or flashers in those days, and the traffic indicators had to be partly blacked out. We pushed on as fast as we could go before it got dark. Then, it was a case of gluing one's eyes on the white dashes on the road and, with a bit of luck, seeing two, or at the most three, at a time. 'Cats eyes' had only been introduced a year or so previously and only a few counties had installed them; even though we were on the A1, we only came across them on a few stretches, when we could really get a move on. We took it in turns to drive but an hour at a time was quite enough and it was with great relief that we saw the eastern sky beginning to get brighter as dawn approached. We arrived at Gran's about 9 a.m.; she started arguing about whether or not to come to York but Father and Uncle Reg (who was staying behind in London) made it quite clear that we were setting off back within an hour and that she and Aunt Ottie were coming with us. We had breakfast and listened to the wireless, which confirmed that unless Germany got out of Poland, we would declare a state of war at 11 a.m. and that they would be compulsory military service for all men between eighteen and forty-one. We then bundled a protesting Gran plus her luggage into the car and got on our way.

The journey back was uneventful, except that Gran kept wanting to stop; we passed an airfield by the side of the A1, on which we saw some Hurricanes, arriving home in the early evening. We were dog-tired as we had had no sleep, so after a meal and a check on the blackout, went to bed, knowing that now, at last the period of waiting was over and we were now at war.

3
Accepted at Last

I was wondering how I stood as regards the RAFVR. Posters appeared outside the Mansion House and at other places in the city, headed 'Royal Proclamation'. There were four different posters, one was headed 'By the King. A Proclamation. For Calling out the Air Force Reserve and embodying The Auxiliary Air Force' and ended with 'God Save the King'. I read it through but did not know whether I was regarded as being in the Air Force Reserve or not, so, I managed to get through to Brough on the telephone to ask what I was to do. They told me that as I had not yet got a service number, I should do nothing, wait until I heard from somebody, or register when my age group came up if I had not heard anything by then.

A few months previously, the 'Yorkshire' had made me a trainee inspector. I was gradually taking over an area from an old inspector who was about to retire. It was a very pleasant area centred on Malton, some days I went out on my own and some days, we went together, but now I was called back into the office for two or three days a week as they were short of staff now that the Territorial boys had gone.

At home, we were busy sticking brown paper tape on all the windows that were not leaded lights, getting any combustible material out of the loft, equipping the air-raid shelter, and keeping out of Gran's way. Before dusk, we would watch the black Whitley Bombers from Linton heading east like black cigars with a drooping nose, laboriously climbing on their way to Germany, often, we later learned, carrying leaflets and not bombs. During the night, we would hear them coming home, trying to count them to see if there were as many as we saw go over earlier.

Study for insurance exams was now 'kicked into touch' so I enrolled at the local 'ARP' post; I was issued with a tin hat, a better gas-mask, and an armband saying 'Warden'. The retired chaps manned the post during the day and others did evenings and nights on the roster system. Usually, there was an old ex-service type in charge of each shift who instructed us on firefighting and first aid, how to get our reports through in the event of an air raid, and generally what to do. We then went off on our patrols, checking on the blackout and compiling lists of how many people lived in each house, particularly older people on their own and children. The post was in the basement of a large house in Clifton where there was always a pot of tea on the go and somebody by the telephone. Father joined the ARP too, but we were never on the same watch; soon, Mother joined the volunteers who served tea and 'wads' (food) at the canteen on York railway station.

Billy Fearn called to see me at the office one day to tell me that Peggy was in York. Heather's father had insisted that she should leave London and she had come up by train on the day war was declared; she was now living with them in Clifton and was working at the probate registry with her uncle, just around the corner from our office. I told Billy to get something arranged so that I could meet her again. I would have loved to have taken her to one of the 'dos' at the Assembly Rooms but they were all off now, at least for the time being, but we soon got something fixed up. It was not long before I was going up to Heather's place in the evenings. We would play 'Newmarket' together. When they started having dances at the ballroom at the Clifton Cinema, Peggy seemed to prefer dancing with the cinema manager, Tony Lister, as he was a professional dancer, more to her standard, and she would keep calling out 'one, two, three' as we were trying to do the modern waltz, although we did do the old-fashioned waltz rather well and I did not mind as long as I was taking her home. Very soon, I was spending most evenings with Peggy unless I was on the ARP duty or she was 'fire watching' at the office. I was spending more time at Heather's house than I was at my own, Heather's mother and father soon became Auntie Muriel and Uncle Tommy and I would go out with Uncle Tommy for a few drinks at the Grey Mare or the Conservative Club. Unfortunately, Father would not come out for a drink with us but he rather liked Peggy. Mother was quite nice to her but not exactly enthusiastic; I think she sensed she was going to take me away from her or lead me astray.

Now and again, the air-raid sirens would start wailing and I would set off to the ARP post but they all passed over without anything happening. I got to know every step in the pavement and obstruction you could bump into in the blackout between our house and Peggy's. The wireless kept us informed of what we were allowed to know: British troops in France; sinking of the *Royal Oak* in the Scapa Flow; scuttling of the *Graf Spee* after the Battle of the River Plate; invasion of Denmark and Norway by the Germans; our troops in Norway; withdrawal of our troops from Norway; withdrawal of our troops from Flanders; British Troops in Iceland (which did not seem to mean much at the time); withdrawal of all our troops from Dunkirk; Paris occupied by the Germans; France packs up; and air raids over Britain stepping up. Throughout all this, I was still waiting to be called-up. My cousin, Mary, had joined the Woman's Auxiliary Air Force while her brother and younger sister had been evacuated to relations in Canada.

In the meantime, I had registered for National Service, having taken all the correspondence from the RAFVR with me. About a month later, I was called to an interview board where I was told that I would be accepted for the RAF and that I should shortly be called to attend an Aircrew Selection Centre where I would spend about a week. In July, I spent a week at Padgate in Lancashire, appearing before different selection panels; doing written exams, on maths, general knowledge, geography (one bright wag kept telling the rest of us that if you want to be a pilot, make sure you do not do well on the trigonometry paper, otherwise they will make you a navigator; we did not see him again after the first three days); and several medicals and eye tests. The main thing in the medical seemed to be the blowing up of a column of mercury to a certain point and holding it there as long as possible while the M.O. took your blood pressure. Then, we had to do it all over again after having jumped on and off a chair for so many times. At the end of the week, I was told that I had been selected for training as a pilot/ navigator, which meant that I would start training as a pilot but if for any reason I fell down on the course, I would be transferred to the navigator's course. 'Collect your rail warrant from the orderly room, go home and wait to hear from us.' This was great; I could not wait to get back to tell Mother, Father, and Peggy that I had been accepted for pilot training.

The weeks came and went. On the wireless, we heard about more and more raids 'over south-east England', the air battles and the number of bombers shot down, listened to Tommy Handley in ITMA and 'Workers Playtime', and programmes about how to grow your own vegetables and recipes to make the food rations go further, but the RAF still did not seem to need me, although more and more Whitleys were passing over in the evenings with bombs now, not leaflets.

People at the office and those I met kept remarking that I was still here, as if I were trying to 'con' them about having been accepted for pilot training. I really wanted to get away except for one thing—I had got very fond of Peggy and from time to time, I wondered whether she would still feel the same about me after I had gone away.

My twenty-first birthday on 15 September 1940 came and I was still at home. We still had a little petrol for the car so Father took Mother, Peggy, and I (as well as our little Fox Terrier 'Jeff the 2nd') to the Wombwell Arms at Wass for high tea. In spite of rationing, they produced some delightful gammon and even Father had a drink that day. Mother really never drank alcohol but would never refuse one, would drink it straight down, and then ask what it was.

A couple of weeks later, the papers arrived. I was to report at No. 10 Reception Centre at Blackpool on 10 October.

4
A Slight Hiccup

The town of Blackpool appeared to be swarming with RAF and Polish Air Force personnel marching about in squads or drilling on the promenade.

We were billeted in requisitioned boarding houses all over the town. I was in a small boarding house in Warley Road with seven other lads. We were all on the same course and during chat on the first evening, I discovered that they were all hoping to become wireless operators. I learned, next morning, when we reported to the squadron office, that this was a recruitment centre for Signals and that for the next twenty weeks, we would be on a wireless operator's course, after which some of us would go on a further course and become wireless operator/air gunners while others would go on ground wireless operator's jobs. Naturally, I was a bit crestfallen when I learned this; however, they seemed a nice crowd of lads and I was not in any position to argue. We were introduced to the corporal who would be in charge of our squad (all thirty-six of us), taken to be kitted-out, and told that half of each day would be spent on Morse practice and the other half being drill, P. T., lectures, and other instruction.

At 8 a.m. every morning, the street was filled with lads disgorging from the houses, forming up in threes in the road, tallest on the left, shortest on the right, an inspection by the Corporal, and then marching off to our duties. Morse practice was done in big corporation tram sheds on long tables with nine Morse keys and earphones along each side plus a key and earphones for the instructor at the end. We would march back to the billet for lunch then out again. If it had been Morse in the morning, the afternoons would be drill, P. T., or lessons on wireless equipment, codes and ciphers, wireless procedures, aircraft recognition, plus a few general subjects, or a visit to Derby Baths. Evenings were taken up with cleaning buttons, badges, and boots, writing letters to Peggy, or going for a drink at the local Gynn Hotel.

It was now getting into winter and the nights were getting dark much earlier so we had to carry a Hurricane lamp at the front and rear of the squad as we marched home in the evening. Sometimes, the notorious Blackpool winds would blow so strongly that we had to march along the back streets instead of along the Promenade or even fall-out altogether and fight against the wind the best way you could. When the winds blew while we were in the tram sheds and the corrugated asbestos sheets on the roof were rattling, a flight sergeant would order us to 'Put on your caps to protect your 'eads.' By now, we had all settled down to service life and even got used to Miss Hibbert's breakfasts of runny porridge, soya drinks, and some watery red stuff that she bought in gallon tins called 'tomato'. However, some of us were having a bit of bother with the Morse.

Then, we were lucky. We had a change of Morse instructor who told us to forget trying to think of Morse as being dots and dashes but to learn a rhythm for each letter. He gave us a word, or a little phrase, for each letter, which, when said in a certain way, gave the right rhythm and you recognised the letter right away. In the billet, we would be chattering away to each other saying 'baby-bit-it', 'linoleum', 'flat foot flugie', and other daft phrases, checking that we had got the right rhythm. It worked and soon, we were all getting our speed up without any bother.

In December, Mother, Father, and Peggy came over for the weekend. They stayed at the Raikes Hotel and it was great to see Peggy again. A couple of months later, Peggy came over on her own and, this time, stayed in the billet; the lads had agreed to shift round so that she could have a room and Miss Hibbert agreed, provided there was no funny business. Every time I went into Peg's room, however, she would bang on the bottom of the stairs with her walking stick and shout up saying 'I know where you are. I'll be up if you're not down soon', and she was.

By February, we were getting to the end of the course. We were now doing Morse pretty fast with simulated interference in the background, had mastered the Aldis lamp, and the final exam tests were coming up. Then, the CO sent for me. I was trying to figure out what I had done wrong—have the RAF Police seen me out after 11 p.m., or has somebody 'shopped' me for having Peggy at the billet? However, it was none of these. After saluting and standing to attention, he told me to 'Stand easy' and then informed me that he had heard from somewhere that I should not have been sent on this course; I should have gone to an 'aircrew reception centre' and then on to a pilot's course. He saw I was obviously delighted but pointed out that my posting had not yet come through; all he had been told was that at the end of the course, I should not be posted with the other chaps. There were ten days of the course to go. We had completed our exams, had a squad photograph taken outside the Savoy Hotel, and a party at one of the bars in the Winter Gardens at which we gave the Corporal a beer mug as a present. The next morning, the rest of the lads went off to Yatesbury or Compton Bassett and I was left behind. In a couple of days, my posting came through—report to Reception Wing at Babbacombe on 15 March—so I was given my rail warrants and given three clear days leave. I went straight to the telephone to tell Peggy to make sure she was not on 'fire watching' for the next four nights. The train journey took hours, waiting for ages at Manchester and Leeds.

At Reception Wing, Babbacombe, we were all in one big hotel overlooking the sea. All but four of us were new recruits so it was pretty easy for us—bags of drill and P. T., kit inspections, lectures on basic Air Force admin, who to salute and what to polish, and more medicals, including blowing up the mercury and eye tests. Spring was in the air, and the gardens and walks on the cliff top opposite the hotel were perfect for evening strolls, when we were not on open 'fatigues'. The Flight Sergeant seemed determined to show me and Ken Frost (another lad who had been 'in' about six months) that pilots under training had no special privileges by putting us both on fatigues twice within the two weeks we were there. My first time was for not having a close enough haircut and the second for having my 'button stick' the wrong way around at kit inspection. Ken's was for not shaving, although he had such a thick black quick growing beard that, if he did not catch him in the morning, he would get him later in the day. The 'pet' fatigue was picking a bucket-full of wood shavings, which the Flight Sergeant chucked on the pile of coke in the boiler house. He would smile and say 'Right lads, I'll be back in a couple of hours, at nine o'clock, to see that you have picked them all up and put them back in the bucket'. The second time Ken and I were on together, we thought, 'Sod this, again' so crept around to find where he got the shavings from, found them, and got a bucket of fresh shavings. We waited a while, then kicked the coke about until most of the shavings disappeared into it, sat down for a couple of fags, then, as it approached 9 p.m., slowly set about picking up a few pieces of shavings that were still in sight. The old Flight Sergeant turned up at 9 p.m., looked at the almost full bucket, and, with a knowing smile, said, 'Well done lads, you're learning—you've just got time to go to the pub and wash all that coal dust down.'

It was now down the road to Torquay to the Initial Training Wing and another hotel—a very large one this time with its own large gardens and palm trees. We now had to wear white flashes on our caps and white webbing belts (not, as some people thought, to give us any special privileges but the very opposite) so that we stood out as trainees and the RAF police could watch our behaviour and pick us out if we were out later than we should be. They also gave us more to clean as they had to be 'blanco'd' every night.

The eight weeks at Torquay passed very quickly. Plenty of interesting lectures: theory of flight, airmanship, elementary navigation, aircraft recognition, meteorology, and Morse with the Aldis lamp (we did this in pairs and I was always in demand as a partner, having been on the course at Blackpool). Of course, there was always the drill and P. T. There were also several 'one-off' affairs too, such as jumping into Torquay harbour wearing a 'Mae West' (life jacket), inflating, and getting into a rubber dinghy—thank God it was not the middle of the winter, but the water can still be damn cold in early May.

I wrote to Peggy for her twenty-first birthday and told her how that day, I had just been issued with my flying kit, comprising a one-piece flying suit, helmet, goggles, three pairs of gloves (leather gauntlets and silk and woollen gloves), long-johns, and a pair of flying boots. We had our photographs taken in the hotel gardens, wearing our spanking new flying kit and felt we were intrepid aviators although, so far, we had not been near an aeroplane, or even on an aerodrome. Shortly after, we learned that we were to go overseas for our flying training. We were not told where but speculate: Canada, South Africa, Rhodesia, or even America. Somehow, it seemed wrong that we were to leave the UK and go somewhere 'safe', especially when we knew that Rommel was attacking us in North Africa, the Germans had taken Greece, and things looked pretty black, but we were assured that most of us would be back, fully trained by the end of the year. We all pushed off on one week's 'embarkation' leave.

That week went very quickly. I would take Jeff for a walk during the day, then meet Peggy leaving work. I spent every evening with her at her house or mine (Gran had gone back to London by then as she had been so damned awkward) or we would go for a drink with Uncle Tommy. Before the week was out, Peggy agreed to get engaged (what a daft term, 'engaged', it sounds as if you are a public lavatory, but we knew what it meant). On the last day of my leave, I went to Darling, Wood, and Anfield for a ring. I think Father was rather proud that I was going to train as a pilot and I kept thinking that I will have a lot to talk to him about when I get back but I could not make out how Mother felt about it as she never showed her feelings about anything. It was the same over my engagement to Peggy, Father was rather tickled and said they would soon be calling her the 'Sergeant's Mess' but Mother seemed to think I was too young.

It was time to go back. Peggy and Father came to the station to see me off. I had checked on the train times during the day, which were always approximate as trains could be delayed due to troop trains or other military train movements. We arrived in the late evening as it was getting dusk and the station was only dimly lit because of the blackout. It was packed with soldiers and airmen, all waiting for my train. I kept wishing the train would come as there is nothing worse than repeating 'Look after yourselves', 'Don't forget to go in the shelter if the sirens go', 'Look after Jeff for me', 'Do you want a cup of tea?', 'Don't forget to write', all the time looking at Peggy and thinking what a cracker she was. Then, we heard the train coming, about half-an-hour late. Around the curve of the platform appeared a big, dirty-green engine, belching clouds of white steam from each side and more white steam or smoke from the funnel, which glowed red as it passes over the cab and catches the light from the fire-box. The engine rumbled by, hissing and clanking as it slowed down, carriage after carriage passing by with people opening the doors till finally it stopped—what a long train. Soldiers and airmen piled out to get a cup of tea and a wad from the girls with trolleys on the platform, or dash to the canteen, others struggle out with kit bags, while others struggled on. I said my goodbyes, got on, and stood by the open window, wishing it would go. Eventually, after bags of shouting, whistle blowing, door slamming, and flag waving, we started to move and I waved to Peggy and Father as they receded on the dimly lit platform, Father in his Mac and trilby hat and Peggy in her ocelot fur coat.

'Better find a seat,' I thought. What a hope—every compartment was packed, blinds down because of the blackout and thick with tobacco smoke. People are pushing about in the corridor trying to find a seat and eventually, I finished up sitting on somebody's bag at the end of the corridor, sharing it with an ATS girl. She soon fell off to sleep and her head dropped on my shoulder; soon, I was asleep too. We woke up several times, usually when the train stopped and folks were walking over us; we had a fag together to add to the general fug, but we hardly spoke, except when she said: 'Have you left a girl?'

'Yes, I've just got engaged.'

'I've left a fella too. He is in the Navy'.

Back at Torquay it was, 'Stencil "E.A.T.S. CRESS" on your kit-bags, parade at 8 a.m. tomorrow and be ready to move off.' We speculated that E.A.T.S. stood for 'Empire Air Training Scheme' and that 'Cress' probably meant Canada. We boarded a train at Torquay at about 9.30 a.m. and after seeming to meander all around the country (no stations had their names up as these were all taken down in case they should assist any paratroopers or spies) and stopping for long periods outside stations, we detrained and were taken to a transit camp, which we were told was 'on the Wirral'. Next morning, after a few formalities, we were told to parade at 5 p.m., ready to move off again. We anticipated a short journey to Liverpool but as it got dark, we could see we were heading into the Pennines. We carried on all night with frequent long stops and as dawn was breaking, we could identify Glasgow. After more long stops and eventually, on a beautiful summer's morning, we saw the Firth of Clyde, the sun shining on the surrounding hills with lots of ships moored in the river. We came to a halt in Gourock station. We surveyed the scene on the river while having our tea and wads for breakfast on the station, picked out two large passenger liners, and said to each other 'I hope we are going on one of those'.

After lots more hanging around, we then boarded a Clyde ferry steamer, which headed out towards the two big liners. 'Which one are we heading for?', I asked one of the sailors.

'The *Windsor Castle*,' he replies, 'that's the nearest one, the one standing high out of the water, the black one behind her is the *Empress of Japan*—she's full of prisoners, took them out yesterday'.

5

Off to Canada

There already seemed to be hundreds of lads on the *Windsor Castle*, mostly RAF but some Navy, a few Army, and a handful of civilians. We were told to sort ourselves out among some cabins on a particular deck, then report to a certain place where we were given cumbersome life jackets with two big lumps of cork at the front and another two lumps at the back; we were told that we must wear these at all times except when in our cabins or at least keep these slung over one shoulder so that they were always at hand. We were allocated 'boat stations', told there would be boat drill twice a day, and that the first would be within an hour or two. We would be allowed on deck unless instructed otherwise but must stay on the same side as our 'boat-station'. There was to be no smoking on deck and anyone throwing anything over the side would be severely dealt with. 'Any questions?'

'Yes, when do you eat?'

That evening, boat drill over and well-fed, I was on deck, up forward, overlooking the forecastle, looking at the ships around, and admiring the view as the sun was getting low and glinting on the water when an old seaman came up and leaned on the rail besides me. 'Been to sea before, lad?' He enquired.

'No, not really, only to the Isle of Man, a day trip to Boulogne, on those boats around the Clyde and over to Bute and two-hour trips along the coast from Scarborough, but never on a big ship like this.'

'Going over to do your training, are you?' he enquired.

'Yes. Do you know where we are going?' I asked.

'Yes, Halifax, Nova Scotia', he replied.

'How long will it take?' I enquired.

'Maybe ten days, maybe longer—all depends—we are standing by to move out tonight'. Looking down at the forecastle, I enquired about a pile of sandbags and some pieces of twisted metal. He replied, 'That's where we were hit by a bomb on an African convoy and that's why we have a bit of a list, but this is a lucky ship. I've been on her for six years when she was on the Cape Town run'. He moved off. Very soon, the warning went for another boat drill and I told the other lads that we were definitely going to Canada.

The other lads seem to want to stay in their cabins but I wanted to see what was going on outside so went back to the deck. The sun was just setting; we were moving very slowly and so were some of the other ships. Soon, it was almost dark, all the ships were blacked out but you could just see some faint outlines. I had the feeling that we had stopped moving so felt my way back along the dark deck, through a double set of doors into a dimly lit stairway and back to my cabin; the other three were already in their bunks. For the rest of the voyage, we were not allowed on deck after dark.

The next morning, we were moving slowly, in company with about fifteen other ships but land was visible on both sides, which we assumed would be Scotland and Ireland. It was sunny and calm and towards evening, we were joined by two destroyers and a small naval vessel. There was no sign of land now.

The following morning, however, to my amazement, when I went on deck, there was no sign of all the other ships but a great big battleship, which, with its great long foredeck and chopped-off aft, I recognised it as either the *Nelson* or the *Rodney*. It turned out to be the *Rodney*. She was sailing almost abreast of us on our starboard side and only seemed to be a few hundred yards away. I went below to fetch the other lads from the cabin to have a look at this magnificent big, long, low battleship steaming alongside us in this calm sea. Towards early evening, one of the lads spotted an aeroplane some way away, which we identify as a Whitley. It came closer and then all hell let loose. The *Rodney* started pumping off with 'pom poms' and two guns on our ship followed suit; empty cartridge cases came rattling down from the deck above. The Whitley fired off a coloured signal and the firing stopped, but it made me think that I would never get near the Navy unless I was certain they knew who I was.

All the next day, we steamed on in good weather with the *Rodney* in exactly the same position. The following morning, however, we felt the ship rolling and pitching; going on deck, I found it raining. There was white spray blowing off the surface of the sea, big rolling waves, and the sea breaking over the forecastle. You just could not believe that the weather could change so quickly. It was fascinating to watch the *Rodney*; we were rolling and pitching, the bow rising and then plunging down into the sea, but the *Rodney* just seemed to keep level and go straight on. She just went straight through the water; sometimes, the water was completely over her foredeck and you just saw the superstructure moving through the water, then the sea would recede and water would pour off the sides of the deck. Sometimes, she was out of sight from us, behind a big wave, to then appear again looking as steady as if she were running on a concrete road.

This weather kept up all day. It was still the same the next morning, but there was one big difference; there was no sign of the *Rodney*. Word gradually got around that the *Rodney* was on her way to Halifax for repairs to her engines and that she had been forced to slow down due to the heavy weather so we were going on alone as we had more speed and speed meant safety. The following day, the weather eased. It became quite good before the end of the journey and from the stern, we could see from the wake that we were frequently zigzagging. After twelve days, we saw land and were soon tying up in Halifax.

At the time, we did not know that the *Rodney* had just been involved in one of the major naval battles of the war. The *Bismarck* in company with the cruiser *Prinz Eugen* had been spotted coming into the Atlantic through the Denmark Strait between Iceland and Greenland. The *Bismarck* had sunk the *Hood* with virtually all hands, almost with her first salvo. There was then a three-day chase by our battleships, cruisers, and destroyers plus aircraft from the *Victorious* and the *Ark Royal*. The aircraft had damaged the *Bismarck* with torpedoes and after dashing for a day and a half at full speed, the *Rodney* and the *King George V* had intercepted the *Bismarck* and sank her on 27 May. The *Prinz Eugen*, however, being a fast cruiser of 32 knots, had got away and was somewhere in the Atlantic; it was later established that she made Brest on 1 June. The *Rodney* had fired 380 16-inch shells in the action so her guns required re-fettling and she needed a lot of work on the engines, which was why she was going to Halifax. I wondered whether that little A.T.S. girl's fella had been on the *Hood*.

For one more night aboard the *Windsor Castle*, we were moored along the dockside; there were no more blackouts, lights were on all over the ship, the dock and town were a mass of lights, and there was no more wearing life jackets. Everyone was in high spirits. After our evening meal, there was a lot of singing and Ken Frost appeared in the cabin with some bottles of beer, which he got off a member of the crew.

By the next afternoon, we were on a train waiting to set off to Toronto. What a train it was with big wide, high, luxurious rail-cars, open-plan seating (no grubby little compartments as in England), and two seats each side of the central aisle facing alternately forwards and backwards with a table between. No platforms as in England, you just climb up steps from track level. As for the engine: this was a great long, rugged affair, with four driving wheels each side, a big 'cattle catcher' on the front, diamond-shaped funnel and a tender about the length of three English trucks. Ken Frost, Pete Corah, Jim Redman, and I (who had 'palled-up' in Torquay and shared the same cabin on the ship) got ourselves settled down together and by about 5 p.m., with a lot of two-tone whistles from the engine, we started to move.

In an hour and a half, we pulled up in Truro. We did not seem to be in a station; it was as though we were in a street with people milling around. We were told we had half an hour here so got down and the folks seemed most anxious to talk to us, asked us which part of the old country we came from, gave us biscuits (which we later learnt were cookies), and shook us by the hand. After some blasts on the whistle, we were off again. A good meal was served in the diner, but when we asked if it was possible to get a beer, we were told 'not until we get into Quebec, there is total prohibition in the Maritime Provinces'. Just after dark, we stopped for another half an hour in Moncton and the reception was just as it had been in Truro; word must have got around that there was a troop train of English lads coming through. It was almost entirely RAF chaps from various ITWs in England. We settled down for the night in the comfortable high-backed seats but every few minutes, the engine whistle wailed away and we later learned that this was because there were so many unattended level crossings.

The breakfast was smashing: orange juice, two eggs, lots of bacon and coffee, but we did not know what to do with the Maple Syrup—we did not know that it was to spread on the bacon. We were told to put our watches back one hour as we were now on Eastern Standard Time and at about 10 a.m., we pulled up at Rivière-du-Loup. There was no special reception here and it sounded as though we were in French Quebec. It got pretty hot as we rumbled on all day to the incessant engine whistle, so we drank numerous bottles of iced coke. There was one brief stop in early afternoon, then about 7 p.m., we arrived at Montreal where we were told we would have an hour. Ken dashed off to try to find a phone as his elder brother works for a newspaper in Montreal. He came back to tell us that he could not get him as he was not at the office but they gave him the home phone number; he had tried that but there was no reply. Ken was very impressed with the public phones; there were no buttons to press as in England. We left Montreal about 8 p.m., remarking that everything we saw on the station seemed to be written in French. We settled down to our meal, though as we were on late sitting, we did not get it before we arrived. When we got back to our seats, Peter produced a bottle of Canadian Club Rye Whiskey, which he had managed to buy on the station in Montreal; this was shared with as many of the lads in the coach as possible—one tot each in a paper cup.

Soon after it became light the next morning, we could see water on the left-hand side; it was Lake Ontario, but it looked more like the sea. The whistle was going more frequently than ever now and we passed through places called Newcastle, Darlington, Oshawa (that one sounds rather out of place), Whitby, Pickering, and Scarborough. We pulled into Toronto at 6.30 a.m. The sun was already shining from a cloudless blue sky. We were not in a big station but in a sort of siding in the Exhibition Centre with beds of brightly coloured flowers over in one direction while in the other was the blue water of Lake Ontario with a slight mist lifting. My first thoughts were 'I wish Peggy could be here instead of being in blacked-out England with its food-rationing and bombs—it isn't fair'.

We had been travelling for about thirty-eight hours and covered about 1,200 miles but we were less than one-third across this great country—where were we to go now?

6

Canadian Hospitality

The Royal Canadian Air Force Manning Depot at which we had just arrived was in the Exhibition Buildings, surrounded by lawns and flower beds on the lakeside, overlooking the harbour and Toronto Island on which there was a landing ground for light aircraft with some float planes moored nearby. There were hundreds of people here, as well as hundreds who came over on our ship. We slept in big halls in two tier bunks but it was all very comfortable, marvellous food and everyone so pleasant and helpful. The day temperature was in the 80s and we were issued with our summer kit: a light shade of khaki drill. Life here was easy: a parade in the morning to see whether there were any posting instructions, then the rest of the day off to go where we liked.

We were introduced to a very large noticeboard on which were pinned dozens of postcards. Each of these cards was from a local person who wished to meet and entertain a boy (or boys) from the UK. It gave the person's car make and number along with the date and time they would be parked in the road leading to the Manning Depot; you picked a card, took it off the board, and kept the appointment. Jim and I were certainly lucky with our choice. We picked a Mr Pearson; he was in the plain clothes department of the Toronto police. We drove to his home in the S. Claire district of Toronto in a huge open Pontiac (but all the cars looked huge to us), were met enthusiastically by his wife and daughter, Arlene, and were soon sitting down to an enormous meal with Canadian wine, finishing with thick apple pie filled with big chunks of cheese and heaps of cream. All evening, we talked; they wanted to know what it was like in the 'Old Country' when we left, told us all their history—they both left England when they were young children so did not remember much about it—and of all the things we must do and see while we were in Canada. Arlene slipped out and brought a couple from across the road to see us, so we had to go through everything again. When we suggested it was about time we were getting back, Mr Pearson remarked that he would see we were back by 11 p.m., so we were not to worry as we must have some supper first. He then said, 'it's Sunday tomorrow, so will pick you both up about noon and show you the sights'.

That Sunday, we drove 80 miles to Niagara Falls. It only took about a couple of hours, along the magnificent, recently opened Queen Elizabeth Way, with the top down and Arlene between Jim and I in the back. We went into Hamilton, a big steel town at the western end of Lake Ontario, which was very quiet with it being Sunday, then turned back east along the southern side of the lake, through St Catharines to Niagara Falls. We stopped briefly near St Catharines and look at the Welland Canal, which connects Lake Ontario with Lake Erie. The site approaching the Falls is spectacular: there was a rising pillar of spray in the distance, then a long curtain of falling water came into sight; we pulled up at the side of the road and, with the engine shut off, we heard the roar of the water, but as there was no spray above the falls, where was the spray rising from?

'Ah, those Falls you can see are the American Falls. They are 193 feet high and 1,000 feet wide but only a small proportion of the water comes over them. See that island to the right of those Falls? That's Goat Island and the boundary between Canada and the States comes up the middle of the river and through that island. Those three tall buildings over there are in the States'.

We got back in the car and moved a little way up the river, parked the car, and walked around some rather splendid gardens in which we met two of the other lads on our course with their hosts. We all introduced ourselves and had a little chat, then walked around the corner where we could see what was below all that spray, or rather, we could see some of what was below that spray because, in the middle, the spray obscured everything from about 200 yards in front of the falls from the lower water level up to about 200 feet in the air. The noise is deafening but Mr Pearson is a big fella with a big voice and shouts: 'These are the real Falls. The Canadian or Horseshoe Falls. Most of the water comes over these Falls because they are seven feet lower than the American Falls but the length of the ledge around that horseshoe is 2,600 feet'.

After a while gazing at this mass of tumbling water, we walked back to the gardens where we could have a normal conversation and Mr Pearson explained that the Niagara river between the two lakes was 35 miles long;

now he said we would try to see what we can of the Great Gorge and Whirlpool Rapids. We took the car again and then set off down a path. The water below looked very turbulent and after a while, Mrs Pearson and Arlene said they dare not go any further, so we returned. It was about 6 p.m. Mr Pearson said we would have a meal at a little lakeside place he knew about three quarters of the way home. As we pass through St. Catharines, he remarks that the RCAF had a field near here and it would be nice if we got posted there as we could continue to see each other. Jim and I both wondered whether this meant he had something in mind for Arlene. On the way back from Hamilton to Toronto, we left the main Queen Elizabeth Way and took a little road, which followed the lakeside. It was a beautiful, balmy evening (we ought to have been wearing that summer kit with which we had just been issued), we pulled up at a biggish log-cabin type of building, festooned with coloured lights and coke signs, parked on the gravel beach among trees and log seats right by the edge of the glass-like lake. 'Right', says Mr Pearson 'it's time to eat'.

He ordered steaks and French fries for five 'with the two biggest ones you've got for these RAF boys'. We sat outside until the meal was ready. He told us that this part of Ontario was called 'The Garden of Canada'; they grew grapes, peaches, plums, pears, cherries, and flowers and made wine. Niagara is known as the 'Honeymoon area' as folks from all over Canada go there for their honeymoon. It seems that Toronto was originally called 'York' and that the old Fort York still existed and that he would take us to see it if we were in Toronto long enough. A shout told us that the meal was ready. We went inside, sat at a big rough-cut log table, and the biggest steak I had ever seen, with onion rings and thin chips, was put in front of me. Then, on the side plate came a corn on the cob. We struggled through and then there was the inevitable apple pie with lashings of cream. When the proprietor came to present the bill, he announced that the meals for the 'two boys' were 'on the house', with his compliments. We thanked him; he shook us by the hand and said, 'If you come again you can pay next time, okay?'

During the meal, we had talked a bit about cars and as we were about to get in the car, Mr Pearson asked me if I had driven one of these. To my obvious answer, he replied, 'Well now's your chance take us back, I'll show you the way'. He and I got in the front; he showed me a few things and said, 'Don't forget she's 30 hp', and off we set. It was beginning to get dusk, but still warm so we still had the top down. I had to keep telling myself to stay on the right-hand side of the road. The great long bonnet seemed to stick out miles in front and if you touched the brake she gently pitched up and down. As we approached the outskirts of Toronto, it was nearly dark and I offered to let him take over but he said, 'No. You carry on, you're okay. Better go straight back to the Manning Depot'. It was a bit confusing when we got to where the streetcars started but I managed okay, thanks to him telling me which lane to get in and where to go. We got back just before eleven and thanked him very much for a lovely day. Mr Pearson said they would be off to collect their Fox Terrier 'Nanky-Poo' from the neighbours where they had left him for the day and asked us to promise to phone them next evening to let them know whether we had heard anything about our posting. What a day. I thought of Peggy as I had done several times during the day; I wished she could have been here. Why should I be enjoying all this?

Most days during the week, postings came through and groups got ready to move on to places such as Edmonton, Calgary, Medicine Hat, Moose Jaw, and Regina in the Prairie Provinces of Alberta and Saskatchewan, while others went to the States, mostly it seemed to Texas. We heard nothing until the Friday when most of us who had come from Torquay were told we would be going to Oshawa only 30 odd miles up the lakeside but it was a new airfield and the contractors would not be out for a day or two so we would stay where we were for about a week. The other groups all had long journeys—three or four days or even longer—so we reckoned we would all be starting our courses about the same time.

When I phoned the Pearsons to tell them that we would shortly be moving to Oshawa, they sounded genuinely pleased saying, 'That's swell. It's only 30 miles up the Kingston Road so you can get over on your days off or we can come and pick you up.'

7

Airborne at Last

Some Flying Schools will graduate you provided you can land in a big field, others will expect you to land on a 'quarter' but to graduate from here you will have to learn to land on a 'quarter' and give 10 cents change. Those of you who complete the course, will be here for eight weeks in which you will do about sixty hours flying; we will expect you to go solo in about ten hours but that will not mean that you are going to complete the course; after twenty hours and again after fifty hours you will be checked by RCAF officers; at any time, if we think you are a danger to yourself, or anyone else or if we think you are not going to make a good pilot you will cease training and I do not want to see any of your names on the 'C/T' board. We will commence flying tomorrow and these are the names of the instructors to whom you have been allocated. Find your instructor when you are dismissed and get to know him.

So spoke Mr Weisbrod, chief flying instructor at No. 20 Elementary Flying School, Oshawa. We had previously been addressed by a RCAF squadron leader who informed us that he, assisted by two flying officers and several non-commissioned personnel, was responsible for the administration, discipline, and ground training while the flying instruction was in the hands of the Ontario County Flying Training School Ltd under their manager, Mr Robson, and their chief flying instructor. We would be divided into two groups so that half could be flying while the other half was doing ground training and if training was on schedule, we would be allowed one and a half days off a week, provided we behaved ourselves; also, every two weeks we could apply for a sleeping-out pass for the night before our full day off.

Airborne at Last

The date was 23 June 1941. We were the first course to arrive at Oshawa. There was still some contractor's plant around levelling ground near the building. Everything was very tidy, particularly the white-painted guard room at the smart entrance gate with a tall white flag-pole from which drooped the RCAF flag under a cloudless sky, which was even bluer than the flag.

We settled into our brand-new sleeping block—a single-storey building built of wood, clad with red composite slates so that from a distance it looked like brick, with a nice toilet/ablution room at each end, brand-new beds and bedding, little tables, and clothes cupboards. After a very good evening meal, we wandered over to the hangar and had a look at the Tiger Moths. They all looked new too. I met my instructor, again; he had a very English sounding name—'Carrothers'—but I do not think we spell it that way in England. He told me that he had been a 'bush pilot', flying float-planes up in the North West.

The next day, 24 June, I got my 'speaking tube' fitted into my helmet and we flew for the first time, thirty-five minutes. The grounds school syllabus was pretty much the same subjects that we had started in Torquay also 'Engines' (which I was pleased about) and in the airmanship lectures, we were told that we were under a 'Civil Airway' called 'Red One', which was used by Trans Canada Lodestar airliners so we must not go above 3,000 feet unless we were clear of the Airway and this was shown to us on a map.

Each day, we got about ninety minutes with our flying instructor, mostly on general handling and 'circuits and bumps' but the timekeeper only counted the time we were actually in the air so it only counted as forty or fifty minutes. The instructor was always stressing 'Watch your airspeed' or 'Watch your horizon'. If you came in too slowly, you started stalling but if you came in too fast, you levelled out and carried on floating all the way across the grass field so had to go around again because if you let the wheels touch before you were on the point of stalling, you bounce right up into the air. After a few days, the instructor tells you to pick a spot on the grass and touch down on that—imagine it's that 'quarter'.

One evening, Peter and Ken came back from the town and tell Jim and me that they have seen an old Model 'S' Ford that goes and has four reasonable tyres. The chap said he will sell it for $50 (about £13) but Ken thought he may come down a bit. Peter said it would be okay when we cleaned the chicken shit out of it.

We decided we would all go and have a look at it next evening and asked one of the fitters to come along to see what he thinks of it. We worked out that if we split it four ways, it would only cost us about four quid each. We did not know whether we required Canadian driving licences as when I mentioned this to Mr Pearson when he let me drive, he had just said, 'It's okay, get in', and when Ken asked someone about driving licenses and insurance, they did not seem to know what he was talking about.

We duly got a lift into town the following evening with one of the fitters who had a car of his own and went to see this Model 'S'. It was parked behind a little gas station and sure enough, there was straw and chicken shit all over the inside. There she was, the classic square, four-door saloon, wide running boards, shining chrome radiator, two big headlamps, and wheels with thick solid spokes. The doors all opened and shut perfectly so we had a look under the bonnet. It was a bit stuck up with dirt and dust; we then checked for oil and water to see if she would start. We let the fitter have a go at this and soon, he had her running; there was a bit of blue smoke coming out of the exhaust but it did not sound bad. He said he reckoned she would be okay after a de-coke. He had a look under at the brake rods, cables, and the chain drive, moved it backwards and forwards, and said the brakes needed attention but nothing much. We went into a huddle, the fitter said he could do the de-coke and the brakes for us in a couple of days up at the airfield. We made an offer of $40, which was accepted, gave the fitter $10 for the work he was going to do and everybody was happy—it still only cost us about four pounds each, including the gas we had put in. We let Ken drive us back—what a laugh, with the front pedal gear change; two pushes on the pedal and you go backwards. We must have made all of 15 miles an hour at one stage on the two-mile journey, leaving blue smoke in our wake and the lads all came out of the hut to have a look and passed cheeky remarks about Mr Ford's black Model 'S'. There were no more cheeky remarks three days later after our fitter friend had worked on it. We proudly kept it parked outside the hut and half the lads on the course would have done anything for a ride in our Model 'S'.

We had a half day off on 5 July because we had been working all day on 1 July, which was Dominion Day, a national holiday in Canada so we went for a spin in the car. Running grand now, it would do 30 mph without any trouble and with no more blue smoke. We remarked that it was just the job for running into Toronto or up into the country; we had all noticed a lake about 12 miles north of the airfield, which looked rather inviting. Peter and Ken were in high spirits as they had gone 'solo' the previous day but Jim and I had not and we did not want to see our names on the dreaded 'C/T' board along with two that were already there.

However, the next morning, I went with another instructor. We flew over to a satellite field at Whitby. It was just a grass field about five miles away, right by the side of the lake, which we used along with our own for 'circuits and bumps'. There was nothing much there, just the wind-sock, a hut, and the blood wagon. We did a few circuits and bumps, then practised a forced landing. The instructor then got out and said: 'I'm getting bloody hot so I'm going for a coke in the hut. Take her up and do a circuit. When you get down, take a look at the hut and if I'm not outside waving to let you know I'm ready, take her again and do another'.

So, I was up on my own. I remember letting go of the stick, waving my arms in the air, and shouting 'Yipee', then I thought, 'he'll be watching me so I'd better put it down on the bloody "quarter"'. Not too bad—we floated a bit but better than being short. As there was no sign of anybody waving outside the hut, I taxied back and off I went again. This time, I saw the instructor strolling out of the hut, so taxied over towards him and stopped. He just said, 'you'd better take me back to Oshawa now, we're going to be late for dinner'. I now had total flying time of ten hours thirty minutes, fifteen minutes of which was solo but I knew this was only the beginning.

We are about halfway through the course now. Five lads had left. Ken, Peter, Jim, and I had passed our twenty-hours checks. Some more Tigers had arrived (built in Canada), also some more instructors and a new course were due to arrive. We now seemed to spend most of our flying time doing spins, loops, and rolls. The spins were good fun: 'Throttle back. Keep the nose up. Keep it up. The controls become sloppy, then one wing drops away and you flutter down spinning. After about three turns, stick fully forward and full opposite rudder, slowly the spinning stops, so centralise the rudder—you are in the dive—gently back on the stick and as the horizon appears in the correct position, slowly open the throttle. Now let's climb up and do another.'

Ken had heard from his brother in Montreal, who had invited him to take the other three of us to stay with him in Montreal when we got some leave. We had been into Toronto a couple of times in the Model 'S', with Jim and I going to see the Pearsons while Peter and Ken did something else. I had obtained the address where my two cousin evacuees were staying in Toronto and had spoken to them on the phone. We had only been in Canada about six weeks but it seemed much longer because we had seen so much. Words such as 'candies' and 'cookies'; drapes and shades; sidewalks and streetcars; quarters, nickels, and dimes all became normal, everyday language. The big billboards for 'Canada Dry', 'Coke', 'Lucky

Strike', and 'Camel' were everyday sights; we accepted maple syrup on our bacon, big shiny red apples, and 100-page newspapers just as normal as driving on the right-hand side of the road. We had not seen a drop of rain since we arrived; in fact, we could hardly remember seeing a cloud, just blue skies and temperatures in the 80s.

We kept writing home. I knew Father would be interested in how I was getting on. I also wrote to Peggy and wished she could have been with me. Mail seemed to be so long coming and what news we got from the papers was not very enlightening—just brief reports about bombs being dropped in vague areas of the UK, usually south-east England, and that Germany had attacked Russia.

In August, the sky seemed to be full of busy little Tiger Moths buzzing around like flies. We were trying to impress the lads on the second course with our aerobatics but I was still trying to get the hang of a roll out of the top of a loop. Then came the day of our 'cross-country'—a straight flight of nearly 90 miles to actually land at another airfield. I spent all the previous evening drawing a line on the map from Oshawa to Kitchener, marking distances along it, measuring the track (252 degrees 'T'), variation 8 degrees 'W' (variation west, magnetic best, so that means add) right, so magnetic track is 260 degrees M. Now, I had to get the wind in the morning to work out the course to steer. Then, I studied the map, noting pinpoints.

It was another clear, sunny morning; not a very strong wind but gosh, it would make 20 degrees difference between track and course to steer because we were going so slowly. I checked this twice more but I was sure it was okay so I pencilled some times alongside the line on my map. My instructor told me to make sure I set off on course from directly above the airfield. I booked out, stuffed my map in the pocket on my flying suit leg, got my parachute, and off I went. At 2,000 feet, I could see a good way and, looking down, I could tell I was drifting a good 20 degrees.

'That's Toronto on the left,' I thought, 'that's Malton airfield—quite a lot of planes on it. It's got concrete runways, looks to be about two miles away so that's okay. Little town coming up—must be Brampton—should go right over that, just at its northern tip; looks as if I'm going to be at the wrong side of it. I'll hold this course for a bit and see if I drift across. All that smoke over there on the left must be from Hamilton steelworks.'

We were drifting across a bit too much to the north, going to pass about two miles north of Brampton. 'Yes that's Brampton okay,' I thought, 'can see that dead straight railway line and those three main roads, I'll alter course 5 degrees to the left, that's 235 degrees 'M' and see what happens. This little place coming up is Georgetown, must be, there are the two railway lines crossing, should go dead over that, I'm still going to be a bit to the north but no more to the north than I was over Brampton, so I must be steering the right course now except I haven't got back where I want to be. That big place coming up must be Guelph so bugger the compass for a while I'll go right over that road junction just on the outskirts of the town on the north, that will put me back on track, then I'll steer 235 degrees 'M' again and in twelve miles I'll be over Kitchener. That must be Kitchener, over there on the left—quite a big place. Now, should be a racecourse on its northern edge and then, just a couple of miles due north of that, the airfield. Yes, there's the racecourse but where is the ruddy airfield. Ah, there we are, some Tigers in a big field, almost straight ahead, let's start coming down, there's the wind-sock. I fly over the field, have a good look at the windsock, pick a spot to land and in I go.' One hour and ten minutes had passed. We had set off at ten-minute intervals and three chaps were already there and another two were expected.

We all talked about our experiences and set about working out our courses for the return flight, had a bottle of milk and some doughnuts, then booked-out at ten-minute intervals for the return flight. On the way back, we could cheat as we knew where we were going and knew the landmarks around Oshawa. It was with some feeling of achievement that we turned in on 10 August.

The rest of the course was mainly taken up with flying 'under the hood'. We all felt sorry for one lad who had done very well up till now but he had some sort of phobia as soon as he pulled the hood over, so much so that his ordinary flying went all to pieces and he had to leave the course. On 16 August, I had my fifty-hour check, although I had clocked up sixty-five hours by then and, subject to ground exams being okay, knew that I had, at least, got through this course. We knew that some of us would continue on single-engined aircraft while others would go on to 'twins'. Among ourselves, we discussed what we would like to do. I rather fancied eventually going on to Blenheims, Jim fancied something big, while Peter and Ken wanted to go on Hurricanes or Spitfires.

It was graduation day on 20 August. We were all lined up on the parade ground with the second class behind us. There was an official party consisting of the local mayor, sheriffs, local dignitaries and their ladies, plus a party from the press. The Squadron Leader made a speech that we could not hear very well. Robson, the civilian manager, then inspected us and presented a prize to Percy Proctor as best pupil and that was that. We were then advised of our postings. Jim and I were to go to Brantford to continue on Ansons while Peter and Ken were to go to Camp Borden on single-engined Harvards.

It was a pity that Peter and Ken would be parting company from Jim and I as we had enjoyed a lot of good times together, especially with the car. We sold the Model 'S' to some lads on the second course who had been casting wishful eyes over her. We sold her for $50 so she had cost us nothing.

We were all due at our next schools on 1 September, which meant we had ten days leave, although we were told we could stay another day or two if we wanted to witness the official opening of the school by H.R.H. the Duke of Kent. We did not bother. The four of us caught the greyhound bus in Oshawa for the nine-hour ride to Montreal to see Ken's brother.

8

Wings Parade at Brantford

The town of Brantford did not have much to offer. Its only claim to fame seems to be that it was here where Alexander Graham Bell succeeded in receiving the first telephone transmission of a voice, using the wires of farmers fences to carry the signal. It is in a flat, cultivated area, producing a variety of fruit and flowers, probably because it is in the most southerly part of Canada, on a peninsula bounded by three of the Great Lakes—sixty-five miles south-west of Toronto, with Lake Ontario thirty miles to the east, Lake Erie thirty miles to the south, and Lake Huron eighty miles to the west. Some 100 miles to the north is a bay protruding off Lake Huron (Nottawasaga Bay) but otherwise to the north, it becomes mile after mile of coniferous trees and little lakes, which seem to go on forever and ever.

The Service Flying Training School was about 2 miles west of the town and here, we found a large RCAF station with lots of substantial buildings, with two concrete runways. There were two courses already partway through their training. The thirty-six on our course were split into two as before so that half flew while the other half did ground school. The lads from Oshawa were all kept in the same group as the others all seemed to have done their elementary course in the States. We were told that those of us who satisfactorily completed the course would be here twelve weeks, after which we would get our 'wings' and return to the UK for 'operational training' before going to squadrons. We were allocated flying instructors; there were six for our course: two flying officers, three pilot officers, and a sergeant. I was pleased to be allocated to Sergeant Harry Guest; the officers were all wearing very new-looking uniforms with flat 'gramophone record' hats, whereas Harry looked a bit more 'well-worn' and his wings were not bright and new.

The syllabus looked a bit forbidding; the ground school included several new subjects: astro-navigation; Link Trainer; maps, charts and projections; and instruments and compasses. The flying programme had twenty-six 'sequences' to be mastered.

On 3 September 1941, Harry took three of us up together, each of us having about forty-five minutes in the pilot's seat while he let us get a feel of the aircraft and demonstrated what a 'lazy' aircraft the Anson was by throttling back until she stalled, then taking his hands and feet off. She just slowly dropped the nose, glided a little way, then the nose came up, slowly dropped away again, and so on, just as if she were going down a flight of stairs. He said there was no need to be afraid of the Anson, it was so meek and mild that you would have to be a complete idiot to hurt yourself but, he stressed that, for that reason, it was a poor training aircraft because whatever we flew next would be far less forgiving and therefore for our own sakes, he was going to be very strict and see we did everything correctly. There would be no question of just 'getting by'. I liked Harry right away; he was a bit of a rough diamond, who taught us all a few new Canadian swear words—we were all 'God damn sons of bitches'—but you knew where you stood with him and he could fly.

The next day, we were introduced to the Link Trainer. There were ten of them, all going flat out from 8 a.m. until midnight, with two shifts of instructors, mostly flying officers or pilot officers, and we started instrument flying practice. Sessions lasted an hour, although the last ten minutes or so was probably spent at the plotting table explaining where you went wrong.

The wash basins in the ablutions were arranged in rows, back-to-back, with mirrors mounted on both sides of a board sticking up above the basin. While shaving one morning, about a week after the start of the course, I looked through to see who was at the other side of the mirror and through a layer of lather, I recognised Peter Stembridge; we were members of the same rugby club in York. We were on the same course; in fact, we had the same instructor—Harry Guest—but we had not seen each other before as we were on different halves of the course. Peter had done his elementary flying training in Florida on Fairchilds. Peter and I had a lot to talk about that evening but we did not know then that our futures were to have so much more in common.

On 8 September, Harry sent me up for fifteen minutes solo. A couple of days later, the CO came up with me for an hour and a half; he seemed satisfied but stressed that, from now on, we would be concentrating on instrument flying: flying accurate courses, keeping constant heights and airspeed, doing accurate 'rate 1' turns coming out dead on course without gaining or losing height, and learning manoeuvres on the 'beam'. Things began to get really hectic now. Some days, we would fly up to six sessions in a day, plus, of course, the ground school; by the end of the month, I had completed my first 'cross-country' (two and a half hours) and started dual night flying. I found night flying particularly fascinating, particularly as there was no blackout in Canada. On 1 October, I did my first solo night flying and the next day, about half of us were given four days leave. We had not had a full day off since we arrived; in fact, I had not been off the airfield for a month, but it did not seem as long as that.

Jim's leave was to come later so I phoned Mr Pearson and to ask if Peter and I could go over for a couple of days. We caught the greyhound and were in Toronto by evening. Peter was overwhelmed by the reception we received; he had seen nothing like it in Florida. We spent the first evening at the Pearsons's house, having a big meal. The next morning, we went into town and bought some nylons in Eatons to send home to Peggy, but Mr Pearson asked us to be back soon after midday as he was having the afternoon off. We drove down to the lakeside just out of Toronto, where we had a 'weener roast'—that is a sort of picnic where you roast weeners (little sausages) over a fire made from sticks you gather up from under the trees. The weather was getting a little cooler now but was still very pleasant.

That evening, I called to see my two cousins—Henry and 'Bubbles'—who had been evacuated to Toronto. The relations with whom they were staying (from the other side of the family) were pleasant and put on a very good meal but somehow the atmosphere was not very relaxed and all the time, they were trying to make an impression by talking about their possessions, cars, and how well they were living in Canada—such a contrast to the Pearsons. I do not think they had been in Canada very long. Henry was now seventeen and he was very keen to talk to me about flying, saying that as soon as he was eighteen, he hoped to join the RCAF and become a pilot. I learned that their elder sister, Mary, had just been commissioned in the WAAF back home.

Back on the job, I flew several times a day or night practically every day for the next four weeks. Most of us now had our certificates to carry passengers and I had been 'excused' from ground school for signals subjects (in view of the course I had done at Blackpool). I scrounged flights with other lads, or instructors, so that I could play around in the air with the W/T equipment and also practise map-reading. The Anson was ideal for map-reading as the whole of the side was one long window. We were getting some wet and cloudy weather now so often, even the instructors were glad to have a wireless operator on board. I shall never forget the first time I climbed through a layer of dark grey stratosphere to emerge into another world. There was a brilliant sun in a perfectly blue sky and below an endless carpet of whiter than white cotton-wool, so brilliant that you needed sunglasses. Here and there, little tuft of cotton-wool would stick up above the rest and sometimes you could see the little shadow of the aircraft dashing along on the top of the clouds, now and again encircled in a complete circle of a rainbow.

The daytime flying now was mainly cross-countries or instrument flying under the hood, the night flying either circuits and bumps or cross-countries using marine lights on the lakes or flashing beacons as turning points. Some of the instrument flying involved 'beam flying', but most of the beam practice was on the Link.

The civil air routes in Canada (and in the States) were along beams, which were the 'legs' of radio ranges. A radio range is merely a radio transmitter with reflectors arranged around the aerials so that a Morse letter 'N' (_ .) is transmitted in two opposite sectors and a Morse letter 'A' (. _) is transmitted in the other two sectors. The reflectors are adjusted so that the sector signals overlapped slightly, with the result that where they overlap slightly, the 'N' and the 'A' signal are of equal strength and they interlock to give a continuous steady note, namely, the 'beam'. The sectors need not be of equal size—in other words, the legs need not be at right angles to each other; in fact, they very rarely are. Two opposite legs are aligned along an air route and the other two legs point in directions where they are likely to be of most use. The beam in which the steady continuous note is heard is 4 degrees wide and on each side, there is a twilight zone of about 20 degrees in which the sector letter ('N' or 'A') can be heard with the steady note in the background. The letter gradually fades away as you enter the beam while at the outside edge of the twilight zone, the continuous note in the background fades away, leaving just the clear-cut letter. Each range has its own radio frequency and transmits a call-sign (usually once a minute) so that you can be sure that you are on the correct range; some range stations also transmit weather information once an hour at a predetermined time. The Air Charts show the legs of each radio range, marked with the magnetic course to steer in still air conditions, along the centre of the leg, to reach the range station (known as the QDM) and to fly away from the range station (the QDR) but you never steer these exact courses for two reasons.

Firstly, the air is hardly ever still. There is invariably some wind giving drift, so the drift has to be ascertained and allowed for, otherwise you will be zigzagging all over the place. Secondly, you do not aim to fly in the centre of the beam but on the right-hand edge so, as the beam is 2 degrees either side of the centre line, you aim to steer 2 degrees less than the centre line when flying towards the station and 2 degrees more when flying away, but the actual course to steer is a combination of these two factors.

The reason for flying on the edge of the beam rather than in the middle is that you could be happily cruising along thirty miles away from the station where the beam is two miles wide, getting a continuous note to show you are in the beam but, all the time, you could be drifting across the beam until, all of a sudden, when the beam is getting narrower, you shoot out of it and have a job to find it again, probably also missing flying over the 'cone of silence', which tells you that you are over the station, so you do not know where you are. If, however, you get the drift sorted out and settled down on the edge so that you can just faintly hear the sector letter, you get an immediate indication if you are drifting off and only a small correction is necessary to regain the edge. Although we practised beam flying, it was stressed that we were not to regard this as a lazy way of navigating and we must concentrate on our dead reckoning navigation, as there would be no ranges where we would eventually be operating and beam flying was mainly to help us get used to beams for when we came to using the standard beam approach system later in the course.

Beam flying in the Link was most absorbing. To start with, the exercises were done in still air conditions: finding the beam and settling on the edge, turning out of the beam and regaining it in the opposite direction, measuring the width and thereby calculating the distance from the station, figures of eight and 'extended' figures of eight. In due course, the instructor introduced wind so the appropriate drift had to be ascertained by 'bracketing' the beam before the other manoeuvres could be carried out; eventually, he would be altering the wind at different heights. It was just as interesting watching the plot on the instructor's table while listening on a spare pair of earphones to the noises the pilot was hearing inside the Link as you could then see from the plot exactly what the various noises were indicating. I found the Link so interesting that often, in an evening when some of the other lads were playing cards, I would nip over to the Link, borrow a pair of earphones, and watch plots. If there happened to be a free machine, one of the instructors would only be too willing to give me the odd half-hour. Peter started coming over with me; we got very pally with one of the flying officer instructors, who let us know which evening he would be on duty and we played games on the Link to see which of us could win in a given time. It was all good fun—much better than playing cards and we did not lose money at it. I often thought what a lot I would have to tell Father about when I got back, as you could not explain everything in a letter; in any case, most of my letter-writing time was taken up writing to Peggy.

A few days before the end of October, I flew with the CO again, for about an hour. On our first landing approach, he waited until the wheels were just on the point of touching when he shouted 'Overshoot' so I had to open up and go around again. On the second approach, he suddenly pulled one throttle back and I thought 'I hope he's not going to shout overshoot this time'. As we taxied in, he seemed in a good mood and remarked, 'You won't have to wind the undercarriage up and down by hand when you get on your next aircraft. It will be hydraulic instead of hand-raulic'. I thought that sounded quite encouraging.

Then, half of us got four days leave—how quickly October had passed. I thought 'only another month to go, all being well, then I should be back home with my wings, see Peggy, plus I have so much to talk to Dad about.'

Peter and I went to the Pearsons for a couple of days as we thought this may be our last visit if we left for home as soon as the course finished. Mr Pearson, however, was quite sure that we would be over again. Mr Pearson took a day off and we drove up to Camp Borden, about sixty miles north of Toronto. There was a lot of broken cloud around but when the sun shone on some of the trees, they were a wonderful red colour; autumn was nearly over but there was still plenty of colour from the maples. He called at the ACAF Station at Camp Borden in the hope that we may be able to see Ken and Peter, but we could not find them. The air was full of noisy little Harvards. They made such a terrible raucous noise; it must have been murder being on that station, especially if they were night flying—no wonder they were miles away from any town, otherwise the inhabitants would have been up in arms. The excessive noise was because the prop was a direct drive from the engine without any reduction gear and it was a high-pitched prop too so that the prop tips were going around so fast that they made this ear-splitting noise.

When I was back for the final month, the weather was very mixed. Most days, we had at least one flying session with a different instructor, the idea being that each instructor reported on each pupil. Both in the air and in the Link, we did a lot of blind approaches on the SBA (standard beam approach).

The SBA worked on the same principle as the radio range, although it was not as powerful as it only needed to be picked-up in the vicinity of the aerodrome and it only had two legs (or beams) instead of four. The transmitter was sited on the boundary of the aerodrome so that the centre line of one beam was parallel to the runway, but about sixty feet to the right of the right-hand runway lights when looking down the runway in the direction of the transmitter. This beam, which passed along the runway, was the 'front beam'. The other beam was directly behind the front beam so that the two were in a straight line; this was the 'back beam'. Instead of 'A's and 'N's as on the radio range, the signals of the beam were dots and dashes—dots on the left when approaching the airfield on the front beam and dashes on the right. The beam width was the same as on the radio range, 4 degrees with a 20-degree twilight zone on either side.

When approaching on the front beam, there were two marker beacons to indicate the distance from the touch-down point. The outer marker was usually about two miles out and as the aircraft passed directly over, low pitched signals at a rate of two per second were heard. The inner marker was on the airfield boundary and emitted a high-pitched signal at the rate of six per second. All final approaches were made on the front beam as there were no marker beacons on the back beam, which was used for manoeuvring or maybe holding. The beam was off-set to the right of the runway because a first pilot always sits on the left of the aircraft; also, some aircraft have long noses and a long nose may mask the runway lights if an aircraft got over to the left. A slightly different technique was used from flying on the range in as much as you tried to settle in the centre of the beam or, if there was a little drift, on the upwind edge. In practice, you would not expect much drift, otherwise the crosswind on the runway would be such that you ought to be using another runway. In the aircraft, there was actually an instrument with a 'kicker' to show whether or not you were on the centre line of the beam and also a needle to show whether you were on the correct angle of descent, but we had these covered over: firstly because the CO was adamant that we must be able to fly listening to the sounds only, rather than being obsessed with this instrument and overlook other important things like airspeed, artificial horizon and height; and secondly, the 'glide-path' to show the angle of descent had not yet been proven reliable enough for service use.

It was by the middle of the month that a squadron leader, who none of us had seen before, appeared and started taking us, one by one, on our instrument test. A couple of days later, the CO took me on my 'wings test'. All this time, we were busy with oral and written exams. We carried on flying, mostly night flying and cross-countries, but we knew by now that we had either passed or failed; it is just a matter of waiting. One day, I flew with Harry again; he said we would go up and 'have a bit of relaxation'. It was very windy; he took me over Lake Erie to show me 'wind lanes', white streaks on the surface of the water, roughly at right angles to the waves, which showed very clearly the direction of the surface wind. I asked him whether he knew if I would be getting my wings, to which he replied, 'of course you will, you son of a bitch, those that weren't going to make it have already gone'.

Then, the big day arrived. On 20 November, a notice went up saying that a wings parade was to be held the following day; it listed the names of the twenty-seven of us remaining on the course, in alphabetical order.

The wings parade was a very 'domestic' affair—no bullshit like there was at Oshawa. We paraded in a hangar with another course that was halfway through, behind us. In front, there was a table covered with a green baize cloth on which were laid out twenty-seven pilots wings in neat rows. The instructors took up their positions behind the table; we were then called to attention and in came the CO with a RAF group captain. After an introduction from the CO, the group captain said a few words, congratulating us on completing the course and wishing us all the best for the future. Then, our names were called out, so we went up and saluted the group captain. He pinned a pair of wings on our tunic. Then, a photographer took a picture of him doing it, which later cost us a dollar. We took a pace back, saluted again, and that was that. We were then told that we would all be promoted to sergeants; also, some of us would be commissioned, but we would be advised about this when we arrived at our next station. Posting instructions would be coming through in the next day or two and it was anticipated that we would be going to the Manning Depot in Toronto, which would arrange our return to the UK for operational training.

That evening, we were all busy sewing our wings on our tunics. The following day, we were issued with our sergeant's stripes, so that was another sewing job. Then a notice appeared on the board instructing (in alphabetical order), me, St John Hawkins, Cyril Payne, and Peter Stembridge to report to the CO at 9 a.m. and the remainder of the course to parade at 10 a.m. for posting instructions. We wondered what the devil this was all about and after some discussion, we all dreaded that it may mean we were being kept in Canada to be instructors; none of us wanted to be instructors. The CO informed us that we had been chosen to go on a G. R. (general reconnaissance) course at Charlottetown on Prince Edward Island, and that we should be very pleased about this as it was a much sought-after course. We asked him what it was all about and he advised us it was an advanced navigation course for those who had already qualified as pilots or navigators. When we asked why we four had been chosen, he informed us that the instructions came from Training Command but he could tell us that the four of us had all come in the top six in all the subjects on the course and it was not often that they got anybody into this course and this time, they were delighted to get four. We could not resist mentioning that three of us (Peter, Cyril, and I) had been pupils of Harry Guest (the only sergeant instructor), but this CO quickly pointed out that Ground School subjects were equally important. We asked what we were likely to finish up doing after the course; he did not really know but suggested we would probably be on long-range aircraft on which the pilot could relieve the navigator. A posting date had not yet come through.

We found Harry to tell him about the posting to Charlottetown and he was over the moon to think that three of his pupils were going on this course: 'you God, damned sons of bitches, been trying like hell to get on that course myself. Tonight we're all going into town to get drunk, be at the gate at 20.00 hours'.

I wrote to Peggy and to home to say I would not be coming home as soon as I thought. The other lads kept asking why we were not going with them. Then, Peter, Cyril, and I went to a hotel in town with Harry. Harry kept pulling Cyril's leg about his name, saying it sounded like a silly girl's name: 'as for that other one, that's going with you "St John"; he should be in a church with a name like that'. The local beer was very pleasant—in any case we had hardly had any drinks since we arrived in Canada so it soon started having an effect—so we went on to Canadian Club, which was quite a palatable whiskey. To finish off, we each had a good thick steak—now we were sergeants, we were on twelve shillings and sixpence a day, which was pretty good pay. Harry kept on about wanting to get off the instructor's job and get 'over there' to England; he swore he would be seeing us over there one day and I think he meant it.

Just before the end of the month, our posting came through to be at Charlottetown by 13 December. We were given rail warrants and left to make our own way there so we had almost two weeks leave. There had been nothing much to spend our money on at Brantford so we were all feeling quite well off, and we had just got a rise, so Peter and I decided we would have a couple of days at Niagara Falls as Peter had only seen them from the air, then a day or two in Toronto, and carry on to Montreal for a few days, where we would meet up with Cyril and St John for the journey to Charlottetown. We rang the Pearsons from Niagara Falls to tell them we had got our wings and that we would like to call in and say 'cheerio' on our way to Charlottetown. The response was, 'Great. Try to get over tonight. How long can you stay? Your beds are waiting'. We only had one night at the Falls and moved on to Toronto.

9
Across the Frozen Water

Mr Pearson was as excited over us getting our wings as if we had been his own sons. First thing in the morning, he insisted he had a photo taken with us on the steps in front of the house; he was so tall that Peter and I stood one step above him so that we looked less like dwarfs.

We asked what he knew about Charlottetown. I told him that, according to the guide book I had looked up, it said:

> The Capital of the Province of Prince Edward Island. The Province being an island 120 miles long by 35 miles wide situated in the Gulf of St Lawrence, renowned for its rich red soil and lush farmland with huge beaches of golden sand.

He laughed, and replied, 'that's in summer. In winter, it will be under feet of snow—they get about 112 inches; here in Toronto, we only get about 55 inches and that's plenty. The Gulf will be frozen solid—that's why Montreal port is only open for six months of the year. The temperature won't rise above freezing until the end of March or April and it will go down to about 10 degrees F; that's 22 degrees of frost, but you probably won't feel it as folks from the old country don't seem to feel it the first year as it's dry cold but you feel it alright the next year when your blood gets thin'. We wondered what we were in for.

The second morning, we woke up to find that the snow had started. It snowed most of the day, so we took Nanky-Poo for a walk and he loved romping around. We also had a chance to catch up a bit with the news, looking through a pile of newspapers. They did not make very happy reading: the usual vague references to air raids over England; American forces in Iceland; British troops in Persia; German attack on Moscow; British Army on offensive in Libya; the *Ark Royal* sunk; the *Dunedin* sunk; the *Barham* sunk; and points rationing scheme and clothes rationing in the UK. I wrote to Peggy, wishing that she could be here, away from the danger of air raids and the austerity at home—here, where the lights were still shining, the shops were full of good things, and everyone was carrying on as normal.

We told the Pearsons that, on 8 December, we would have to move on; we could then have a couple of days in Montreal. During the day, Peter and I usually went into town, which was preparing for Christmas. A little more snow fell each day. The big stores were dressed in fancy lights; coloured lights were hung in the trees. Darkness fell about 4.30 p.m., and then the whole town became a mass of lights, mostly from some enormous flashing advertisements, and with the snow on the ground, the effect was most spectacular. The snow did not turn to a dirty slush as it did in England; it stayed clean and white. The roads were kept clear by snow ploughs and traffic was moving quite normally. We understood that at night, big wagons collected the snow pushed up by the snow ploughs and dumped it in the lake. In view of what Mr Pearson had told us about Charlottetown, we took the precaution of checking with Canadian National Railroad that it was still possible to get onto the island. They assured us that it was okay as during the winter, an ice-breaker replaced the summer ferry.

One evening, we all went to see the Toronto Maple Leafs play ice-hockey against a team from Montreal; it was in a huge covered stadium with lots of razzamatazz. On leaving, Mr Pearson asked if I wanted to drive; I pointed out that I had not driven in as much snow as this. 'Nothing to worry about,' he told me, 'just start off in top gear, slip the clutch a bit, and keep the handbrake slightly on until you get going—works like a charm—you never saw folks having any bother getting going in Canada like you do in England with wheels spinning and folks pushing.'

Mr Pearson had booked at the Old Mill for the night of 7 December, our last night. There was great commotion on the radio all that day because the previous day, the Japs had attacked Pearl Harbour. Reports and opinions seemed very confused. Some reports made out that practically the whole American Fleet had been sunk, while others referred to only minor damage. Some commentators seem stunned to think that anyone could have the audacity as to attack any part of America, almost as if it were some sacred land. They talked of treachery by the Japanese and what to do about the large number of Japanese living in the States; in fact, we got the impression that they were in a real panic at the thought that there was a risk of America herself being attacked. The tone now was very different.

Until now, when listening to American radio, it was all talk about what they were doing for others under Lend-Lease (provided that we could get the aircraft and equipment across the Atlantic) and the fifty old destroyers, which they had taken out of moth-balls and let us have (but no mention of the fact that in exchange we had given them air bases in the West Indies and British Guiana) but no suggestion that they would ever get actively involved. Now, they would have no option; it could no longer be just Britain and the Commonwealth, plus a few folks who had escaped from occupied countries, standing up to aggression (admittedly, Russia was fighting Germany and the Russians were an unknown quantity). It was obvious that something was being cooked-up by the Japanese when, only three months after the fall of France, Vichy France invited the Japanese into French Indo-China. The Japanese clearly wanted to damage as much of the American fleet as they could, for starters.

In spite of the news, we had a really good night at the Old Mill. The Canadians took it as just another development in a war in which they were already involved. It was snowing hard, which all added to the pre-Christmas atmosphere. This time, we were joined by a young couple we had met before at the Pearsons's house—the lad was on leave from the Army and expecting to go to England very soon; in fact, he did, and later spent quite a bit of time with my mother. The meal was good, as was the wine, and the band was in good form too. However, we should have guessed it—after a roll of drums, the band leader announced that there were two English boys who have just won their wings: 'yes, there they are over there, everybody on your feet for a big "high" to these boys from the old country.' Peter had not come across this before and was even more embarrassed than I was, but the Canadians meant well, so you could not really get cross. However, there were a party of Yanks who got on our tits; they kept coming to our table, wanting to shake hands and say, 'we're all in this together now, buddy'.

The next morning, we duly moved off to Montreal, with promises to write, keep in touch with, and get to see them again before we left Canada. It had stopped snowing as we made our way along the 350 miles to Montreal. We noticed that the snow seemed to be thicker; now and again, we passed the snow plough travelling in the opposite direction and the sun shining on the snow made it difficult to see outside without screwing your eyes up. The train was most luxurious—there was a damn good meal in the diner and a very attentive attendant, but everywhere you went, you had to step over folks playing lie-dice (or crap) on the floor (I could never understand what was wrong with the tables; perhaps the dice shot better on the floor).

We booked into a small hotel for a couple of nights. There was already a good level (18 inches) of snow in Montreal and it was well below freezing all day but the streets were clear except for maybe an inch of hard, packed snow; here again, traffic was quite normal. We had a look around the town, bought ourselves some good sunglasses and fur ear-muffs, and then went up to Mount Royal to watch folks skiing. The view with all the snow on the ground was even more spectacular than it had been when I went in August with Jim, Ken, and the other Peter. Luckily, it was not snowing but a bright sun shining in a perfectly blue sky; it was a good job we bought those sunglasses. We did ourselves well that night in a French restaurant, but it was very cold when we came out—about 12 degrees below—so the ear-muffs came in useful. Someone in the hotel told us that in January, it got down to 8 degrees 'F'—gosh, that was 24 degrees of frost.

The next day, we met Cyril and St John at the railway station and get ourselves organised on the train due to leave about noon for Halifax. We were going to get off at Amherst, which was about 700 miles and should have taken about twenty-three hours. In view of the snow, we felt glad to know we had kept a day in hand; it was the 10th and we were not due at Charlottetown until 13 December, but the officials seemed to regard the snow as quite normal. The engine was most impressive and this time, there was a snow plough on the front.

The only complaint about the train was that it was very warm and you could not adjust the heating, but it was better than being cold. As we steamed on, with frequent stops at small halts and incessant whistle-blowing, we talked about what we had done on our leave; the news about Pearl Harbour; news from home; what this course was going to be about and the aircraft we would like to fly when we eventually got back home.

We could only speculate as to what this course was all about. An advanced Navigation Course. What did that mean? Why do pilots require an advanced navigation course? Surely, that is a job for navigators. There had been some talk of 'relieving navigators on long flights' or 'having two pilot/navigators instead of a pilot and a navigator', but we could not think of any aircraft in service where this might apply—possibly some long range bombing jobs—then we decided that as there was a lot of water around Prince Edward Island (even though it was frozen at the time), it may have had something to do with Coastal Command. Cyril suggested flying boats and we all remarked, 'Surely not, lumbering slow flying boats'.

As for the type of aircraft we would like to finish up on—we knew they would not be single-engined—we thought through the ones we had come across in 'aircraft recognition'. Peter fancied something like a Wellington, Cyril a Halifax, St John did not seem to mind, and I plumbed for a Beaufighter.

After a very long dinner in the diner, we settled down for the night but were awakened about 3.30 a.m. by a lot of noise to find we were in Campbellton station and it was snowing again. We stopped here about half an hour so got out but soon got back in as it was damn cold. We got off to sleep again and shortly after it was light, we stopped at Moncton. It was about 8.30 a.m. and not snowing so we had a look outside and saw they were changing the engine. It was at least another two hours to Amherst, so we took our time over breakfast. The scenery outside looked like snow-covered desolation; we were jolly glad we had got those sunglasses.

Amherst was a real back and beyond place—thank goodness, we got straight on another train (a much inferior train to the one we had left)—to take us to Cape Tormentine. It seemed very slow but the attendant told us there was no need to rush as the boat would be late because of the ice. We pulled into a bleak deserted jetty, which seemed to be entirely surrounded by snow or ice. The attendant told us we may as well stay on the train as the boat would not be in for a couple of hours yet and the train would not be going back until the boat gets in. We met four other lads on this train, two pilots, and two navigators; they were also heading for Charlottetown. Their main concern seemed to be whether or not they would hear if they were to be commissioned when they arrived. I did not think that any of our four had given that matter any thought—if so, it was not mentioned. We were more interested in what we would be doing on the course than whether or not we were to become officers.

After a while, we left the train to see whether there was any sign of the boat. Out in the haze, getting on for a mile away, there was a boat, discharging clouds of black smoke out of four tall funnels—two on each side of the boat, arranged in a square, but it did not seem to be moving. As we watched, the boat appeared to move a little way forward very slowly, then stop, go back a bit, and have another go. It was damn cold so we got back on the train.

We boarded the boat about 3.30 p.m. for a nine-mile crossing. All we could see around us was snow on top of ice and but for some trees on the shore, you could not tell what was sea and what was the land. Not a drop of clear water to be seen, even where the boat had come in, the slabs of ice had drifted back across the water. An area around the jetty, and on routes where the icebreaker had been, were rough, where slabs of ice had piled up on each other and frozen together; otherwise, it was just flat, white disappearing into the haze. We thought the icebreaker's journey back would be easy as it could go back through the route it had smashed up on the way over, but how wrong we were to be.

We shunted backwards and forwards several times before even getting away from the jetty. For the first half hour or so, we appeared to follow the route made by the boat on its way in, pushing big slabs of ice out of the way, although now and again, we came to a standstill and reversed a little to get another run at it, but this did not work for long.

Soon, it became a case of charging the ice. The bow rose up on top of the ice, the boat would shudder to a stop, then there would be a noise like a creaking door as the ice cracked and—thump—the bow fell down into the water. We reversed about a hundred yards, then the engines throbbed away at full power, full speed ahead. In a few minutes, there was a grinding noise as if we had run aground. The boat seemed to stop, then with a creaking and a thump, the bows went down and we started all over again. I had a look over the bows on one of these runs; when the bow had risen up on the ice, the creaking started as the ice began to crack; two cracks opened up like a 'V' till the top of the 'V' snapped off and the outer sides of the 'V' were cracked off as the boat fell into the hole. I did not watch this for long because when the bows fell down, you felt as if you were being left suspended in thin air; also, it was damn cold. It was a funny feeling being inside the boat, too. You had to keep hold of something and having a cup of coffee or Coke was a real performance. After a while, you could tell by the noises what was going to happen next. After the motors dropped away at full blast, you braced yourself for the grinding and then the bow cocked up about 15 degrees. Then, the creaking, so we held on to our glasses as we were going to thump back level any second. It soon became dark. After four hours, we arrived on the island at 8 p.m. where the train was waiting: front cars for Charlottetown, rear cars for Summerville. We pulled into Charlottetown about 10 p.m. and you would have thought we had gone back in time about 100 years.

The four lads we had met were dying to get to the aerodrome and off they shot. However, Peter, Cyril, St John, and I had previously decided that we would find a place in town for the night as we were not due until the 13th. The hotel was only a few yards from the station so we set off through the snow and nearly got knocked down by a sleigh; it was being pulled by a pony so you could not hear it coming. St John pulled me out of the way. When we arrived at the hotel, the two occupants of the sleigh were in there, the pony and the sleigh having been tied to a rail outside. The hotel must have been built when the first settlers arrived in Canada, but the beds were great. There were no drinks though; there was prohibition on the island.

10

Christmas Wonderland

On arrival at Charlottetown, Peter and Cyril learned that they had been commissioned as pilot officers; St John and I had not, so we moved into a room together. The accommodation was very splendid: rooms for two, nicely furnished with double-glazed windows and hot water radiators. The rooms were in two-storey blocks and we were on the upper floor. The Sergeant's Mess was very comfortable too, and there was a bar, but no drinks to be taken out of the bar because of the local prohibition laws. I soon had the room organised with Peg's picture prominently displayed and dashed off a letter to let her know the new address.

The Instructors here were nearly all RAF; some had come from a G. R. School at Squires Gate near Blackpool. Most of the pupils were RAF, a few Canadians, and one or two from other parts of the Commonwealth. There were twenty-four of us: twelve pilots and twelve navigators, of which sixteen were pilot officers and eight were sergeants. The course was to last two months so now it looked as if I would be getting home about the end of February, if we were not snowed in.

This course was to be mainly ground work but there would be thirty to thirty-five hours practical navigation in Ansons but most of the flying would be done by staff pilots. The ground subjects sounded interesting; dead reckoning navigation, astro navigation, meteorology, signals (again), compasses, instruments, coding, reconnaissance, photography, ship recognition, and visual signalling. We were to get one and a half days off a week, but where can you go when the snow gets 112 inches deep?

St John and I were getting along fine together. We had fun purposely saluting Peter and Cyril whenever we met them, much to their embarrassment, but we soon found out we had a real 'character' of a station commander. One evening, we returned to our room to find the door had been removed; one or two other lads' doors were missing as well. We learned in the Mess that the group captain had been on a round of inspection and he must have found our door open because when he did, he got the chippie to take the door off. We knew not to worry; we would find it back on tomorrow, which we did. Apparently, on the same inspection, he saw a ladder against one of the blocks, so he veered off, leaving his retinue standing, climbed the ladder, paused at the top for a while, then came down, and carried on without saying a word. His wife was living on the station and sometimes, he would take her with him on his inspections so it was advisable only to have respectable pin-ups in your rooms.

The chief navigation instructor introduced himself to us as follows:

You can all navigate overland, or near the coast, where there are easy to recognise features, otherwise you would not be here. We are going to teach you to navigate over the sea, may be a very long way out to sea. You will learn to keep a continual log, regularly ascertain the wind speed and direction and to know your position at all times. You will be taught how to obtain fixes when you can—by Astro when you can see the stars and by radio bearings when you can. You will not rely on radio aids—remember they are only 'aids'. Those of you who are pilots will have to fly accurately, as well as navigate accurately, fly accurate courses at constant airspeeds. You will learn to read the weather, so that you will anticipate changes in wind speed and direction. From now on it is no longer Left and Right, but port and starboard, not miles per hour but knots, not statute miles but nautical miles. That's to make life easier because a nautical mile is one minute of latitude on your chart and a knot is one nautical mile per hour—but don't let me ever catch anybody referring to knots per hour. Any questions?

'Bloody hell,' we thought, 'where are we going to find any sea round here? It's all bloody ice.'

By Christmas, I had done four practical navigation exercises. I had been teamed-up with a pilot officer navigator by the name of Williams. A staff pilot flew while we both sat at navigation tables in the back and kept passing the pilot notes as to the course to steer and other bits of information, which he carefully put on a clipboard. These flights were all over the Gulf, which was a solid sheet of ice as far as the eye could see. We had 'landfalls' in various parts of the Magdalen Islands, about 100 miles from Charlottetown—a long narrow strip of six or seven islands that appeared to be uninhabited. In two places, they rose to about 500 feet, but it was impossible to see any definitive coastline as the white landscape just rose in a sort of bump; there were hardly any trees but we did spot the ruins of what looked to have been a church. The chart showed some marine lights but these were not working as there was no shipping at that time of year. I could never make out whose chit the pilot took notice of because I did notice that our two chits often differed considerably; in fact, on one occasion, the navigator forgot to apply variation and as it was 27 degrees west, it made a lot of difference. We took drift readings but as we were over ice, we did not use smoke or flame floats; we dropped canisters containing dye, which made a big coloured smudge on the ice. It was damn cold—sometimes 10 degrees F—and if you got too near the window, your breath just froze on the Perspex, so you had to scrape it off with your Douglas protractor, a piece of square celluloid. Fortunately, we had now been issued with Irvin jackets—sheepskin leather jackets with a nice big collar. We could also change our flying boots, if we wished, for a pair of fur-lined suede with a zip up the front, but I preferred to hang onto my leather and canvas ones as I had heard that the loose suede ones shot off your feet if you had to bale out; this may be an advantage if you were over the sea but damned inconvenient if you were overland.

On Christmas Eve, the others decided to go into town. It was 3 miles. The road had been kept clear with snow ploughs and transport picked us up at the Mess. The scene in Charlottetown was out of this world. The little square was decked in coloured lights. Folks were coming in on sleighs pulled by little ponies, which had colourful rugs on their backs. The folks kept warm under brightly coloured blankets. Everywhere was covered with white Christmas snow, which was so dry that it did not wet you; it just shook off like cotton-wool. In one corner, a group were singing Country and Western-type songs to the accompaniment of two guitars. After a while, we went to the hotel, which was packed with people singing. One old chap, who was swaying a bit, came up to us to tell us where we would find a 'bootlegger', but we were not interested in that—we had heard what this methylated spirit coloured with boot polish could do to you.

Back in the square, everyone was now singing carols and some folk had lit torches. It was a remarkable scene—a truly white Christmas—and I began to feel very sentimental. At home, it would be about 4 a.m. on Christmas morning; Peggy would be in bed, unless she was fire watching or there was an air-raid alert. How I wished she could be in that square with me, away from the blackout. It did not seem fair that I should be enjoying this fairyland Christmas Eve. I was the one who should be where the war was, but for the last six months, I had been away from it all and having a good life. Gosh, I just wanted to put my arms around Peggy and I felt a tear starting to freeze in the corner of my eye, so I said to St John, 'let's go and get a coffee in that drug store'. I had to snap out of it. When we were back in our beds, I said to St John, 'Singe, are you awake?'

'Yes', he replied.

'Singe, you know that star we were singing about tonight—the Star of Bethlehem—which star was it? Because the light from the nearest star takes sixteen years to get here, so if it did shine extra bright that night, it must have all been arranged at least sixteen years previously.'

St John replied, 'get to sleep; you're getting too involved with the Astro'.

Christmas Day was a good day in the Mess, bright and sunny outside too: a real day for the sunglasses and earmuffs.

Back in class, we were now spending a lot of time on map and chart projections. All projections seemed to have drawbacks of one sort or another because it was impossible to portray the surface of a sphere on a flat sheet without distorting it in some way. On the Mercator chart, which was the standard plotting chart for navigation, the lines of longitude were shown as parallel instead of converging to a point at the Pole; therefore, the east-west scale increased as you moved towards the Pole so, to keep the north-south scale in step, the parallels of latitude were spaced progressively wider apart as you moved towards the pole. This type of chart was obviously useless in the Polar regions. A straight line on this chart represented a rhumb line, which was a constant track, but it does not represent a straight line on the Earth's surface, therefore it is not the shortest distance between two points. The shortest distance, known as the Great Circle, would be a curve on the Mercator Chart, arching up on the Pole side of the rhumb line. That is where the Gnomonic chart comes in. On this chart, the reverse applies. The Great Circle is shown as a straight line, the rhumb line being a curved line on the opposite side of the Great Circle but, the Gnomonic Chart cannot be used for plotting. So, for a long trip, where you wished to follow the Great Circle route (because it is the shortest), you would first draw a Great Circle track on the Gnomonic Chart as a straight line, then pick off the latitude and longitude of a series of points along this track, transfer these to the Mercator Chart, and join them up to give a series of short rhumb lines approximating the Great Circle route. The Gnomonic was also useful for plotting bearings from distant radio beacons, as radio waves travel in straight lines (i.e. along the

Great Circle); consequently, if the bearing was plotted on a Mercator, there could be considerable error unless a special 'half convergency correction table' is used. The limited use of other projections (Conic, Pollyconic, Azimuthal, and Bonne's) was also considered.

The navigation moved on to the plotting of various search patterns: creeping line ahead, square searches, rectangular searches, and sector searches, all based on both fixed and moving datum points, taking into account the visibility, height being flown, size, and maximum speed of the object of the search. This was when it became very clear that there must be a lot of cooperation between pilot and navigator and for each to know exactly what the other was doing if searches were to be done accurately and thoroughly. It was becoming evident that our training was leading up to fairly long-range Coastal Command work.

Meantime, the practical work continued, when the weather allowed. By now, there were banks of snow on both sides of the runways where the snow ploughs had blown the snow. It was fascinating to watch the big snow ploughs at work—a big rotating fan blew the snow feet up into the air to land well clear of the runway. If the sun was shining, there would be dozens of rainbows in the blowing snow. The banks of snow were now high enough to hide any aircraft on the runway and as they landed, they just seem to disappear in the snow. Most of the aircraft now had skis fitted on the undercarriage. There was a slot in all the skis through which just a little of the tyre protruded to give a bit of braking. I persuaded one of the staff pilots to let me land a couple of times on the skis; it was just like landing on wheels, the back of the skis touchdown first, then there was a bit of a 'clap' as the front came down. The oddest feeling was seeing the banks of snow on either side, like being in a railway cutting.

We had four trips at night so that we could practice our Astro. I was absolutely bewitched with Astro. On a clear night, I would gaze up at the stars—they say you can see 2,500 with the naked eye—and pick out the ones we were to use for navigation. They were mostly bright ones, spaced around the sky so that you could get three position lines, which would cut each other at suitable angles to give a nice 'cocked hat' on the chart (a little triangle around your actual position). Looking up at the sky, it would appear as if all the stars were painted on a flat black disc, slowly rotating round a point near to Polaris. It was almost impossible to comprehend that they were all different distances away; the nearest one, Altair, was so far away that it took the light sixteen years to get here, Rigel (in the top left corner of Orion) so far that it took 900 years for the light to reach us, and Deneb (at the top of the cross of Cygnus) so far away that the light has been on its way 1,500 years before it reaches us. In fact, those stars are not where they seem to be at all, we are seeing where they used to be 16, 900, 1,500 years ago respectively. So, Deneb may have 'gone-out' 1,000 years ago and we would not know for another 500 years. The distances and time are so vast that it makes you feel so insignificant. Then, to think of the size of some of them (Betelgeuse for instance) at the bottom right of Orion is supposed to be so big that if its centre was in the same position as the centre of our Sun, its circumference would extend to the orbit of Mars. Then, the thought goes through your head that if all the stars are suns, surely they must have some planets whizzing around them on which there is some sort of life because surely nobody would have created all these suns just so that we can look up on a clear night and admire the stars. Back to Earth, it seemed hardly credible that you could take a reading on where a star was maybe 900 years ago and from this, establish your position as being somewhere along the line on the surface of the Earth. Also, although the light may have been 900 years getting here—so that star is far enough away from that spot by now—you must note the time the sextant reading was taken to the minute before referring to *The Air Almanac* to work things out. How in the world the boffins worked out all those day by day tables for the Air Almanac I will never understand, especially when it is all based on the point in space that does not exist: the first point of Aries. Looking up at the stars never ceased to make me marvel; none of those stars were now where they looked to be and they never have been in those positions in relation to each other because the light has taken such vastly different lengths of time to get here; it's all a big optical illusion and yet, with the aid of a sextant, an Air Almanac, an accurate watch, you can tell where you are on the surface of our little planet.

On clear nights, St John and I would go outside with a bubble sextant and take star shots, and then retire to our room to work them out. At first, we often used to get one position line that was obviously miles out; this was usually because we had shot the wrong star or made a cock-up reading the tables, but we gradually got better. It was easy on the ground but in the air, you cannot stand still while you take three shots of different stars so you have to transpose two of the position lines along your track to allow for the distance you have travelled between shots, which makes it a bit of a longer job. Also, in the air, the bubble in the sextant tended to wobble about a bit if the ride was a bit bumpy and the astrodome usually seemed to be in a position so that you had to be a contortionist to see through it properly; also, shots must only be taken with the sextant in the middle of the astrodome, otherwise you got refraction, which would upset the reading.

Cyril, Peter, St John, and I were all thoroughly enjoying the course. Often, Cyril and Peter would come over to our room in the evening; sometimes, one of us would get a bottle of Rye from our Mess. We would talk about letters from home; Peter's parents were in touch with mine so we got quite a lot of cross information. Cyril had had a letter from Harry Guest at Brantford, who said his present lot of pupils were a shower of big-headed sons of bitches with no chance of them getting on a G.R. course. He wanted to hear from us so we all wrote a bit and sent him a combined letter. Peter and Cyril were rather shocked at the amount of their Mess bills and uniform. We worked out that, with our smaller Mess bills, we were better off than they were. We all got orderly duties; ours came around more frequently than theirs because there were more officers on the station than sergeants, but they seemed to have more to do as orderly officer then we did as orderly sergeants; we told them that this was all part of their officer training.

We awoke one morning to find we could not get out of our building. It had been snowing hard during the night and the wind must have swung right around because it had piled up above the door at both ends of the building. As it was Sunday, nobody was in any hurry to dig us out and we could not shift the door at all as they opened outwards. Anyway, there was no bother over getting a late breakfast in the Mess. By noon, it was a beautiful day—clear sky and sun shining—so we went for a short walk, though not far as it was too heavy going in the deep snow. We did not feel the cold at all, so we did not even wear our greatcoats. In one place, I went down into a deep snow drift and it was a hell of a job to get out. St John came to help me; he sunk in too. The snow was so dry and powdery that you could just push it out of the way; it did not even wet your clothes, but it made you think how nasty it could be to get stuck in a big one. We spent most of the evening asking each other questions about meteorology and compasses and instruments, as some of the end of course exams were due to start the next week.

Soon, almost every day, the sheet appeared on the course noticeboard, giving the results of one or more final examinations. The first to appear was 'compasses and instruments'. To my amazement, I was top of the list with 93 per cent. Peter was eighth, St John ninth, and Cyril twelfth. Nearly all the top half of the list were pilots and the navigator who had flown with me was bottom with a cross against his name, denoting 'to be re-examined'. The lists kept appearing: I came second in reconnaissance; fourth in astro; sixth in ships; first in signals; second in coding; equal ninth in photography; second in meteorology; and first in visual signalling. I could not believe it.

Then, quite late one evening, there was a bang on our room door and in came Peter and Cyril with a bottle of sparkling wine. Peter says, 'You old bugger Jack, you've come out top of the course. The lists have just gone up in our Mess. You're top, another sergeant pilot—Hakala—second, then me, Cyril, and St John. We've shown those navigators how to navigate. Where are the glasses?'

We soon polished off the bottle of wine and discussed how long it could be before we got home. We had heard that since the middle of January, U-boats had been operating almost right up to the coast from the entrance to the Gulf of St Lawrence down as far as Cape Hatteras, south of New York, and had sunk over a dozen ships, so we hoped something would be done about that before we set off for home; in fact, Peter suggested it would be safer to fly. We also knew that the Japs were on the move, having landed in Malaya, sunk the *Repulse* and the *Prince of Wales*, and taken Hong Kong, but we were unlikely to come across them yet. Anyway, it seemed as if we should be getting home and doing something towards the war effort. 'Who's going to write to Harry and let him know the results? It will make his day.'

Well, we were not to return home yet. Ten of us——five pilots and five navigators—were told we were going to stay in Canada for our operational training on Hudsons at Debert, near Truro in Nova Scotia. One of the Canadians was going right across to Vancouver for flying-boat training and that the remainder, except for three who were to stay behind for re-examination, were to go to the UK to complete their training. The five pilots for Debert were the four of us from Brantford, plus Hakala. Now, Debert was only about 75 miles from Charlottetown as the crow flies (or should we say, on the Great Circle) and it would only have taken about forty minutes to fly us over in the Ansons, but we had to go by train, icebreaker, and two more trains.

It took us ten hours to get to Amherst, where we had to wait three hours to pick up the main line, Montreal to Halifax, for a two-and-a-half-hour journey to Truro, totalling nearly sixteen hours. Transport was waiting for us and as we drove the four or five miles out to the airfield, all we could see was snow and trees, thousands of them, fir and spruce trees; we seemed to be in the middle of a ruddy great forest.

11

Slush, Mud, and Prangs

We were a cosmopolitan bunch. About half were RAF from the UK, the others Canadian, Australian, Norwegian, and a Pole. The Norwegians had escaped from Norway in a small boat, been picked up by our Navy, taken to Scotland, and continued their training with the RAF; they were already in the Norwegian Air Force. They had no idea what may have happened to their families. The instructors were RAF. Most of them had completed a tour of operations and were on this job for a 'rest'. They had all been on Hudsons, some operating from the UK and some from Iceland. There was a fair sprinkling of DFCs among them. We pupils were pilots, observers (they rightly preferred their proper title, instead of navigator) and wireless operator/air gunners.

Whoever thought of building an airfield here, God knows. We were about 50 miles from the coast of Nova Scotia, near the tip of one of the forks at the head of the Bay of Fundy and surrounded by thousands, nay, millions, of fir trees. The airfield was merely a clearing in the forest with a strip about 1 mile wide and 3 miles long, trees felled and cleared at the end of each runway. There was just one road out, leading to Truro, which was 4 or 5 miles away. It had only been open a few months. Everywhere was covered in snow except for the black-looking trees, which extended as far as the eye could see.

We could look forward to twelve weeks in this place, the first half to be spent learning to fly the Hudson, understanding its equipment and systems, and learning how they work. The second six weeks would be taken up flying as a crew so that when we left here, we would be ready to go straight on operations. So, we all started calculating, thinking we should be back in the UK sometime in May; however, some of the instructors said they were operating from Iceland and it was just our luck to get sent there. The idea of two pilots taking it in turns to navigate seemed to have been 'kicked into touch' as we were to be crewed up with an observer and wireless operator/air gunner.

The Hudson looked rather splendid. A big bulbous, all metal, fuselage, with twin fins, four long pairs of runners on the trailing edge of each wing to carry the big 'Fowler' flaps, and two 1,200 horse power Pratt & Whitney Twin Wasp radial engines. The wingspan was only 9 feet more than the Anson, but it could manage about three and a half times the power. The loaded weight of 20,500 lb (over 9 tons) was two and a half times that of the Anson and she was about 60 knots faster. The instructors had warned us that the Hudson had a reputation of being 'a bit of a bastard' because the high wing loading meant she had a vicious stall, some nasty characteristics at slow speeds, and she would also ground-loop if you did not watch it, but that, if you treated her with respect, you would soon get to like her.

Inside, everything was neatly laid out, as might be expected in an aircraft, which was really a military development of the Lockheed Model 14 Super Electra airliner, but, what a hell of a lot of tackle. We recognised the standard instrument flying panel (just like it was in the Anson) but by the side of it was the automatic pilot control panel plus a mass of gauges (boost, revs, fuel-flow, fuel, oil pressure, oil temperature, cylinder head temperatures, hydraulic pressure, oxygen pressure and lots more), loads of levers (throttles, pitch, flaps, undercarriage, bomb doors, mixture, trimming tabs, fuel levers, and de-icers), buttons (for feathering the props, fire extinguishers, and bomb release), clusters of warning lights, and rows of switches. Above and behind your head were knobs and dials for radio equipment, although the main radio equipment was at the wireless operator's position on the port side just behind the pilot. Some of the flying instruments were duplicated in the nose for the observer.

Once again, Peter and I had the same instructor—Flying Officer Rees. It was several days before we flew. The three of us spent a lot of time in an aircraft going through the cockpit layout and cockpit checks, which we had to learn by heart, learning the fuel, oil, and electrical systems, flap mechanism and use, emergency systems, and correct airspeeds for take-off, cruising and landing. The instructor impressed on us that we must get used to viewing groups of gauges as a whole and not individually; just like when reading, you look at the word as a whole, you do not read each separate letter, but if one letter is wrong, it stands out and hits you, provided you can spell.

We were getting along quite well, learning what the various gauge readings should be, the airspeeds required, amount of flap, and readily finding the right lever but those ruddy switches—they were all so neatly arranged on the side of the box down by the pilot's right leg, but you could not look down and read what the little name above the switch said; what is more, in the dark, all you would see would be a row of luminous dots, so we had to learn the order off by heart and practice touching the right switch without looking. Peter and I used to sit in the aircraft many an evening, taking it in turn to sit in the pilot's seat while the other called out switches till we found we could touch them automatically. In the Anson, there were by no means as many switches but those that there were, were stuck in all different places so that there was no chance of mixing them up; however, here, there were so many more and all within an inch of each other—it looked neat but was not the safest arrangement.

On 24 February, the instructor decided it was time we took to the air. He took Peter and me up together and we took turns in the left-hand seat to get the feel of it. Then, over the next few days, when the weather allowed, because the weather was pretty bloody awful, we each did 'circuits and bumps'. On 8 March, the CO gives us a 'solo test' and up we go to do half an hour each of solo landings but they were not really solo because there always had to be someone else aboard in case you need to get at something that you cannot reach from the pilot's seat; it just meant that the instructor was not with us. For the next fortnight, it was 'circuits and bumps' and then more 'circuits and bumps' with a different pairing nearly every time, plus the odd flight with the instructor for single-engined landings, overshoots, instrument flying, automatic pilot practice, low-flying, and bombing. By 21 March, we were night flying; this time, I was teamed up with Cyril.

When we were not flying, it was 'synthetic' flying in the Link; standard beam approaches and yet more standard beam approaches, or perhaps lectures. Most of the lectures were now on engines, engine handling, and graphs showing combination of boost and revs at different aircraft weights for normal cruising, maximum endurance, and maximum range. There were other graphics linking these with airspeeds because flying for maximum endurance did not give the greatest range. We also started doing twenty-four-hour shifts as duty pilot, which meant running the control tower with the help of a duty airman.

I discovered that one of the fitters was a chap from York by the name of Collingbourne, who lived in Acomb and worked at the N. M. U. His folks sent him *The Yorkshire Evening Press*, which he passed on to me, but no newspapers made very happy reading: Singapore had fallen, Java had surrendered, the Japs had occupied Burma, U-boats were operating off the coast of Florida, heavy losses in the Atlantic, the Army had suffered defeat in the Western Desert, parts of the UK kept getting bombed, and we were bombing German towns.

St John and I went into Truro about twice a week on the bus. We would go to the picture house and then to a restaurant called the Belvedere, where we always had a good slap-up meal, but no drink, of course, not in Nova Scotia. One evening, they even had a trial blackout in Truro. We were in the Belvedere at the time. It only lasted half an hour. The manager brought out oil lamps and electric torches. Oddly enough, the film we had just seen was *Pacific Blackout*. Other films we saw in Truro were *Son of Fury*, *Babes on Broadway* with Mickey Rooney and Judy Garland, *Quiet Wedding*, *The Lady is Willing* with Marlene Dietrich, and *Sergeant York*. Some of these films were not at all suitable for a lad over 2,000 miles from home who wanted to get back and get married.

On 18 March, I received the first of Peggy's letters addressed to Debert. She did not seem too bothered about me staying on in Canada and sounded to be having quite a nice time with the other girls who worked at the Probate Registry, so that was great; I hoped it was only with the other girls. That same day, the thaw seemed to have started. The snow was melting and becoming a mucky slush, just like in England. The triangle between the runways was just a sea of reddish mud. There was a Hudson marooned in the mud; it had ground-looped off the runway and sunk in up to its axles. The road to Truro was all pot-holes filled with muddy water, the bus service was suspended so we took a taxi. The same day, the inspector general decided to visit us so there were parades and inspections and with the damp, it felt a damn sight colder than when it was colder but dry. For the next three or four weeks, it was just like a miserable English winter: more snow, then a thaw, everywhere wet and slushy, then some rain and low cloud; it was diabolical. It was certainly a good experience for us towards the end of our training. We could not really have timed our training better; those beautiful, cloudless, hot sunny days at Oshawa; then Brantford, which started nice but deteriorated a little towards the end; lovely dry snow at Charlottetown; and now this atrocious weather, with ice in every cloud, to wind up with. Pity Collingbourne and the other ground crew lads who had come from the UK and only been here in Nova Scotia where it was said that they had nine months winter and three months summer. You could hardly credit that we were on the same latitude as the middle of France. I thought, 'By Jove, I'll have something to tell the folks at home about and Dad will be ever so interested to hear about the Hudson—that it's more powerful than his tank'.

In the letters I got from home, I heard that several Canadians had been to stay with Mother and Father as a result of giving my address to folks I met through the Pearsons and I thought this was great; after all, the Pearsons did well for me and one of them had told Mother that Debert was a very desolate place. I was surprised to think that anyone had ever heard of it. I received a letter from Harry Guest telling me he has been made a flight sergeant so I wrote and told him he deserved it. He wanted to know how 'his boys' were getting on.

During these first few weeks, we had got to know the other lads quite well and we were chatting each other up thinking who we would like to have on our crew. It was not etiquette for us to ask anyone to fly with us, they should approach us and as it was not leap year, I felt like I imagine a girl feels when she wants someone to propose. However, there was no harm in dropping a few hints. I had my eye on a sergeant observer who had been with us at Charlottetown. He was no oil painting, rather well-built, nearly bald, had one tooth missing at the front, and a broad Cockney from Battersea. He came somewhere in the middle of the course at Charlottetown; in fact, he got rather bad marks for his log-keeping on the exercises but he had a very dry sense of humour, was a good darts player, and never seemed to let anything worry him. I thought, 'he'll do for me. Couldn't imagine anyone I'd rather be with if we got into a spot of bother'. So, I kept having a drink with him in the Mess and the odd game of darts, at which he always beat me and then, one night, he proposed. He said he did not want to fly with an officer so he asked if he could fly with me. We were having a drink when a Canadian WOP/AG joined us and asked if he could join the crew. So, that was that. I had my crew: 'Tug' Wilson and 'Goldie' Goldberg.

We now moved to another flight with different instructors and used mainly the aircraft that were not fitted up for dual control. We were now allowed to log our flying hours in the 'First Pilot' column of our Log Books; up to now, we had to show them as either 'Dual' or 'Second Pilot'. We start flying as a crew, the first exercise being low level bombing (observer release) and Tug seemed to be making a lot of smoke over the target, so that was okay. Later in the day, we went up so that Tug could take some photographs—handheld obliques—and I could practice some 'vertical line overlaps' with Tug's co-operation. Then, we did some navigation exercises, some up to about five hours, and Tug seemed to be spot-on all the time, so I thought, 'I've got a good 'un here', but he was always getting told off when we got back for not having enough in his log. As well as flying with the crew by day, I also had night 'circuits and bumps' with one of the other pilots, usually sessions of one and a half hours each, but sometimes, our turn did not start until midnight or later. There were also late afternoon air tests to be done before an aircraft was used for night-flying. My instructor flew with me now and again to demonstrate low level bombing (pilots release), dive bombing, and more single-engined landings; he always brought his dog with him: a Fox Terrier called Prune (after Flying Officer Prune), which went up on the bunk in the back and went to sleep. I seemed to always find Fox Terriers: Jeff, Nanky-Poo, and now Prune.

On 9 April, it was a lovely, clear, bright, sunny day—such a change from all the rubbish we had been having. We were flying back up the Bay of Fundy on an exercise that had taken us down off the coast of Maine. We were on auto-pilot, I was looking down at the small port of St John on the port side and thinking, 'These are bloody grand aircraft, now I've got you licked,' when a red light started to flicker indicating low fuel pressure on the port side. I checked the fuel cocks, they were okay, and the fuel gauges, they were okay, but the boost gauge went to zero and the port engine faded away. I took the auto-pilot out, increased boost and revs on the good engine and re-trimmed the aircraft as we had been told to do. I swapped over tanks and try to get the engine going again without success, so I feathered the prop and Tug came up on the intercom.

'What have you feathered the prop for?'

'Because the bloody engine has stopped,' I reply, 'better give me a course straight back to Debert.' Tug soon came up with a course for the 110 miles back to Debert; there was nowhere near to land anyway as Halifax was about the same distance and we did not know what the approach was like. I told the WOP to send a message to base telling them that we were 20 miles south-east of St John, returning direct on one engine, and would contact them when in voice range. Tug could not care a toss. I was thinking that we would cause a bit of a stir when we came in on one engine, that I had better nurse the good one and not let it overheat or over rev, but it seemed to settle down nicely. The hydraulics were okay as they came off the good engine and there was a generator on the good engine too. It could be trimmed to take the pressure off the stick and I was soon able to re-engage the auto-pilot. I studied the fuel position and decided to open the cross feed so that the good engine could get fuel from both sides. There was nothing else to do but just remind myself of the single-engined landing procedure: come in a bit high, do not let the speed drop, leave undercarriage a bit later than usual, off with the trim as you throttle back, then bags of rudder to stop it ground-looping. I could only hope the other bugger kept going; I never did fancy single-engined aircraft.

When we got within voice range, the flight commander was on the R/T, asking, 'have I tried this, have I tried that, what is this reading, what is that reading, what fuel system have I got on?' He seemed satisfied that everything was under control.

I gave him an estimated time of arrival and ask what the weather was like and the runway was in use. The weather was okay and he asked if I wanted to do a circuit before landing. I said 'No. I'll come straight in'. He then reminded me about coming in high, watching my SP, leaving the undercarriage until I was sure I was getting in, taking the power off gently and the trim. The airfield comes into view so I altered course, against the good engine doing almost a 270-degree turn to line up with the runway; out of the corner of my eye, I saw the other fuel pressure warning light beginning to flicker.

By now, Tug is nonchalantly sitting beside me on the canvas seat, which is his position for landing and I thought, 'All those bloody trees.' Fortunately, we had just got to the beginning of the clearing at the lead-in to the runway when the starboard engine faded out. Now, the Hudson glided like a brick, so the only thing to do was to put the nose down to stop it stalling, dive down, and do a crash landing. I just had time to press the R/T button on the stick and say 'Other engine gone. Putting her down', then level out. There was a thunderous noise of tearing metal and breaking Perspex. Tug shot down into the nose like a bullet from a gun and the next second he was flashing past me in the other direction towards the tail. I flipped all the switches off and followed him, quick as I could—the WOP had already gone, the door was open, and I jumped out. It seemed to take ages to hit the ground as the tail was cocked up in the air about 12 feet. Tug was waiting on the ground and we both said simultaneously, 'Better run like buggery, before she blows up'. It was a bugger running as it was muddy; the WOP was well ahead of us. When we got to a safe distance, we stopped and expected her to catch fire as the Hudson had a terrible reputation for catching fire, but she did not. Tug asked if I had a match. I said, 'you're not going back to set light to it.'

'No, you silly sod,' he said, 'I want a bloody fag'. Well, we decided to wait where we were rather than walk about in the mud or try to climb back in the aircraft to get our things out. In due course, the flight commander arrived in a truck, followed by an ambulance; he seemed surprised and relieved to see we were okay. He said he was watching us come in with binoculars and saw the other engine pack up. At that instant, he was sure we would bury it and expected to see a column of smoke any minute. When he was satisfied we were okay, he took the truck up to the aircraft from which we could climb back in. He had a good look around as we collected our gear. Some ground staff arrived to look after it and we set off in the truck. The flight commander said they would get some accident investigator to strip it down to try to find what caused the engine to cut. It was only later that we realised how lucky we had been—if that engine had cut thirty seconds earlier, we would have been over trees; if thirty seconds later, I would have had the undercarriage down, so it would have gone up through the fuel tanks and caused a fire without any shadow of a doubt. We thought that if that sort of luck holds out, we were going to be okay and we had lots of confidence in ourselves after that.

Shortly after we got back and had all had a cup of tea with the flight commander, he said, 'there's an aircraft wanting a flight test before night flying. Do you fancy taking it?' I took it on a couple of circuits; Tug and Goldie asked if they could come with me. I thought that was great. As we came in each time, we looked down at our crash and Tug remarked that we only had just missed those trees. I remarked, 'Good job your course was spot on, otherwise we would have been in them'. There was a lot of talk in the Mess that night about being the first Hudson on the station to crash without catching fire and cracks about 'no engine' landings. Three days later, all the aircraft were grounded for checks on the fuel system; it transpired that the investigation team had found some foreign matter in the fuel that had clogged the filters. The CO said it was a lucky thing that it did not catch fire, otherwise they would never have found the cause; maybe, if I had not used the cross feed, the second engine would have kept going, but the CO did not seem to think so.

There was no flying for a few days but it did not matter as the weather was so awful; the snow seemed to be coming back but it was the English kind—wet and mucky. Then, the flight commander told me they were a bit concerned about my observer as his logs were so sketchy—only about a quarter of the length of the other observers, winds shown without any indication how he arrived at them, and Astro fixes appearing out of the blue. He seemed to infer that we were cooking things up, perhaps cheating by using radio and then making things fit. I assured him we were not clever enough to do that; in any case, we would be only heading for eventual trouble if we did, but that I too had noticed his brief logs and wondered how he did it. I suggested that he, or one of the instructors, should come with us on our next night navigation exercise to check up; he said he intended to do this anyway.

The flight commander came with us on our next night exercise—a trip lasting four and a half hours down to Grand Falls in the States, up to Campbelltown, and back to Debert. It was a bit of a bugger of a trip; we were sometimes above cloud, sometime below cloud. Also, there was a fair bit of icing in the clouds so we had to keep shining the Aldis lamp along the wings to see if there was ice on the leading edge; we would let it build up a bit, and then operate the 'de-icing boots' to crack it off, keep giving the props a squirt of alcohol to keep the ice off the tips. For long periods, poor old Tug could not see a thing: neither stars, nor the ground.

We just carried on as normal. The flight commander and I took turns at the controls, which was mainly watching the auto-pilot. Tug kept giving us instructions, some of which, in Tug's usual way, were 'alter course to ... I'll check it in a minute'. He would come back shortly and say, 'that course I gave you is okay, stick on it'. Then, 'At ... hours, alter course to ...'.

I would say, 'Tug, I'm going up a couple of thousand feet to 10,000 feet to try and get out of this cloud, starting now, I'll let you know when we're settled'.

His reply would be, 'okay when you get there, alter a couple of degrees to port on to ... If we broke cloud, in case he wasn't looking out, I would tell him and perhaps say, 'you can get some good shots on some stars if you want them'.

To this, he would probably grunt and say 'okay'. The flight commander was certainly seeing Tug at work. When we got settled on the long leg to Campbellton, Tug came up and joined us for a coffee from the flask and had some sandwiches, had a pee in the back, and then announced the wind had changed so he should go down and give as a new course; how the bloody hell he knew I do not know but in a few minutes, he gave us a new course. Shortly afterwards, I decided to come down to 5,000 feet, as from what I could see of the cloud, I thought we would be better down there. He gave me an alteration of course and we could begin to see odd lights on the ground. We should have seen some lights at Campbellton but if we were above cloud when we got there, I decided we should carry on over the Gulf and let down over the water before turning back to the Debert. However, we saw the lights of Campbellton approaching, slightly on the port bow, but they stayed in that position, so that meant we were okay; if we stuck on this course, we would drift right over them, and we did, dead on ETA. When we got back, the flight commander collected Tug's log and as he looked at it, he said to me, 'I don't believe it'.

I said, 'I'd go anywhere with him. His mother must've been a pigeon'.

We were now in the middle of April. We seemed to have seen the last of the snow but still got a lot of rain and low cloud. We did some navigation exercises at maximum height, about 22,000 feet, to get used to using oxygen and keeping the aircraft in the correct attitude because, as you approach maximum height, the aircraft is in the climbing attitude with the tail down; when you cannot climb any more, you do not want to be 'mushing' along at this attitude causing unnecessary drag, so you have to get tail up and do a shallow glide, then level out keeping to tail up. It was quite a job, like trying to keep balanced on the tip of a pin. At the other extreme, we had low-level exercises, then exercises on search patterns over the sea.

As there had been U-boat activity off the coast, it was decided that we may as well do some of these exercises where there was some shipping so, before starting the exercise, we would fly over to Dartmouth, the airfield at Halifax, for briefing. These exercises meant that Tug really had to work—and so did I, for that matter—but they seemed satisfied when we returned for debriefing. Calamity struck again on one trip, however. As we were taking off at Dartmouth for the thirty-five-minute hop back to Debert, there was a hell of a thumping on the starboard side just as we were lifting off. I was about to move my hand to the undercarriage lever to retract the landing gear but as I applied the brakes to stop the wheels spinning, the thumping stopped, so I hesitated and thought, 'there must be something wrong with the undercarriage so I'd better not retract it, in case it jams up.'

I could not see the wheel from my side but Tug could and said, 'there's a bloody great strip of rubber hanging off the tyre'. I flew close to the Control Tower so that they could have a good look. They told me to stay up and another aircraft would formate with me to have a closer look. I was 'holding' in the figure of eight pattern for nearly an hour, then another Hudson appeared and formatted on me—it was the chief flying instructor from Debert.

He told me that the tread had shred itself from the tyre so, 'you know what to do. Try to keep the weight off that tyre as long as you can, don't brake too hard and be ready for her 'ground-looping'. I asked whether we should go back to Debert but he thought it better to land here so he went in first and I followed a few minutes later. Fortunately, we were fairly light, so I came in a little slower than usual. We touched down OK. For a few instances, there was this thumping, then it stopped. I had to apply a little brake, otherwise we would be off the end of the runway, then, off she started. I banged the starboard engine full open, putting the wheel hard over to port, hoping this would lift the starboard wing up a bit, full port rudder, and brake.

We came to a halt, miraculously still on concrete. There were two runways, intercepting about two-thirds of the way along the runway on which I had landed. I had shot down the other runway. The tyre had blown but the undercarriage had not collapsed. We left the aircraft at Dartmouth for the undercarriage to be checked and the tyres changed and flew back with the C.F.J. I thought, 'what else is going to happen in these Hudsons. First the fuel packs up and then a tyre goes.' However, strangely enough, I had got to like them and thought I had 'got them beaten', even if it was with the help of a large chunk of luck.

A day or two later, we had the unhappy experience of attending the funeral of two pilots who had recently arrived on the next course. They were flying together and had come down in the trees shortly after take-off. The aircraft just blew up and caught fire; the black smoke was seen from the airfield.

We all seemed to be feeling a bit depressed for some reason, but Tug went around whistling 'the shrine of St Cecilia'. The newspapers surprisingly mentioned the names of actual towns bombed—Bath and Norwich—instead of just referring vaguely to areas. The weather was still cold and wet. The novelty of the Link was wearing off—we were getting fed up with those dots and dashes on the SBA approach—and all wishing we could get back to the UK or wherever we came from. We had heard a rumour that some of us may go up to Goose Bay in Labrador for operations and we felt sorry for the Norwegians and the Pole, whose homelands were occupied.

Then, on 1 May, four of us—Tug, St John, his observer, and I—went down to the Belvedere for a meal and picked up the morning paper. A big banner heading about three inches high said, 'YORK BOMBED', and underneath 'Hundreds of casualties: 10,000 homes destroyed or damaged'. I immediately knew that my father had been killed, he must have been, he would be out in his ARP duty (air-raid patrol) and knowing Dad. he would have been out with his tin-hat on, pulling folks out of houses, but what about Mother and Peggy? The paper said the raid was in the early hours of 29 April, so Mum would have been in the shelter in the garden with Jeff, but what would Peggy be doing? I hoped to God she was not fire watching; if she was at home, at Heather's, pray God she got downstairs into the Morrison shelter.

Strangely, I felt no animosity against the Germans. We had started this bombing of cities so it was obvious that they would retaliate. I thought, 'what a bugger for Dad, going through the First World War and then getting killed on his own doorstep'. I was quite certain he was dead and thought back to when he and Peg saw me off at York station, standing there in his Mac and trilby hat. The next morning, I saw Peter. He had also heard the news, as had Collingbourne, and we promised to let each other know if we received any news. Letters were taking three to four weeks, but maybe we would get a cable; yet over there, they would not know that we knew that York had been bombed.

On 6 May, most of us were going up for formation practice. This did not involve the observers, so three pilots were going up in each aircraft to do an hour's flying each and swapped over in the air. I was flying with two Norwegians—Quartermasters Rasmussen and Myran—and while we were getting our gear on in the crew-room, Peter came over and said, 'you didn't tell me about your Dad, Jack. I am sorry'.

I replied, 'I didn't know for sure till now, you mean he was killed in the air raid'. Peter felt most embarrassed but I reassured him that somehow, I already knew, but I was pleased to know for certain. He had received a cable from his father that morning, his family were okay and as he did not mention my mother or Peggy, I felt relieved to think they must be okay. I pushed off with the Norwegians to the aircraft and just as we were about to start off, the Tower told us to wait for an instructor. The instructor with the little dog came out; he and Prune got in and he told me that the flight commander had sent him out as Peter had just told the flight commander about my father and if I did not want to fly, it was okay. I told him that I would rather fly; in any case, what are these Norwegians going to think if I do not, when they do not know what has happened to any of their families?

He replied, 'Okay. Mind if Prune and I come along for the ride?' When I was not flying, I was playing around with Prune on the bed in the back and giving him biscuits; he was just like Jeff.

Nearing the end of the course, when training on the link, some of us were doing synthetic trans-Atlantic flights using the radio beacon and range at Lough Erne in Ireland and the Prestwick and Valley radio ranges, making us think that we were going to find our own way home but not in Hudsons with only 6.9 hours endurance. Shortly, all was revealed. Six crews—including Peter, Cyril, St John, and I—were going to Montreal and Ferry Command.

12

York, after the 'Baedeker' Raid

[After that eventful first Hudson crossing from Gander to Prestwick on 3–4 June 1942, Jack sought leave to see Peggy and comfort his mother following the death of his father. He asked for fourteen days but was granted seven.]

As the train steamed into York station, I could see the blue sky of a June evening through the twisted iron work of the station roof; I supposed it must have been glass before, but with it having been covered in salt and grime, I had never noticed what it was—piles of rubble and twisted iron work neatly pushed out of the way and a canteen doing a roaring trade in 'tea and wads'. There was no Father or Peggy on the platform this time, just the smell of steam and service people standing about and grimy looking coaches. Military police and RAF service police were everywhere, checking passes.

With my kit bag on my shoulder, I walked over Scarborough Bridge—that seemed okay—then up Queen Anne's Road, where there were a few damaged houses. Coming up towards Bootham, I noted that the pillar supporting the corner of the chemist's shop at the corner of Bootham Crescent and Bootham was still standing and thought, 'Father would have been pleased about that' because, when his firm were altering that building and he did the plans for a pillar supporting the corner of the building, some folks had said it would not be strong enough. The air raid had given it a good test.

Going down Bootham Crescent, I saw a tarpaulin over part of our roof and, getting nearer, I noticed that some of the leaded lights had been replaced by clear glass and other windows must have been replaced too as they had had brown paper strips stuck on them when I had left but they were not there now. The main structure looked okay though.

Mother seemed to be taking everything in her stride. She spoke about how she and Jeff (the dog) had gone into the shelter as soon as the siren went and very shortly after, bombs were falling, some of which sounded very close. The shelter was a small brick building with a thick concrete roof, which Father had built in the garden at the end of the brick garage and partly let down into the ground and fitted with a couple of bunks. The concrete roof of the garage was damaged but the shelter was okay. Father had been away on duty at the post at Bootham Grange, just opposite the top of Bootham Crescent. She told me that Father had been killed instantly, she believed by machine-gun fire (but this turned out to be incorrect), that she had not seen him as he was identified by Lesley (my cousin Mary's Father), and that he was cremated at Lawnswood near Leeds. She seemed more concerned over the fact that a Labrador dog belonging to Col. Innes Ware, the local coroner and in charge of the post at Bootham Grange, had turned completely white overnight as a result of the raid. As Mother seemed all right and she had a girl 'digging' with her, I went to see Peggy.

I could not make out whether people were pleased to see me or not. People seemed different, or maybe it was me. I had just returned from a year of 'the good life' in Canada, enjoying good food, seeing interesting places, no air raids or blackouts to bother about and become engrossed in flying, yet I had done nothing so far for the war effort, except deliver one Hudson. On the other hand, these people had grown used to two years and nine months of blackout, wailing sirens waking them at night, making the best of meagre rations, and doing nightly stints of fire watching, or at the civil defence post, after a hard day's work. Nevertheless, they seemed to be taking it in their stride and had their social lives organised—dances had started again, the cinemas had re-opened, and most folks were talking about how the vegetables were coming along in the plot they had made by digging up the lawn or a flower bed.

Mother assured me there was nothing I could do. The damage to the house was all being taken care of by Lesley and somebody else was dealing with the 'War Risks Claim' for the cost of repairs, so all I could do was some gardening, take Jeff for a walk, and put the car up on bricks to save the tyres as it may be a long time before we could use it again. Lesley informed me that cousin Mary had been commissioned in the Woman's Royal Auxiliary Air Force and that cousin Henry (the one I saw in Toronto) was hoping to join the Canadian Air Force in a few months' time, as soon as he would be old enough. The blackout was not much bother at this time of the year and I noticed that in the evening, it was Halifaxs flying out from Linton now, instead of old Whitleys.

I called at the D1 post in the basement round the back of Bootham Grange—where I had put in a bit of time before joining up and where Father was deputy in charge—to see whether there was still anyone there I knew. They all told me what a grand chap my father was, how he would tell them when he heard from me, and how pleased he was when I got my Wings. Col. Ware happened to be there. He told me that on the night of the raid, he did not get a 'purple' warning; the first he knew was when the sirens were going and incendiaries were falling at the same time. It was about 2.30 a.m. He got on his bike to come to the post. Part of St Peters School was burning and just as he arrived at the post, Father was setting out on patrol; he had already alerted the fire service. Almost straight away, a stick of high explosives straddled the road just by the bridge over the Scarborough railway line at the top of Grosvenor Terrace and Father was killed instantly by shrapnel. Eddie Moat (the grocers) said Father must have suffered a direct hit because no trace whatsoever was found of him. It was a moonlit night and with fires in Bootham Crescent, Burton Lane, and Queen Anne's Road, it seemed as light as day. The top of the Minster stood out, illuminated by fires all around. They had an unexploded bomb to deal with in Clifton (Peggy had told me about that); it was just near them and many people were trapped. I enquired about anti-aircraft defence and was told there was none—no anti-aircraft guns and no fighter aircraft until, after about ninety minutes, one Free Frenchman flying a Hurricane came from Elvington arrived and shot down one plane—they were Ju 88s and He 111s.

From the post, I crossed the road to call on Eddie Moat the grocer, hand in my week's ration card, and collect my rations. I did not need a very big bag to carry them: 4 oz bacon; 8 oz sugar; 2 oz tea; 2 oz butter; 6 oz marg.; 2 oz marmalade; and 1 oz cheese. There was also one egg to follow if I called tomorrow. That lot would have gone down in one meal in Canada but Mother seemed to make do somehow. Bread and potatoes seem to be plentiful and she had some tins of beans and 'spam' but whether or not they were rationed, I do not know. She took my card to the butcher's, which entitled me to one penny's worth of meat (about 8 oz) but one day, she was able to get some liver, as offal was not rationed but not available every day.

Walking around town one morning, prior to meeting Peggy at lunchtime, I noticed quite a lot of fire damage to the Art Gallery in Exhibitions Square in Davygate, New Street, and Coney Street. The Guildhall behind Coney Street was a write-off and St Martin's Church looked pretty bad, but the clock was still there, even if it had stopped. I remember that clock well—

on my driving test, just after we passed the clock, the examiner asked me what time it was by that clock; I am sure he wanted me to look back and then fail me. The warehouses on the riverside looked a bit knocked about too. Everywhere, there seemed to be sandbags and big open topped iron water tanks, labelled E. W. S. (emergency water supply).

I called in at my old office (the Yorkshire) but most of the familiar faces were missing, just the old men and a lot of young girls were left, the lucky old devils. I learned of two of my old pals who had been killed with the Yorkshire Hussars.

One afternoon, taking Jeff for a walk on the Ings, I sat, looking into the river, thinking. I thought there was something bloody peculiar about that raid. You cannot blame the Germans for bombing York. Churchill had made speeches, gloating about how we had destroyed and fired their ancient cities of Lübeck and Rostock and he threatened many more, so the Germans must retaliate to try and stop it. They had even given notice in broadcasts that they would select places mentioned in the *Baedeker Guide* and they had already been to Exeter and Bath so it did not need any special intelligence to know that York would be on the list. Also, they must have especially avoided the Minster because any idiot in an aeroplane could have hit the Minster if he wanted to on a moonlit night with the whole thing illuminated by fires. Also, it looked as if the railway station was the main target. This was a legitimate target—that stick of bombs that got my father was by a railway bridge and it looked to me as if most of the damage, even that in the city, was not all that far from the railway or the bridges so, it did not seem to me that the bombing had been all that indiscriminate. However, the peculiar thing to me was 'where were our ruddy night fighters?' Those damn big masts at Staxton were supposed to give warning of aircraft approaching but even if they did not, or we chose to ignore it, those aircraft were over York for damn nearly two hours and it was ninety minutes before one solitary Free Frenchman appeared in a Hurricane and shot one down. As he only came from Elvington, it looked as if he woke up and saw the glow over York, so took off on his own bat to do something about it. Where were these Beaufighter night fighters and Havocs I had heard about with radar equipment to pick up enemy aircraft? Have we really got any or are we just being kidded because even if they were miles away, they could have got here in two hours, if only to bring some down on the way home? At least this would have been less aircraft to come back and bomb somebody else another day. It all seemed very odd but none of the people I had met seemed to think anything about it; they just regarded it as part of the war.

My leave was nearly over. It was obvious that I was not going to get married on this trip; in fact, I began to wonder whether we ever would. I wanted to but something seemed to have changed. The only person who seemed the same was Peg's Uncle Tommy. He took me to the Conservative Club one night and we had a good night with his pals but what surprised me was the way that folk would come up and tell you little snippets about things they had heard—'They are bringing a new type of radar out, different wave-length to prevent jamming ... the Halifaxes at Linton are carrying some new navigation equipment, they tried it out the other day, accurate to a hundred yards'. This may or may be a lot of bullshit but I vowed there and then, not to tell anyone anything about what I was doing—maybe just the type of aircraft I was on, or roughly where I was, but no more.

Mother seemed perfectly all right when I left; she even told me off for not emptying the rubbish in the right bins, as she had one for tins, another for paper, and another for waste food for pigs. 'Got to help the war effort with the salvage', she said.

13

A Testing Time

Sixteen hours in the cold, draughty, noisy, windowless bomb bay of the North Atlantic Return Ferry Command Liberator is enough to put anyone, other than a complete fanatic, off flying for the rest of his life. 'What the hell are we doing here?' I thought, 'Have Tug and I missed our postings because I asked for that leave, or is it because we have no wireless operator?'

As we walked out to the Lib, which was to be flown by a British Overseas Airways crew, I had visions of sitting in a comfortable seat and enjoying the ride, even though one of the passengers, who had been before, told me to put all the clothes on I had with me, including helmet, gloves, and flying boots. As we clambered in, I saw no seats; there were a couple of wooden benches in the rear part and forward, in the bomb bay, a plywood floor littered with mattresses and rugs, and some green rolls called sleeping-bags. The wooden floor must have been a foot or so above the bottom of the aircraft in order to get the advantage of the full width; consequently, there was not enough headroom to stand upright, so you moved around in a semi erect posture, holding onto the vertical pillars that formed a double row running fore and aft, then grabbed yourself a mattress and a bit of floor space.

The captain wanted everybody in the bomb bay for take-off but said some could go to the rear half an hour after take-off, but he did not want too many in the rear together. It was bloody eerie in that bomb bay, hearing each engine start, listening to the run-up, listening whether each engine sounded right, then rocking about as we taxied, then another run-up as we taxied again. You could tell we were turning, then a pause, all engines run-up together now, then a rock. Full power was going on now; it would not be so bad for anyone who did not know what was actually happening up there. You could tell we were starting to roll and instinctively you start counting. The take-off run seemed to be endless so you kidded yourself that you had been counting too quickly, then you could feel you were airborne. You listened for a little thump as the wheels came up, but you did not hear it, then the engines noise decreased a little, so you knew he had come down to normal climbing revs and boost, so you could relax a bit.

All you could see was a bit of light through the opening in the front bulkhead at the top of which is the flight deck and the backs of the two crewmen sitting sideways, presumably flight engineer and wireless operator and, at the rear, through an opening in the rear bulkhead, another bit of light. Wind seemed to be blowing in from all directions and when I pulled my helmet off my ears to try to hear what Tug was trying to say, all I could hear was wind whistling and the drone of the engines, which sounded as if they were only inches away through the thin bomb bay walls. All communication became a matter of mime. I thought, 'I hope to God they can't open these bomb bay doors'.

Fortunately, we did not go very high. We knew that, usually, a westerly wind tended to increase with height, so that going west, the winds were usually more favourable at lower altitudes. After a while, the captain sent a chit down, which we passed around and read with the aid of a torch; it said he was planning on going at 5,000 feet direct to Dorval. Soon, it was completely dark, one or two had gone through to the rear, and we tried to get comfortable on the floor. I think, eventually, I did doze off, but we were so close together that you were constantly getting jostled or kicked and damn cold. You hardly dared move in case of putting your foot in someone's face; it was the longest day of my life, or rather the longest night. When, after an eternity, a bit of light appeared, bodies started moving about, trying to stretch in the confined space, going to the rear for a pee, and diving into a crate of sandwiches. Three or four were sitting on the wooden benches in the rear near a pile of sacks, which presumably carried mail—at least, at the rear, you could look out of some little side windows and could even see the sea as we were below cloud, a big black wing looked reassuring. A couple of fellows were invited onto the flight deck but they must have been senior chaps, not sprogs like us, but it was better than nothing. The coffee in the Thermos flasks has gone cold by now.

We crawled back into the bomb bay and tried to get warm under the rugs. Another chit came around and told us our ETA for Gander and Dorval and said we had climbed to 7,000 feet; there were another six hours to go. We made sure we realised what a difference a westerly wind made. There was continual stretching and going to the rear. You could see land through the little windows at the rear. We were going down the St Lawrence; it had been a very smooth trip but bloody uncomfortable.

We pile out at Dorval—tired, stiff, hungry, and miserable—but it was 80 degrees so we peeled off our flying gear and got some heat into our bones. We paid a quick visit to the admin building, where they checked us off and phoned the hotel. We then had a coffee in the airport cafeteria until the transport arrived. Then, we were off to the Mount Royal, into the bath, then down for a meal. That meal tasted good.

After a day's rest, I thought I had better get along to Dorval and see what is going on. It seemed to be packed with aircraft—Hudsons, Liberators, Venturas, one or two Mitchells, and a Fortress. I wondered around, looking at names on doors—such as 'field operations' and 'crew assignments'—and thought, 'That's where I want to be'. They told me it would be a few days before they had an aircraft for me so would fix me up with some flying in a day or two. When I asked how it came to be that I had come back whereas the other lads had gone to squadrons, all I got was that my instrument and range ratings were quite good so the boss would hang on to me as long as he could, but it probably would not be for long. I thought that sounded a bit odd as I was sure that Peter's ratings were as good, if not better, than mine. I felt sure it was due to getting that leave, they probably told Coastal they had given me fourteen days when in fact, they only gave me a week, to get one more trip out of me.

That night, I thought that, with one trip under my belt, I dared venture into the Piccadilly Bar on the ground floor of the Mount Royal, where the ferry crews congregated. Tug was eyeing some girls. I told him the only doll I was interested in at that moment was a paper one as everyone was humming a tune roundabout that time called 'Paper Doll': 'I'm going to get a Paper Doll that I can call my own, the Doll that other fellows cannot steal.' I was thinking about Peg and wondering really just how we had left things because I was damned if I knew, and I did not want to lose her.

I wondered whether to phone the Pearsons but decided not to. I had dropped them a line from the UK and thought it best to leave it at that. I would drop them a line from time to time.

I was told, 'Now you are back, we had better get you checked out for a full instrument and range ratings. You were okay on the checks in May but those were only "one tripper" standard.'

To get in a bit of practice, a Canadian flying officer and I got the use of a Hudson for four hours. Tug came with us and we spent the time flying up and down the Dorval and Ottawa ranges. We spent two hours each with one flying while the other looked out and worked the R/T. It was a lovely summer's day with hardly a cloud in the sky. Then, the next day came the tests.

This included take-off and landing, followed by an overshoot, then climbing to 5,000 feet and on with the hood so we could not see out. First of all, he would take the controls over and put the aircraft into some crazy position—like a steep turn, followed by a diving steep turn—and then just on the point of stall, each time saying, 'You've got her; put her back'.

Then, there was a bit of straightforward instrument flying, rate one turns, rate two turns coming out onto specific headings, then turns either losing or gaining height at a specific rate. He asked how I calculated the bank for a rate one turn; I replied, 'divide the airspeed by ten and add five', but got no answer. I was just thinking that this was going okay when he slapped a disc over the directional gyro, in the middle of the bottom row of the instrument flying panel, and said, 'keep her straight and level without that ... Now turn 45 degrees to port ... Now 315 degrees to port.' I counted off another 105 and straightened out. He uncovered the gyro; I was 6 degrees out. He says nothing, I say nothing, but slide gently 6 degrees to starboard to put us back on the original course.

'Now we'll find Dorval Range. I'll tune it in for you'. Clear 'N's came through my earphones, then the identification call-sign. 'That's not Dorval', I tell him, 'you want 248 K/cs.' I got no answer, but he re-tuned, still getting 'N's, but this time the identity was 'UL', the crafty so-and-so. I realised I must not take for granted anything he said. The 'N' meant we were in either the north-west or south-east segments. I figured that we were most likely to be in the north-west from the courses we had been flying, although we had been turning about all over the place. He told me that Dorval was reading 160 degrees relative on the loop, but did I believe him? That meant we were flying away. I applied that 160 relative to our actual heading, so that would check we were in the north-west sector.

'Which leg do you want me to find? The 169 or 100?'

'The 169'. I turned starboard onto 079 to hit the beam, counting as we went through it for sixty-two seconds, and then volunteered the information that we are about 40 miles from Dorval to no answer. I went through the usual bracketing procedure and got settled on the right-hand edge of the beam. Now for his next diabolical trick: 'Imagine your pitot head (measures aircraft velocity) is frozen-up and you have lost your pressure instruments', whereupon he puts discs over the airspeed indicator, the altimeter, and the rate of climb indicator; yet there were not just blank discs, but were discs that had faces like the real instruments with daft readings on them. Trying not to be distracted by the phoney discs, I concentrated on the 'little aeroplane' on the artificial horizon and the directional gyro, while listening to the range, then he took over and put us in a shallow turning dissent and told me to put it right. I climbed up to where I thought we were before and when the discs came off, we had lost 600 feet—but nothing was said. Now, it was a procedure turn and back down the leg, away from the airfield.

I was just beginning to think that we must be getting to the end when, without me being able to see, he cut the fuel from one engine. I could not see the engine instruments; my first thought was 'which one is it? I'm needing a hell of a lot of starboard rudder, so it must be the port one'. While trimming the rudder to get some of the weight of my foot, I told myself 'take your time – don't rush, open up the good one, that's starboard, bit of boost, increase the revs, trim a bit more. Now for feathering, must get the right one or we'll be right up shit creek without a paddle.'

I reached for the port red feathering button and paused with my hand on it. I was quite sure that was the right one; I firmly pressed it down. As the blade came to rest, the pressure on the right rudder eased, I could now trim it right out and then play about with the revs and boost to maintain safe single engine speed of 120 knots and get back on the edge of the beam. Finally, I opened the fuel cross feed so all the fuel was available to the good engine.

After a while like this, we were off again: 'Procedure turn on to the reciprocal with half rate turn towards the duff engine,' so off we went, 30 degrees turn to starboard, which needed quite a lot of pressure towards the good engine, but instead of counting, I used the directional gyro as this gave me time to think 'if I can only do a half-rate to port, I had better carry on off the beam longer to give me more room to complete the turn, or shall I keep this first turn on beyond 30 degrees. No, I come out now at 30 degrees but double the time on the straight bit to ninety seconds so start counting'.

Ninety seconds seemed a long time. It was now time for the half rate turn to port, 8 degrees of bank for 140 seconds. I watched the airspeed, not letting the bank increase as it was trying to do. 'Bloody hell,' I thought, 'we are getting back in the beam and haven't anything like completed the turn. Don't be tempted to increase the turn, not against that duff engine or we'll be in real trouble. I'll keep gently turning like this, no point in bothering to count now.'

I tried to visualise what would be happening to the trace if we were doing this on the link—we were through the beam now; then we were about parallel with it; then we were closing with it. The 'N's were fading so I started taking the turn off. We were nearly there so I gradually turned the other way. There we were, straightening up on 167. I asked him what my engine instruments were reading as I could not see them—cylinder head temperature, oil temperature, etc.

'Now get that fan working again'. It was just as long a job as getting it stopped. 'Throttle and rev settings, mixture, fuel cocks, booster pump, now for the feathering knob—must be sure to push the right one—don't want to feather the other one.' I thought. 'Think, pause, yes, that's the right one, push and hold in. Trim as the turning prop creates drag, she's fired and running, throttle back to allow to warm up. I ask him to give me the cylinder head and oil temperatures every thirty seconds. When they are okay, gradually increase to cruising revs and boost, adjust the trim, get steady on the edge of the beam.' I thought, 'pity I made a bugger of that by going right through the beam'.

'We'll just cover the artificial horizon for a while, carry on to the cone of silence' (which was directly over the range station where momentarily the noise built up, then went quiet, then built up again before going back to normal). 'Then, a procedure turn and standard let down to 500 feet'. He gave me the artificial horizon back just after the procedure turn. At 500 feet, with wheels and flaps down, he pulled off the hood. 'Right, do an over-shoot, and then bring her in on one zero.'

He walked off without saying a word.

14

Trans-Atlantic Captain/Navigator

Back in the Pic (the Piccadilly Bar back at the hotel), those civvy chaps were so different. In the air, they hardly said a word, maintaining a strict instructor/pupil relationship, but they were true professionals and over a glass or two of iced beer, they would chat away, answering questions and giving you tips. I learned I had done okay on the instrument/range check but would have to do some Astro fixes in the air to get my full captain/navigator rating.

I learned one night about the origins of Ferry Command. When it was realised that someway would have to be found to get urgently needed aircraft to the UK other than by sea because this was taking too long and the losses were too high, some Imperial Airways pilots were rounded up and with the help of the Canadian Pacific Railway Air Services Department, set up an organisation called ATFERO (Atlantic Ferry Organisation). This was in the spring of 1941. They recruited 'contract' civvy pilots from Canada and America. The name did not last very long however as President Roosevelt insisted that military aircraft should be delivered to a Military establishment and so the Organisation was renamed the Royal Air Force Ferry Command although the change was purely cosmetic as far as flight personnel was concerned. The first winter crossings were made in November 1940 by Hudsons as it had been shown that, by fitting additional fuel tanks, this was a feasible proposition although pessimists had predicted a 50 per cent loss rate.

After a couple of days, I spent a day at Navigation School. That night, four of us went up as passengers in a Fortress to take Astro shots and plot Astro fixes. They chose a Fortress because it had a proper astrodome—why they did not fit astrodomes to the Hudsons I could not understand, it being much easier than trying to take shots through open windows to avoid parallax. We handed in our plots, charts, Almanacs, and chronometers and dropped off to sleep on the half-hour ride back to the hotel. The next day, I decided I would have a rest and that they could call me if needs be. Tug was nowhere around; I reckoned he was fixed up with some bird. We had a couple of lazy days, then a phone call came, 'this is crew assignments, will you and your navigator come out tomorrow? Got a Hudson for you'.

In crew assignments, I saw my name on the board as 'captain/navigator, Hudson' so, I must have passed those tests okay, but nobody had told me. We were introduced to another 'wet-ear' radio operator, looking very nervous. We were even more particular on this flight than on the previous one because the more you talk to other chaps, the more you realise what can go wrong and being aware of it is half the battle. We even swung the compass in the air after all the freight was on. One of the ground bods remarked that nobody could fly to within one degree anyway; I agreed but pointed out that one degree over 2,000 miles could mean thirty-five miles off course so one degree either way was seventy miles and there was no point in having unnecessary errors, so he shut up and helped us to get away. We swung with the undercarriage up, the aircraft in normal flying trim, and with the radio on, also noted any difference with the interval lights on. After Gander, I told the radio operator to do nothing, except to listen out and log what he heard. Tug watched 'George' while I sent the routine reports to Gander and Prestwick; I also worked the loop, which was so much easier with a serviceable loop.

I spent another long horrible flight back, curled up in the bomb bay, but there were no chits sent around to tell us what was happening this time. It was ever so cold. Sometime, while it was still dark, the body next to me gave me a dig and in the light of a torch, I saw him putting on his oxygen mask. He mimed to me to do the same and indicated to pass the word on. I found the spot to plug my oxygen tubing and turned it on, trying to see if the little bubble looked okay. It was hopeless trying to lie down and sleep now and the mask seemed to smell of raw rubber—I had never noticed this awful smell before when I had been busy flying.

After an eternity, it seemed to get light. I took my turn to go to the rear and plug in by one of the little side windows. I had no idea how high we are, except that it was damn cold and the sky was clear and blue but I was fascinated to see great long streams of white vapour, forming a foot or so behind each exhaust and extending rearwards as far as you could see through the little side windows. Against the clear blue sky, they were really striking—must be what they call vapour trails, the exhaust gases condensing in the cold air. What were we doing right up here? The engines seemed to be making rather a funny scrubbing noise, which I later found out was because the 'variable pitch' on the propeller sometimes froze up, thus making them fixed pitch so the revs fluctuated and the props got out of synchronisation; this apparently was quite common with the Curtis Electric props as fitted on some Libs.

It was not until some days later, when one evening someone mentioned the crashes on the return ferry service, when I learned that three Libs had crashed last year: two within a couple of days of each other in August—one flying into high ground shortly after take-off from Prestwick, the other on take-off at Prestwick—while the third crashed trying to land at Gander in bad weather. In all cases, all the crew and passengers were killed. Ferry Command lost nearly a quarter of all its contract pilots in those crashes and it seemed to cause a lot of controversy among the contract pilots as to whether BOAC crews should operate this service. They argued that, as far as the Gander crash was concerned, British crews did not have much radio range experience whereas American and Canadian pilots were brought up on radio ranges. As a very junior bod, I refrained from becoming involved in the argument but thought that, you really want both on this route: basic dead reckoning navigation and Astro on one hand with range flying on the other, you could not rely on only one.

I did however, willingly get involved in an argument about pay. An RAF officer was holding forth about the contract pilots getting $1,000 a month whereas he was only getting his normal Air Force pay. I pointed out that I was getting twelve shillings and sixpence a day (about $75 a month) but I was quite happy—I was living free in a first-class hotel, getting all my meals included, had plenty to spend and buy my round of drinks, I had only started to fly some thirteen months ago and the RAF must have spent thousands and thousands of pounds training me. The contract pilots, however, had paid for their own training, they had to pay for all their accommodation and meals so, all in all, the RAF were getting their services on the cheap. This brought me quite a few drinks from the contract pilots.

These were hot July days but not without a little rain. There did not seem much for Tug and me to do. I felt a bit sorry for him as, being the navigator, he was not particularly interested in 'pilot' talk; the pros and cons of different aircraft meant little to him and if you could navigate one, you could navigate them all. A pilot, however, wanted to get qualified on different types, which made life all that more interesting. However, he seemed to be doing all right with the girls; he was missing most evenings, although one night he did go with me to the cinema to see a new film

The 49th Parallel, all about German spies in North America. I kept looking out for Zig, my Czech friend, but he always seemed to be away when I was around.

During my time at Dorval, I had many interesting chats with Mitch, who worked in field operations, checking the aircraft over as they came in to see if everything was there, checking calibrations, fuel consumption, and that sort of thing. 'I'm doing a Lib tomorrow. Do you want to come with me?'

'Sure, great.' I replied.

'Okay, see you in the lobby at eight o'clock'.

When driving out to Dorval in Mitch's open convertible, I thought, 'What a lovely morning. I ought to get up early more often'. Mitch explained that the Libs coming through were now B– 24Ds, different from the Return Ferry Libs, which were LB-30As, having a longer nose, oval engine nacelles, and exhaust-driven superchargers, known as 'turbos'. The nacelles were oval because the oil coolers had been moved from the wing and positioned in the sides of the front cowling, also the supercharger intakes were in the 'cheeks'; the turbos were big spinning discs under the nacelles, driven by the exhaust gases. The engines were a bit modified but they were still Pratt & Whitney Twin Wasps, fourteen cylinders in two rows, 1,200 hp.

'When we go through field operations, grab yourself a head-set and keep plugged into position four "inter" on the interphone, you'll find a "jack box" at each crew position. Stand behind the co-pilot to start with, you will be out of the way there but later if you move about, plug-in. We will be pretty busy but I'll give you a few minutes at the controls later on. Okay?'

We flashed our passes and drove into Dorval. We met another four chaps in field operations but, as nobody wore brevets, I had no idea what rank they were. Mitch picked up a great pile of papers and we were on our way to a big black Lib. I followed Mitch while he had a good look around, then we bobbed under the open bomb bay doors and sprung up onto the 'catwalk'. Standing on the catwalk, which was the 'keel' of the aircraft, the bomb bay looked huge—plenty of room to stand upright—the wooden floor in those return Libs must have been several feet above the catwalk. I could see no sign of the bomb doors to start with; they ran up inside the aircraft like the top of a roll-topped desk. We clambered up forward onto the flight deck. One chap had been all around, making sure all the hatches were closed; Mitch and his co-pilot were switching things on and off and making marks on the papers they have in front of them. I tried to make myself inconspicuous, standing behind the co-pilot and making sure that I did not knock any switches. When it came to starting the engines, I realised that, the way the cockpit was set out, made this a two-man job, as most of the switches were on the co-pilot side, well out of reach of the Captain. I tried to follow what was going on during the run-up as more ticks and figures were made on those papers. As we taxied, I thought that this nose-wheel undercarriage arrangement seemed to make it look very easy, but, of course, Mitch was a professional. There was more running up and more marks made on the papers. Everybody, except me, seemed to be very busy. During take-off, I heard, over the intercom, the co-pilot calling out airspeed, then boost, revs, temperatures, and pressures; another chap, who I deduced is a flight engineer, is busy noting these on his forms. We climbed, did two turns, slowed down, and put some flap down; we then airswung the compasses and feathered each engine in turn while I was trying to follow what is going on. Mitch said I could have a look in the nose so I climbed down and crawled forward, under the flight deck, past the nose wheel and squatted down, looking out of the glazed nose. It felt a bit funny at first, but soon, I was enjoying the view; we were about 10,000 feet, so you could see for miles. We were just north of Ottawa and I could relax knowing a professional was in charge.

'So, this is where the navigator lives,' I thought, 'not bad at all, plenty of room, a decent table, a compass to check up on the pilot and, above all, a decent astrodome.' I asked Mitch if I could have a look at the rear end.

He said, 'Sure, have a look in the turret.' I made my way along the catwalk, noting plenty of vertical struts to hold onto (in case he opens the bomb doors). I had a look around the spacious rear, noting control cables running to the tail-plane. I looked at the turret; it looked a bit dicey in there. Anyhow, I plucked up the courage and squeezed in. I did not like this at all—sitting here, looking backwards, I could not see any aeroplane at all. Some yards behind, I saw something trailing behind, going around and around in small circles—it must have been the weights on the ends of the trailing aerial. I looked sideways at the huge fins and rudders; they seemed to be bending up and down. I got out of the turret as soon as possible—thank God, I was not an air-gunner. I plugged into a jack box in the rear and spent a while looking out of the side window to get over the experience of being in the turret. I heard chatter over the intercom from which I deduced they were calibrating the loop aerial. We kept altering course and I tried to figure out how they were doing it.

We had been airborne for over three hours now but it did not seem that long. They still all seemed to be completing forms. They seemed to be concentrating on the auto-pilot now—a different make from the one in the Hudson: this was a Norden, an American make. After a while, the co-pilot left his seat and Mitch beckoned me to sit down. When I get plugged in, he said 'Have a feel of her for ten minutes, auto-pilot is out'. It was so perfectly trimmed that it was flying straight and level without doing a thing. He invited me to do a turn or two and finish up on the reciprocal. There was a full instrument flying panel on the co-pilot side, so I just watched this and forgot I was in a Lib; she turned beautifully, just a little bit heavier than a Hudson. There were also a lot more engine instruments but I did not bother about these. I thought 'I'd like to fly one of these'. I stood behind for the landing and it looked so easy, but these chaps were professionals.

I asked so many questions of Mitch on the way back to Montreal: what is the technique for these nose-wheeled aircraft on take-off and landing? What was all that about so many inches on the turbos? I decided to keep out of the Pic that night in case he was there and was bored with me.

These civvy chaps would go out of their way to help you if you asked questions; however, the odd RAF officer could be quite different. A night or two later, I was in the Pic. It was pretty full and the tables were all taken. I was wearing my summer uniform shirt with sergeant's stripes on the sleeve and talking to a grand guy from Texas, known to us all as 'Tex', when, behind me, I heard 'Excuse me sergeant, I believe this is an officer's bar'.

Tex looked over my shoulder and said, 'This sergeant is a North Atlantic Command captain/navigator, we are just discussing the effects of icing and carburettor heat on gas consumption. Pull up a chair if you want to join us'. I turned around to see two RAF officers walking away. Tex then said, 'Why in God's name don't the RAF make all qualified pilots officers? The Canadians do.'

I replied, 'We can't afford it, can't even pay for our own aeroplanes'. Incidentally, to an American, a 'Command' pilot is merely the first pilot, or captain, as so many of the aircraft are designed for two pilots, but if we built our aircraft to require two pilots, we would not have enough pilots to go around. Shortly afterwards, two chaps who we did not know joined us and started asking questions. I think we had both recently seen *The 49th Parallel* and thought they were spies so we left and had a look in the basement where a heaving mob were jitterbugging to a jukebox. As it was too noisy, we decided to go to Tex's room, where he had a bottle of Brandy. On the way, we met Mitch, who said I could go with him in the morning on another test: 'be in the lobby at eight'.

Crew assignments gave me another Hudson then three days to wait for the return trip, so I dashed off then posted a few letters, spent a dingy evening in Ayr, and one morning had an interesting chat with a girl—yes, a girl pilot of the Air Transport Auxiliary who was collecting a Hudson to take it to a maintenance depot near Burtonwood. She seemed to fly just about anything—quite a girl. I thought it was about time I got qualified on a few more types.

Then, back at Dorval, crew assignments gave me a new card they had started to issue called a 'competency card'; under the heading of 'command pilot', mine showed one type only: Hudsons. Some of the civvy guys had type ratings on damn nearly everything, which made my solitary Hudson look pretty sick. I was not very keen on a Ventura, but a Mitchell or even a Fortress (they say they were just like overgrown Ansons) or perhaps even a Lib would be very nice; I wondered how Peter and St John were getting on with their Wellingtons. I would have liked to have a go on a nose-wheeled job. While I am walking along daydreaming, I hear 'hi,' and looked around to see Mitch. 'Doing a short test on a Lib in the morning, a few things to check back on. Do you want to come as co-pilot?'

When we get settled in, Mitch explained what I had to do on take-off: 'Follow my hand through on the throttles, when I take my hand off hold them there and tighten-up the tension nuts with your other hand. Soon, as we are starting to roll, brace the rudder pedals firm so that I can operate the toe brakes. I'll tell you when to take your feet off the pedals, then start calling out the airspeed every three or four seconds. When I say "gear up", stop calling airspeed and shove in that knob on the top of the undercarriage lever and move it right up. Don't touch the flaps. Keep an eye on the revs on take-off; if they go over 27,000, bring them back with one of those switches, and bring a throttle back if it goes over 52 inches. When the undercarriage lever pops back to neutral, select "Up" again and hold it there for a few seconds. I'll tell you when to reduce boost and revs and what to. I'll tell you when to start bleeding the flaps up, only five or ten degrees at a time. Those are the gill switches on the side there, I'll tell you if they want opening, but don't open them more than a third or we'll get tail-buffeting. Later, I'll tell you when to switch off the fuel and hydraulic boosters—those five switches there. Right, just run over that. Now let's get the show on the road. All the starter and ignition switches are on your side—we'll start number three first, then four, two and one; but first the preliminaries.'

We adjusted our throat mikes—a band that went around your neck with two little pads, one resting each side of your Adam's apple. Our voices sounded like two different people. Mitch checked with the flight engineer, who had come to squat down between us. He checked the hatches and bomb-doors were all closed and the tail support removed. He then started calling things out and either doing it himself or pointing to them for me to do if they were on my side:

Gear lever	Down
Auto-pilot	Off
Oil dilution	Off
Instrument power	On
Battery switches	Off
Acc power	On
Generators	Off
Ignition master switch	On
Mixture	Idle cut-off
Parking brake	On
Hydraulic booster	On
Main fuel cocks	On

He signalled to the ground crew, who signalled back, indicating that each engine had been turned over by hand and that the outside accumulator was plugged in:

Props	Set to maximum rpm position
Superchargers	Off
Inter-coolers	Open
Gills	Open
Fire extinguisher	Set to number No. 3 engine
Throttles	Quarter open

He then asked me to confirm nobody was near No. 3 prop. Then, it was time for No. 3:

Both ignition switches	On
Fuel booster	On

I lifted that number three starter switch up for twenty seconds, still holding it there till the hum became constant. I came to central for a second, then now pushed it down to MESH and also pushed No. 3 primer switch. Mitch moved the throttle a bit and, with a big puff of blue smoke, the engine fired. 'Okay, release both switches.' Mitch moved the mixture to auto-rich very slowly and she runs smoothly at about 500 revs. We set the fire extinguisher to number four and went through the routine again, then for number two, but number one would not fire, so it was a great long performance.

Switch off
Check that the flywheel has stopped by engaging MESH
Have prop turned half a term by hand to make sure not engaged
Open throttle full and get ground crew to turn prop several times to blow out
Ignition switches on
Go through the routine again

This time, she fired okay, so all four engines now running:

Generators	On
External accumulator	Off

Mitch was talking aloud to himself and to me: 'Oil pressure is okay. Revs, thousand. Switch off fuel boosters, 15 lb, that's okay. Flaps down, pressure is okay, now half flap, see whether they "creep", no, that's okay, flaps up. Move each turbo slowly through full range, wait ground crew signal that they are all turning, exercise up to 47 inches boost, generators charging, throttle back, open up and check each generator cuts in at 1,200 to 1,400 rpm. At 25 inches, boost, check prop pitch operation through full range three times and leave as maximum rpm, open throttle till the back edge of lever is between "R" and "O" on quadrant and slowly open turbo to give 48 inches of boost, go back to first one to check it has steadied, leave turbo set, throttle back to 25 inches, now check mags, they are on your side, we'll do 1, 2, 3, and then 4, forward switch off, okay, rear switch off, okay, drop mustn't exceed 75 rpm. Now drop to 23 inches and check them all again: fuel pressures, okay; oil pressure, okay; oil temperature, okay; cylinder head temperature, okay; vacuum pressure, okay; hydraulic pressure, okay; de-icer pressure, okay; and brake pressure, okay.

'Now, you hold the controls locked with this lever while we taxi.' He was chattering away to control while we taxied and it all looked so easy, just using the outboard engines. It was then time for the checks at the end of the runway:

Hydraulic booster pump	On
Trim	Rudder 3 degrees starboard, elevator and ailerons, none
Intercoolers	Open
Mixture	Auto-rich

Props	Maximum rpm
Turbo is	Already set
Fuel	Engineer confirmed cocks on. Booster pumps on.
Flaps	Third down
Flying controls	Lever unlocked, check full movement in all directions
Auto-pilot	Off
De-icers	Off
Gills	Closed
Engines	Open up to clear at full revs. Check mags again

After a thumbs-up to the flight engineer, we taxied onto runway and lined up before un-caging the gyro.

I braced the rudders, while Mitch opened the throttles. I followed his hand as he released the brakes and we were off. It went like a dream and Mitch did not bawl me out so I felt pretty pleased.

It turned out that the object of the test was to check a new turbo that had been fitted to one engine as on the first test, it had been playing up, so the boost had been fluctuating. After a while, the flight engineer took over my seat and the two of them kept altering and checking this turbo right up to 24,000 feet, so we soon had to put our oxygen masks on. I stood behind, trying to understand what it was all about. Eventually, they both seemed satisfied and Mitch motioned me back into the seat, but told me not to kick some switches. He let me handle her for a good twenty minutes and explained that, on the landing, the main thing for me to do would be to call out the airspeed on the approach and brace the rudders as we slowed down on the runway, but he would tell me when and also tell me what to do on the approach. On the down-wind leg, he started:

Hydraulic boosters	On, and as before, I repeated whatever concerned me
Brake pressure	1,000 that's okay
Gills	Closed
Intercoolers	Open
Undercarriage	Down when we touch 145 knots, right, now
Fuel booster	On
Mixture	Auto-rich
Props	Fully fine

He pulled one throttle back and the horn blew to check undercarriage down. The engineer re-appeared and said, 'Gear okay, visual check'. We were now turning across wind and starting the approach.

Flaps at 130 knots, 20 degrees down, wait, right, okay now
Start calling airspeed
Full flap
As we touchdown, hold the throttles back
Now brace the rudders.

As we came to rest, it was okay raise the flaps, open the gills, turn superchargers, all boosters, and the generator off, then lock the controls. In no time, Mitch had taxied back and we were at rest but, we were not to use the parking brake yet—let the drums cool. We let the engines idle a while to let the cylinder cool, then put the mixture controls to idle cut-off and the props came to rest. With all ignition switches and battery switches off, we set the undercarriage lever in the down position while the Engineer got out to fix the tail support. Mitch collected his papers and said, 'We'll make a co-pilot out of you yet'. Coming from him, I liked to think that this was a compliment. On the way back to the office, I was asking questions about the turbo settings, how they work, about oil dilution, and when you use it. However, we arrived at the office all too soon so it was a quick, 'Thank you very much for the ride, I really enjoyed it,' but he had disappeared.

15
O. P.'s Little Black Book

Tug seemed to be doing all right with his girlfriend as he was never around in the evenings and sometimes did not wait for dinner so he must be on to a good thing. I was thinking that it would be a good thing if we could get posted to a squadron and start doing something positive instead of getting nowhere here; Peter and St John were probably making names for themselves by now. On the other hand, I had picked up a lot of good gen from these guys.

One evening, I got involved with the chap who flew for Prairie Airways before joining Ferry Command. He had already had quite a few drinks; I ribbed him that I had heard that Prairie Airways pilots thought that a 'track' was two parallel strips of metal on the ground running from town to town and, from time to time, obscured by a line of box-cars. We had another drink and he started talking about 'pebbles in the bucket'. I asked him what the hell he was talking about and he carried on about the Good Lord handing you a bucket when you started to fly. Everybody's bucket weighed the same but some were filled with big rocks and others with tiny pebbles. Every time you left the ground, it was a rock out of your bucket. If you were lucky, you had lots and lots of little pebbles, but if you were not, you had some big rocks—you can't see what's in the bucket. I enquired what happened when the bucket was empty, to which he replied, 'You kick it'.

'Charming', I thought and told him he was a silly bugger as his was full of sand, thousands of grains of sand. He seemed to believe me and we had another drink.

Looking in crew assignments to see if anything was in the pipeline, I was told to call to another office. There, a gruff guy chucked a thick, dog-eared manual at me and said, 'Get all that into your head in a week, then we'll see about giving you a check-out'. I looked at the cover: 'Consolidated B–24 E Heavy Bombardment Aeroplane'. I thought, 'Christ, that's the Liberator'. 'Yes, sir,' I replied, 'One week'.

For the next seven days, that manual was only out of my hands when I was asleep and even then, it was probably on my bed, or on the floor, where it had fallen when I dropped off.

For two days, I hardly left my room. I was quietly studying skeleton drawings, diagrams, and photographs to locate all the bits and pieces; making sketch drawings to see whether I had got the fuel and hydraulic systems right; converting capacities from US gallons to imperial gallons as the former can be dangerously misleading; memorising temperatures and pressures; tracing the electrical system; following the pneumatic system; the braking and undercarriage systems; use of the turbo superchargers; de-icing system; starting procedure; preliminary checks; pre-take-off checks; take-off procedure; climbing revs, boost and air speeds; cruising settings and speeds; limitations; actions before landing approach and on the approach; emergency actions; and so on.

The third day, I dragged Tug out to Dorval with me to have a good look round a Lib with my book in hand and find out exactly where everything was. I then sat in the seat to get the feel for where everything was around me how high I was above the ground, identify all the levers, switches, and dials, and finally got him to take the book and ask me to touch levers and switches to make sure I could find them without having to look.

That night, I decided to give it a break; it was perhaps one of the best things I ever did, for, in the Pic, I plucked up courage to speak to one of the BOAC pilots on the Return Ferry Service. An Irish man with a Welsh name, known to everybody as 'O. P.'. He was a quiet man; you would almost call him 'reserved', but not in the least standoffish. Of medium build with a dark beard, he was usually smoking a cigar. An ex-Imperial Airways captain with thousands of hours behind him, in my book, he was the 'number one gentleman of the air'.

'Excuse me, sir. I wonder whether you would help me. I am checking out on a Lib in a few days time—from Hudsons—I haven't flown a nose-wheeled aircraft before, I'm studying the manual but there's nothing much in it about nose-wheel technique'.

'Certainly, let's go and sit down. Call me O. P., all the other pilots do. What's your name?' For over two hours, over two brandies, numerous cups of coffee, and the odd cigar, we talked—not like the experienced airline pilot and a mere sprog, but like old friends.

He explained that the nose-wheel arrangement was better in crosswinds; the tail, being already up, reduced the take-off run; on landing, you lost the slowing down drag as the tail came down but you did not get that blanking off effect on the tail as it was coming down when the tail-wheel arrangement was likely to want to swing off. On take-off, you got your co-pilot to brace the rudders so you could use the brakes until about 50 knots, then you would have enough airflow over the big rudders to keep her straight. 'Just ease the nose-wheel off and keep it there until you lift her off at 105 knots. Do your approach just as you would in a Hudson except turn on to finals a bit further out to give you a bit more time to get things settled down. If over 47,000 lb, approach at 120 knots, otherwise, at 103 knots, you should already have 20 degrees of flap, put full flap down when you are sure you are going to get in, then just keep the nose-wheel about 6 inches off as you take the power off and let her settle on the main wheels.'

This was where some opinions differ—some chaps kept the nose-wheel up until it sank down on its own but in the Lib, you could sometimes get a nasty nose-wheel shimmy. If you did, the whole aircraft shook like the very devil, so much so that you would not be able to read anything on the panel—not that you would want to—but it was not very nice and did not do the aircraft any good. 'If the nose-wheel has sunk on her own through lack of flying speed there is nothing you can do about the shimmy and you may even go off the runway so, what I do is, lower the nose–wheel gently onto the ground while I still have enough speed to ease it off again if she starts to shimmy, then let it down again and hope it doesn't do it the next time.'

A shimmy was usually caused by unequal pressure in the two shimmy dampers so he told me always, when looking around the aircraft before getting in, to have a special look at the nose-wheel; if it was not pointing dead ahead, it could mean faulty shimmy dampers, which could be caused by previous pilots not moving straight forward far enough to straighten the nose-wheel before stopping.

I asked about taxiing. 'You must remember that, with a nose-wheel set up, the centre of gravity is forward of the wheels, in a Lib it is only very slightly forward so that is why you see them rocking while taxiing and some people call them "pregnant ducks". If you were to break hard, she could rock back and hit the tail on the ground—making you very unpopular with the gentlemen on the ground—so, if you have to break hard, give her a burst of throttle as you stop to keep the tail up. Also, never try to turn from a standstill, always start moving forward first, put a bit of power on before turning to compress the nose oleo and never try to castor through more than 35 degrees. I use the outboard engines for taxiing as that is easy on the LB-30s, the throttles being a split spade arrangement, but in yours the throttles are all in a straight line so I don't see why you should not use the inners, it would be easier, in any case your hydraulic pump is on number 3.'

We talked about the 'Davis' wing on the Lib. It was a fairly new design, supposed to cut down the drag by 25 per cent at low speeds and 10 per cent at high speeds and possibly the reason why it had such a wide range of speeds from 265 knots maximum, to 150 knots for maximum range, and 108 knots for maximum endurance, although O. P. reckoned it would not be easy to handle below 125 knots for very long unless in very calm air.

I asked about the bit in the book about the 'elevator load being reversed at 70 degrees of bank' (not that I anticipated ever banking that steeply). He explained that with the wings on the Lib being further back than on a tail-wheeled aircraft, the centre of lift was also further back, so no lift was required from the tail-plane; in fact, the tail-plane was actually pushing downwards to keep everything in balance. Over 70 degrees placed a lifting pressure on the tail-plane and as the tail-plane was virtually sitting on the top of the fuselage, just held in position with a few bolts, it was not a good idea to risk lifting it off.

Then, there followed some very useful tips. He told me how he always carried his 'black book' in his breast pocket. This was a little book containing all the data about the aircraft he was likely to ever require, all arranged so he could turn to what he wanted quickly. Then, he had his little 'red book', which listed position, call-sign, and frequency of all radio aids; details of navigational lights; sketches and details of all possible airfields; radio frequencies; and call-signs. He also said he had a small chart covering both sides of the Atlantic, copied from a school atlas, showing a number for each radio beacon; a cross for each range; a triangle for each airfield and high ground marked in red. He had this on a small board covered with a piece of thin celluloid in which he drew the track with red chinagraph pencil, and the weather pattern in black chinagraph. You could always wipe off and re-draw the weather as you go along. It was no use for navigating on but it gave you a constant picture of where you were as you go along and if anything cropped up, you could tell the navigator immediately what you were going to do.

Never take anything for granted in this job. Get to know your aircraft. Plan every trip as if it were your first. Learn your emergency systems. Look after your engines and study your Cruise Control Charts. Always watch the weather and try to appreciate what's happening. Keep listening out for the weather at your destination and alternatives. A 'Dalton' Computer is very well for working out the triangle of velocities but the most important computer is the one in the top of your head. Don't forget the ground crew—they are most important. Good night. All the best with your check-out.

What a grand old man (anyone over about forty was old to me). I went to bed thinking how lucky I had been to talk to O. P. He made that take-off and landing sound so easy. I thought that I must get started on my little 'black book' tomorrow; it should help me to remember all that data.

Straight after breakfast, I slipped out to buy my little book, only it was a brown one. Shut away in my room, I then set about compiling my little brown book. The first few pages were the checks, right through from getting in, to shut down after landing. I tried to condense everything that mattered, but everything seemed to matter. I spent another half day sitting in the Lib going through everything as I talked to myself and referred to my little book. Sitting in my room, eyes closed talking myself through take-offs, climbs, descents, engine failures, approaches and landings and moving my hands on imaginary controls—I was pretending I was O. P.

On check-out day, a big guy in a greasy leather jacket, closely cropped hair and a poker face asked me a lot of questions about critical speeds; stalling speeds; emergency procedures; engine limits; pressures; temperatures; and how the trail alters with undercarriage and flaps. Eventually, he said, 'Okay. You seem to have swallowed the book. Let's see if you can put it together'. We picked up another guy who was a flight engineer and marched swiftly out to a Lib, packed closely between two Mitchells, in stony silence.

He seemed to be heading straight to climb in through the bomb-doors but I veered off and made a point of slowly walking all around, looking at the control surfaces, around the engines for leaks, up at the turbos and then a long, exaggerated look at the nose-wheel. He followed me around, but still, not a word. On the flight deck, he at last spoke, 'First, a whirl with you as co-pilot then we'll change over. Okay? Let's get the show on the road.'

At this point, I thought it essential to clear up how we were going to work, so I asked him whether I was to deal with the undercarriage, flaps, revs, boost, gills boosters, and what have you, on my own or whether he would call out what he wanted. He said he would call out, just as he expected me to do when we changed over—so that was okay—but I was glad I had already had a go as co-pilot with Mitch. He asked me to call out the preliminary checks, then told me to start the engines. I was relieved when all four started the first time. Then, I had to call the warm-up checks, check the mags., and call out the pre-taxiing checks. He got control clearance and then told me to taxi out.

That was when I started to make a real bugger of the job. The brakes seemed very keen and we were rocking up and down, more like an old hen than a pregnant duck. I was aware of 55 feet of wing sticking out at each side and scared of hitting something, telling myself that I must not try to turn from stationary, nor caster more than 35 degrees. I knew I should keep the oleo compressed, then apply a burst of power to stop the tail hitting. Eventually, we lined up on the runway and my poker-faced companion said, 'You did that like a wet-ear in diapers but at least you got here'. It all seemed so 'cack-handed', sitting in the right-hand seat and using toe brakes.

The take-off, circuit, and landing went off okay, with no choice North American swear words, so I presumed I did my job all right. Then, we changed seats and felt much more home on the left. The taxiing was easier too. 'Now I'm just a dumb co-pilot so you have to tell me what to do. I'll only come in if you are going to wipe us out' he said.

I said to myself, 'Just imagine you are O.P, he wouldn't rush. Do all the checks in full each time'.

We lined up for take-off, opening up the throttles while still on the brakes. I said, 'Come on, you should be following me through.' I felt his hand behind mine, opened up fully, let off the brakes, and we started to roll. 'Right, feet off and give me airspeeds'. At 105 knots, I eased her off, braking the wheels. 'Undercarriage up'. The nose came up a bit, so I trimmed her down 130 knots. 'Start bleeding flaps up.' The nose came a bit lighter, so I trimmed her down. 'Open gills one third; switch off fuel and hydraulic boosters; bring back boost to 43.5 on superchargers; drop revs to 2,550,' and so on. I thought to myself, 'This is great, took off like a dream and you have someone else to fiddle about for you and your Engineer to watch the engine instruments, while I just fly it'.

Before landing, we climbed away to do a bit of 'air work'. We reduced speed to get the feel of undercarriage and flaps coming down and up again, how this altered the trim, feathering one engine and then two engines—it felt a bit funny looking out and seeing the two inboard stopped together— we did some climbs, descents, and eventually, went in for the landing. There was about a 20-knot, 25-degree crosswind and I was thinking that I must not drop a wing with this bloody great 110-foot wingspan, but the drift kicked off a treat. As I let the nose-wheel settle and called for 'Brace the rudders', I waited for the swing but it did not come and we gently rolled to the end of the runway.

After four more take-offs and landings—she was taxiing much better now—my poker-faced co-pilot said, 'Okay, taxi back; that will do for today.' I make a big point of leaving the nose-wheel straight. Eventually, we get out and walk back to the office but there was not a word about how I had done. Back at the office, he said, 'We had better do a couple of night circuits. We'll do that tomorrow—be here at 22.00'.

I thought, 'Well, he can't have washed me out yet, or he wouldn't bother with any night work. I like night flying and I haven't done much lately, at least take-offs or landings.'

The night's work was great. I felt a bit apprehensive about the size of those wings when taxiing in the dark but as soon as I was in the air, she seemed to come down to normal size. The strip resin lighting in the cockpit made the mass of instruments fluorescent green and could be varied in intensity. We made one extended circuit over Montreal to look at the lights. I would have liked to have stayed up much longer. Walking back to the office, he spoke: 'Okay, you're checked-out but get a bit of practise in if you can scrounge an aircraft from field ops. Good night'.

Left on my own, I found a phone and rang for a taxi. Arriving at the hotel about 3 a.m., I thought I would knock Tug up to give him the news. I knew he would have a bottle of Canadian Club in his room. All I got was, 'Who is that? Sod off, I'm busy'. I knew what that meant.

Wanting a drink of some sort before turning in, I took the lift downstairs and a night porter promised to get me some coffee. While waiting, who walks in but the guy who had been checking me out. He was quite a different guy now; he actually talked and could even smile. He asked what I was waiting for; I tell him coffee. He said he wanted something better than that—leave it to him and he will organise it—but I can pay, at least for the first one. We had a couple of double brandies, then did it again, and talked a while. I asked him how I did; he said, 'Not bad, not at all bad' and we weaved our ways to the lift and up to our beds. On the way, I asked him how he got back; he said in his car. I remarked that he could have given me a lift; he replied, 'You never asked me'. It had been an expensive night, but worth it. I muttered 'Tug, you old bugger', as I passed his room door.

Having got the Lib added to my competency card, I found a co-pilot and engineer willing to risk their necks with me while we took a radio operator up for a couple of hours to check over some radio equipment that has been newly installed.

After that, I thought I would give myself a rest for a couple of days then crew assignments phoned to tell me there would be a Hudson for me in three days. I dared to suggest that it would be nice if they could find me at Lib, but they said I would have to do another Hudson first or some of the senior chaps would start complaining, as it was usually five Hudsons before you got a Lib.

The day before I was due to set off, I was told that Coastal Command wanted me. They had sent a signal asking where I was, as I was to be posted to a coastal squadron. So, I was not going to get my Liberator—good job that signal did not arrive before my check-out.

So, as the coach took me out to Dorval, we said cheerio to the large 'Chesterfield', 'Lucky Strike', 'Coca-Cola', and 'Canada Dry' posters, picked up our wet-ear WOP, who Tug refered to as 'our passenger', and it was farewell to Montreal. I bumped into Mitch, who said, 'Come back when you've done your tour of ops', and we were on our way. It was much quicker getting away in a Hudson than a Lib.

McFog, the weather man, was on the ball again; it was ten hours thirty-five minutes to Prestwick.

The instructions were that Tug and I were to go to a reception centre at Bournemouth. I thought, 'Bloody, hell, here we go again'. We travelled all night in a stuffy, dirty slow train from Glasgow to London, trying our best to get some sleep. After a shave at Euston, it was across London and another train to Bournemouth arriving in the late afternoon. Instructions were to go straight away to a squadron at Ballykelly in Northern Ireland, taking a boat from Stranraer to Larne.

'What aircraft are they flying?'

'Liberators, only operational squadron on Liberators'.

'Well, we've just come down from damn nearly Stranraer so we must have a night's sleep'.

'Okay, we'll get you away in the morning.'

St John lived in Bournemouth, so I popped to see his mother later that evening. She seemed delighted to see me and rustled up a meal—probably her week's rations. She told me that St John was still at Chivenor and she understood that they were flying mainly at night with a big light, looking for U-boats. He was hoping to get some leave later in the month.

The next two days were a horrifying journey to Ballykelly but we knew we had arrived in Ireland when a chap guiding another to reverse a lorry off the boat, kept waving him back shouting, 'Go ahead, Paddy'.

16

The Battle of the Atlantic

Background

In August 1942, the total size of Donitz's fleet had finally reached what was for him the magic number of 300 U-boats, the pre-war 'grand total', which somewhat arbitrarily he had advised Hitler was required to deliver a 'mortal blow' against Britain. Although repairs and servicing meant that sometimes little more than half this number was operational at any one time, the admiral had grounds for optimism. Between August and November, some 380 freighters were sunk in the Atlantic. These figures prompted Churchill to send an unusually emotional cable to Roosevelt:

> The U-boat menace is our worse danger ... The spectacle of all these splendid ships being built, sent to sea crammed with priceless food and munitions, and being sunk—three or four every day—torments me day and night. Not only does this attack cripple our war energies and threaten our life, but it arbitrarily limits the might of the United States coming into the struggle. The oceans, which were your shield, threaten to become your cage.

Indeed, some considered Britain's shipping situation was becoming untenable by the autumn of 1942. Instead of the expected imports of between twenty-four and twenty-seven million tonnes for the whole of 1942, the figure fell to twenty-three million and was considered likely to be worse the following year. By mid-December, Britain's reserves of commercial oil were projected to fall to 300,000 tonnes. With consumption running at 130,000 tonnes a month, the nation's industrial output—

notably the production of steel and the manufacture of munitions—would soon be in jeopardy. In every year since the start of the war, the Allies had been losing more freighters than they had been able to build.

In the spring of 1941, the Battle of the Atlantic Committee had urged that Coastal Command should be reinforced at the earliest possible date with long-range aircraft, noting especially that 'with adequate air co-operation a U-boat should find it impossible to shadow one of our convoys'. Some months later, in December, aircraft played a decisive role during a convoy battle that lasted six days, which had illustrated the point with compelling clarity, the German offensive being called off only because of a lone bomber. A handful of long-range bombers that Bomber Command had been instructed to hand over to Coastal Command repeatedly forced the wolfpack to take avoiding action. One escort commander, Captain 'Johnny' Walker, formally advised that aircraft were 'absolutely invaluable' to the protection of convoys.

Despite this endorsement, there was a continual battle between the demands of Bomber Command and Coastal Command, with Bomber Command winning out. It was believed by Bomber Command that they could best contribute to the weakening of the U-boat offensive by offensive action against the principal industrial areas of Germany. This opinion was initially supported by Churchill, who was apparently mesmerised by the flair for self-promotion of 'Bomber' Harris.

It was, however, appreciated and recognised by the U-boat commander-in-chief that by systematically forcing the U-boats to submerge, they would lose contact with the convoy in the evening twilight and thus lose the best chances of attack during the first four moonless hours of the night. As a result, their prey usually escaped unmolested. Once forced to submerge, the submarines, which relied exclusively on battery power to propel them underwater, could travel at only 7 knots—no faster, and often more slowly, than their quarry. In daylight, even when they had a good fix, it would take them many hours, travelling at their full speed of 17 knots on the surface, to catch up again; on those very infrequent occasions when a convoy was accompanied by an aircraft carrier, even this was virtually impossible without courting disaster in the form of an air-launched depth charge.

By September 1942, the area of the 'Atlantic Gap killing grounds' was becoming somewhat contracted with medium-range and long-range bombers flying from Greenland, Iceland, and Northern Ireland. This still left an area of 300 × 300 miles where in Donitz's words, 'We can be sure of finding them with no air cover at all'. The Air Ministry's persistent refusal to make very long range Liberators available to Coastal Command in sufficient numbers to make an impact was a surprise and relief to Donitz, who feared a closing of the Gap.

The Western leaders recognised the potency of long-range bombers in nullifying the U-boat threat, but Churchill made it clear he had no intention of diverting the RAF's Liberators from 'the air offensive against Germany'. Roosevelt agreed. They failed to appreciate that the deployment of VLR (very long range) Liberators in the numbers required to subvert the U-boat threat in the North Atlantic was every bit as 'offensive' as the bombing of Cologne. As it was, Coastal Command had only one VLR Squadron of twelve operational aircraft by January 1943. This situation was not corrected until after the Casablanca conference in mid-January 1943, when the U-boat threat became top of the agenda. The defeat of the U-boat became the first charge on the resources of the United Nations. The Battle of the Atlantic became the most important struggle of the Second World War.

17

The Liberator Squadron

Leaving the train at Limavady Junction, we got a lift to Ballykelly Airfield—or rather, Ballykelly Aerodrome, as we were back with the RAF now. Almost touching the southern shore of Lough Foyle with its sandy beach and overlooking some 7 miles of water across the Lough, this seemed an ideal site for a Coastal Command station. As we approached, we saw several Liberators on the tarmac, but they were not black like the ones we knew; they were all white and it made them look much nicer. When we got up to them, we could see that there were two types: some with a short nose like those used by BOAC, round engine nacelles but with a blister under the fuselage housing the four 20mm Hispano cannon; and others with the longer nose and oval nacelles, which looked very much like the B-24 D. All of them had four tall mast aerials on top of the fuselage, two rows of aerials along each side, a long broomstick aerial protruding from the nose, and long broomstick aerials splayed out under each wing. We assumed these would be for the ASV (anti-surface vessel) radar. Just then, a Lib came screaming over the hangar at the proverbial nought feet, did a steep turn, headed out over the Lough, and then came in for a landing. The flight sergeant who was with us said, 'That will be the Squadron Leader, mad as a hatter is Guy. Thank goodness he's leaving the squadron tomorrow. Nobody wants to fly with him. He ought to be on bloody Spitfires.' An hour or so later, I literally bumped into Guy in a corridor and damn me, it was the Guy I went to school with and who went with me to Sherburn-in-Elmet for a flight in the old Ferry, but his rank had gone to his head; he made out he did not know me, so I too, was glad he was leaving the squadron tomorrow.

In the Mess that night, I learned that 120 Squadron was newly formed in June 1941 at Nutts Corner, near Belfast, mainly with Second Tour

Aircrew, who set about converting to Libs and they started operational flying almost exactly a year ago in September 1941. Libs were very slow coming through at that time but as more Libs arrived, they were able to bring the squadron up to strength and they moved to Ballykelly. Now that the runway at Reykjavík had been extended, we usually had two or three crews operating from there on detachment.

I also learned that the short-nosed Libs (the AMs) were known as Lib Is; they carried 2,500 gallons all in the wings but the tanks were not self-sealing (or non-flam as the Yanks would say), and had an endurance of about nineteen hours. The long-nosed ones (the FLs and FKs) were known as Lib IIIAs but only carried 1,886 gallons in the wings because they had self-sealing tanks, which took up more room, but they had overload tanks in the bomb bay, which gave a total of 2,386 gallons. They used to have some Lib IIs; their range was only 1,800 miles because they had self-sealing tanks so when the IIIAs started coming through, they got rid of the IIs to the conversion chaps.

The lads in the Mess seemed a bit surprised that someone should arrive who had already flown a Lib as they seemed to think that they were the only folks in the RAF who knew anything about them. They seemed to know that I would be second pilot to Norman, whose second pilot had been whipped off to the conversion unit and from what I gathered, most of the second pilots had not themselves checked out on Libs and some had never been given the chance to make a take-off or landing. I did not like the sound of this. It probably meant that Tug and I would be split up. On the other hand, I could not grumble about being a second pilot—as long as it was not for too long—because my operational training had been in Hudsons, not Libs. The lads in the Mess seemed a good bunch and that was the main thing.

The next day, I met the Squadron Commander, a dark stocky Squadron Leader, with a row of ribbons starting with the red with a narrow band of bluish green on either side denoting the DSO; he was a very down-to-earth chap of few words, known to everyone as 'The Bull'. I proudly gave him my Ferry Command competency card but he quickly pointed out that all this meant was that I could fly a Lib from 'A' to 'B', not fly one operationally. He called in Norman and introduced us, then, turning to Norman said, 'you've got your new flight engineer, second pilot, and WOP now, so get cracking, plenty of practise dropping; I want you on operations again by the end of the month'.

When I first saw Norman, I thought, 'Christ, a pilot officer—hope he's not just passed out.' However, I need not have worried. Norman had been an NCO pilot, done one full tour on Whitleys, and been operational on this squadron for about five months. His second pilot had left to go to the conversion unit, his flight engineer had come off-line to be squadron engineering officer, and one of his WOPs was due for a 'rest'. Norman was a great guy—a tall, fair-haired, southerner with a neat little tash—a Bank clerk in civvy street, about twenty-five, friendly, cheerful, and always wore a smile. He seemed delighted he had got a second pilot who had already spent a bit of time over the Atlantic and knew something about Libs.

Freddie, the new flight engineer, was also a great chap, the sort you can tell immediately is going to be okay. Freddie, now a flight sergeant, joined the RAF as a boy apprentice at Halton some fifteen years ago, so he could not have had a better training and he was so enthusiastic about flying. Tall, thin as a rail, and almost bald, he had a very sallow complexion with a very dark beard so he always looked as if he needed a shave. It soon became obvious that he knew every nut and bolt, pipe and cable, in fact everything about the workings of a Lib, which was very reassuring.

Ron, the new WOP/AG, was another 'regular' who I was amazed to find also came from York, St Olaves Road in fact, the very next street to where I lived. He was a small, lightly built lad, kept having a moan about the RAF but was good fun and liked his ale. He was a sergeant.

Fred was the navigator. We had to call him Fred to differentiate him from Freddie. He was another Yorkshireman, from Leeds. A Building Society clerk, he was very quiet and studious, smart, with a head of thick straight black hair. He did everything very deliberately, and could smile but rarely did. He was quite a contrast to poor old Tug, who I had now lost—I wonder what his new skipper will think of him?

Les, a pilot officer, was previously an NCO, WOP/AG, and sergeant. A friendly chap, with dark curly hair, and of medium build, he was quite an expert at using the ASV radar.

Harry was another WOP/AG sergeant. A big cheerful Northumberland chap, he was full of fun and had a mass of curly fair hair.

They were a pretty good bunch; three Yorkshiremen out of seven cannot be bad and the other four seemed nice guys.

I had a look over two aircraft with Norman and Freddie. The short-nosed Lib I only had one pair of bomb-doors as the forward part of the bomb bay was made up and consisted of a nice little gallery and a rest bunk, with, in the middle, the breeches of the four 20-mm cannons and eighteen circular magazines of 20-mm shells each weighing 56 lb, so someone would be busy heaving those mags around when the cannon were being used—probably the poor flight engineer. There was no rear turret, just a couple of doors in the tail, which slid open so a single gun could be mounted on a spigot, the gunner sitting on a canvas seat. Big side panels took off on each side so that a gun could be mounted on a spigot, with the gunner standing up. The bomb bay held eight 300-lb depth charges, four on each side, mounted one above the other.

On the flight deck, sitting sideways behind the skipper, the flight engineer had his own desk with a full panel of instruments; all the pilot's instruments (except the instrument flying panel) were duplicated on this panel and there were a few more besides. Back to back with the flight engineer was the wireless operator's table, complete with ASV viewing screen. Up front, the throttles were unusual; instead of being just a line of straight levers, they were each shaped like half a spade handle with two crosspieces so that, by holding the middle crosspiece, all four throttles were moved; by holding the top crosspiece, the two outers were moved; by holding the bottom crosspiece, the two inners were moved. There were no turbos to bother about, just the two-speed supercharger. A big reflector gun sight for the cannon was mounted in front of the first pilot and swung away when not required. The seating and general finish was superior to the Libs I had flown—no wonder the lads seemed to like the Lib Is and were able to have hot grub, coffee and tea, even though you were flanked by 2,500 gallons of fuel in non-sealing tanks.

The Lib IIIA seemed to be the same as the B-24 D I had already flown, except that in the forward half of the bomb–bays were two extra fuel tanks, holding about 250 gallons each, together with a fuel transfer panel fitted with two open, 'U' tubes, and the pump. There was also additional radio equipment and downstairs in the nose, the navigator had a single forward-firing machine gun mounted on a ball in the middle of the nose fairing below the ASV aerial. There was no place for the poor flight engineer; he had to squat down between the two pilots or just find a place to curl up as best he could. The rear turret was different from the one I had seen before—a British one and it looked much more workmanlike.

There was no heat in either model. I understood that the Americans fitted some sort of paraffin heater but the RAF took them out as they considered them to be dangerous and they were not much use anyway. I was very pleased to see that British Air Ministry compasses had been fitted instead of the American steering compasses, which were not very good, but even more pleased to find radio compasses like we had in some of the Hudsons, instead of the type where you had to rotate the loop by hand. Norman, Freddie, and I spent the rest of the day running over the bits and pieces of equipment, and over our cockpit checks so we each knew exactly what we were to do and getting to know each other.

The following day, we got together as a complete crew and spent the whole day on take-offs and landings, some general flying and 'descents through cloud' using the SBA. Everything went okay—Norman seemed relaxed and to have everything under control. They were all a good bunch of lads and I thought, 'I'm going to enjoy flying with these chaps'. Norman seemed happy and when we packed up, he remarked that there was no need to spend more time on that, we would get started 'dropping' tomorrow.

Armed with two crates of 11.5-lb practice smoke-bombs, we took off to practise dropping on a floating target towed by a small Naval launch on Lough Foyle. Good grief, this was scary but certainly exhilarating. Starting from 1,000 feet, which was a fairly standard height for carrying out a patrol, you would scream down at maximum revs (2,700 rpm) and over 50 inches of boost, 250 feet above the water, trying to cross the target on an angle of about 30 degrees to its course when the pilot would release a stick of four bombs, set to a spacing of 45 feet. There was no bomb-sight, it was just a matter of the pilot getting used to when to drop. The Liberator did not seem very big ,way up in the air, but when you got down to 50 feet and had some twisting and turning to do, you are only too bloody aware of that 55 feet of wing sticking out at each side. Each time we came in, Norman was giving me tips as to how to judge the moment to 'press the tit', Harry in the rear turret kept telling us whether we had, undershot, straddled or overshot. However, poor old Freddie, after every couple of runs, he had to go into the bomb bay and hang up another eight bombs, while we were climbing and turning—no wonder he looked a bit paler than usual by the time we came in for lunch.

During the afternoon session, Norman and I swapped over. On the first few runs, I overshot terribly, mainly because I was far too high, and by Jove, you needed some brute strength on those controls to haul her back as you levelled out. Fortunately, Norman was a good guy and remarked, 'Better to be 100 feet too high to start with than 50 feet too low or you wouldn't get another chance'. It took some willpower to keep pushing her a bit lower but slowly, we began to get nearer.

The following day, a report had come in from the Navy chaps on the results of our drops and although Fred had kept a log of all our drops, there was no need to refer to that to tell which were mine—mine were all overshoots. The Navy launch was not available that day, so we went over to the Aldergrove range with a Lib I to practise cannon firing; this was equally scary as, although the target was on Lough Neagh, the approach was overland and we seemed to be damned low, then the cannons would rip up the water in front of us, but you had to not get too carried away by the splashes and forget to pull up before you hit the water. Once again, Freddie got all the hard work; with choking cordite fumes all around him, he had to keep changing the cannon magazines and with us climbing and turning a bit, they felt as if they weighed far more than 56 lb. As we passed over the target, whoever was doing the stint in the rear window would have a go at it with the 0.5-inch machine gun.

We finished the day with a visit to the armaments officer, where we were shown some charts of the aerial depth charge, drawings of what happens to a depth charge from the moment it left the aircraft, how it could disintegrate on hitting the water if dropped too high or too fast, and shock waves that could catch the tail of the aircraft if the aircraft was too high. I was beginning to understand why we had to come in as low as 50 feet. The aerial depth charge weighed a pound or two under 300 lb, of which 255 lb was Torpex explosive. It was 39 inches long and 11 inches in diameter, with fins on the rear and two little lugs for hanging it to the bomb-bay. The hydrostatic fuse should ensure that it did not explode until it reached 25 feet, which the boffins had decided was the best height for the U-boat just starting a dive. This was a new type of fuse as they had found that the previous type had been going off too deep. The explosions should occur three seconds after hitting the water; if longer, it had gone too deep. Our D. C.s had slightly convex noses but we were told that the new ones were to have concave noses to slow them down a bit in the water as there was still a tendency for them to go too deep before the fuse went off.

We spent another three days dropping. After a while, we adopted a routine whereby we were flying happily along at 1,000 feet on the automatic pilot and Fred, in the nose, suddenly shouted out, 'Target ten o'clock, 2 miles' (or whatever). We would all click into our routine and whichever of us (Norman or I) was in the first pilot seat went in for the attack on the target (the one being towed in Lough Foyle). Norman was very keen on this as he pointed out that you could be flying hour after hour and trip after trip on this job without seeing anything, then when you do spot a U-boat, you could bet one of you is in the back having a 'Jimmy Riddle' and if you mucked about, you would have lost your U-boat.

A session in a Lib I was a bit hair-raising when we combined the cannons with a drop. If you concentrated on the cannons, you could be sure the drop went adrift so, I agreed with Norman that if you were going in for a drop, it was better to concentrate on that and just press the cannon tit in the hope that they would put off anyone on the U-boat's gun and only concentrate on the cannons if you had no D. C.s left, or if the fire from the U-boat was uncomfortably accurate.

On our last dropping exercise, another skipper and co-pilot shared the aircraft with us and we each took turns. While I was 'off duty', Les gave me a run down on the ASV. It could be switched from either forward facing or beam aerials. In ideal conditions, the forward aerials could 'see' 5 miles and the beam aerials 5 miles each side. Peering into the opening like a letter box at the end of a foot-long rubber eye-piece, I saw a square screen with a bright, fuzzy, shimmering green line running from top to bottom, dividing the screen into two halves. As the line reached the bottom, it rapidly spread out to fill the whole width. Les said that the widening at the bottom was reflections from the surface of the sea or land; over a calm sea, it was not so bad, but if it was rough, you got a lot of 'clutter', making it difficult to pick out a 'blip'. Fiddling with the knobs he said, 'we are on beam aerials now. If you look on the left side of the screen, almost up at the top, you should see a good blip. That's Inishtrahull, about 4.5 miles away on the port side. That big area lower down on the other side, is land. Now we'll go over to the forward aerials—don't think you'll see anything but a blip on the left should mean there is something on the port bow, if the blip is equal on each side it is something dead ahead. As we get nearer the blip moves down the screen until it is lost in the clutter at the bottom, probably about a mile away. An U-boat on the surface only shows a very small blip—a big boat would show a bigger blip. Very useful for picking up coastlines too, as ASV beacons, they flash a letter of identification. You won't spot a U-boat at 5 miles unless you are very clever and probably lose it at a mile so it's a fair strain on the eyes after a while'.

After this rather hectic week's work of heaving a Lib about, my arms and shoulders were becoming quite sore so I was glad one morning when Norman informed us that the CO was satisfied with us and we were going on the 'Mayfly'. The Mayfly was the list of operational crews, the crew at the top of the list taking the next op and so on. After a trip, you went to the bottom of the list and worked your way up. It appeared you got to the top of the list about once a week, but the CO was not on the list although he had his own crew; he just slipped himself in at the top when there were some good pickings around.

Later that day, however, Norman informed us of a change of plan. We were getting a couple of weeks leave, after which we were to go to Iceland on a month's detachment. Smiling, Norman says, 'Good show chaps. See you all on 6 October'.

18

A Quiet Wedding

On Wednesday, 23 September 1942, I arrived in York after crossing on the early morning boat from Larne. After a tedious journey, Mother seemed okay and did not mention Father. She seemed very 'full' of the Canadian lads who came to see her and her girl lodger. House repairs were completed except for the two stained-glass windows, which remained boarded up. I thought about phoning Peggy but decide not to; I was a bit afraid of what she might say. I took Jeff for a walk and had an early night.

On Thursday the 24th, I phoned Peter Stembridge's mother; she said he was expected home on leave on Saturday. I was looking forward to seeing Peter again. I went up to town in the morning; most of the damage has been tidied up but a lot of blank spaces. People all seemed cheerful; maybe it was the nice weather. I plucked up courage to call Peggy at the office; she seemed pleased to hear me and I arranged to see her in the evening. It was a nice evening with Peggy, Muriel, Uncle Tommy, and Heather, but I did not get much time alone with Peggy. We seem to be back to normal.

On Friday the 25th, I saw Peggy at lunchtime and again in the evening. We decided to get married on this leave. We realised we would have to get a special licence as there would not be enough time to have the bands read out and we would not be able to get that till Monday. We decided to avoid Tuesday as unlucky things happen to our family on the 29th so settled provisionally on Wednesday the 30th. We told Auntie Muriel and Uncle Tommy of our plans; he produced some drinks and we celebrated. I weaved my way home in the blackout. I woke mother to tell her the news; she was not amused.

On Saturday the 26th, we called on the vicar of St Olave's, Rev F. M. Windley. He agreed to marry us on Wednesday, subject to us producing a special licence, which we agreed to do on Monday when we could make final plans. He did not give us the little talk we expected; he probably thought it would be wasted on a sergeant pilot. We dashed around seeing people, taking tea with mother (who was still not very amused), then see more folk in the Olde Starr in the evening.

Sunday the 27th was an easy day. Peggy came here for dinner, so we took Jeff on the Ings in the afternoon and spent that evening with Auntie Muriel and Uncle Tommy. He and I slipped out to the Olde Grey Mare for a quick one. I phoned Peter and arranged to see him Tuesday to ask him to be my best man.

Peggy was on leave as of Monday the 28th. We called at the office of the Diocese of York to obtain a special licence and find the registrar is Col. Innes Ware, who knew us both well so that sped things up a bit and by noon, on payment of a £2 fee and 10 shillings stamp duty, we were handed a special licence. That afternoon, we saw the vicar and fixed for 10 a.m. on Wednesday. Peg called in her office and I called in the Yorkshire to let folks know the time of the wedding. We rang a few more folks in the evening. Peg fancied going to London for the honeymoon—possibly to do with the lure of the big city. I would have preferred Scarborough (where we first met) to cut down the travelling time. Doubtless though, it would be London. Uncle Tommy was going to give Peggy away. Heather would be bridesmaid and Peter best man, so that was fixed up.

On Tuesday the 29th, Peggy had a lot to do. I saw Peter and we talked a lot of shop. They carried big 80-million candle-power lights under their Wellingtons—called 'Leigh Lights'—named after the bod who invented them. They were contained in a sort of retractable dustbin mounted amidships under the belly and could be adjusted a few degrees in all directions by one of the crew lying on his tummy in the nose. They could only be used in thirty-second bursts, then the batteries had to recharge. The idea was that they home on to a U-boat as far as they can on ASV, then switch the light on and hope to spot it. They had to come down to 50 feet— like we did. Peter said there was a great temptation to get mesmerised by the beam and fly right down it into the sea. This sounded ruddy hazardous to me; it was bad enough in the daylight. Their ASV sounded better than ours; we would have lost the U-boat in the clutter at 5 miles. Peter's squadron is the first one to use these lights and made their first attack on the night of the 3–4 June, a night I too remember. Peter was waiting for his first attack but had done a lot of practice. Most of their ops were in the bay off Brest. I saw Peggy briefly in the evening, when we decided it would be London. Then, we went out for the night with Uncle Tommy and his friends.

Wednesday, 30 September was a nice sunny morning. I polished my buttons, took Jeff for a short walk, made sure I had the ring that I had brought from Montreal, and met Peter at the church after seeing Mother safely inside. Soon, Peter and I were in our seats, not wanting to look around as we heard people coming in. Then, the organ blared forth and Peter said, 'Have you done your cock-pit check?'

Soon, Peggy was standing beside me, looking an absolute cracker in the navy blue dress with an angelic white collar, a navy blue hat at a rakish angle, and holding a big bouquet of bronze chrysanthemums. The service and formalities over, I walked proudly up the aisle. I was pleased to see that a couple of girls from the Yorkshire and one of the lads had skived off to be with us and I reckoned the Probate Registry must have closed down for the morning as they were all there. We then went up to Uncle Tommy's for the reception; considering rationing, they did us really well, serving plenty of food and drink. There were photographs in the garden and soon, it was time for the train to London, but you never knew whether they would be on time.

A little contingent saw us off on the usual train, packed with service folks and full of fag smoke. Of course, we had nowhere fixed to stay; armed with our identification cards and the marriage certificate to prove that we really were 'Mr and Mrs', we took a taxi to the Russell Hotel—no chance, they were fully booked for tonight. They could not suggest anywhere as everywhere in town was full of masses of service folks milling around, mostly foreigners. We made a booking for the following three nights and set off to find somewhere for that evening. Peggy knew her way around London very well so we dived down the tube to find it was filling up with folks who were settling down for the night on makeshift beds. After trying several places with no luck and beginning to get a bit depressed by seeing all these people crowding into the tube and sleeping on the platforms, Peggy suggested that we go to her pre-war digs in Earls Court as some of the girls she knew were still there and they would fit us in. We did get a nice reception there; the girls shifted around so that we could have a single bed for the night (good job we were both slim)—the first night of our honeymoon. We would not have had this bother in Scarborough. Anyway, it was a quiet night; at least there were no air-raid warnings.

On Thursday 1 October, we took the Piccadilly line from Earls Court to Russell Square and moved into the luxury of the elegant Russell Hotel. This was more like it—what a lovely sunny day. We took a stroll down Southampton Row, Kingsway, and Aldwych, did not see much air-raid damage. We booked for the theatre tomorrow, had a very nice dinner, and an early night in a lovely big bed.

On Friday the 2nd, we took the tube and had a walk by the river. We took in the usual sites: Houses of Parliament, Buckingham Palace, and Hyde Park. We had an early dinner, then to the Palace to see Jack Hulbert and Cicely Courtneidge. Threading our way through the sleeping bodies in Russell Square tube station, I thought, 'We must be mad. All the locals are sleeping down here, or in shelters, we, and other visitors, are sleeping four or five floors up'. I soon forgot about it after we had a drink and went to bed.

On Saturday the 3rd, we looked around London more. Peggy certainly knew her way around. We went to the pictures in the evening, had a nice dinner, and made the most of our last night away.

On Sunday the 4th, we returned to York on a very slow, stopping train. Having collected some of Peggy's things from Uncle Tommy's, Peggy moved into Mother's house.

On Monday the 5th, I left York in the early afternoon to get the night boat from Stranraer to Larne.

19

To Reykjavík

It was time to see whether Iceland was as bad as the Ferry guys made out. Instead of going direct, we were to make a detour to spend a couple of hours escorting a ship *en route* from the Faeroe Islands to Iceland until Hudsons from Iceland would take over. We only carried six D. C.s and did not fill the 'overload' tanks because we were also carrying three ground crew, lots of spares, tools, and all our kit. Only Freddie and I had not been to Iceland before.

As we approached from the east, the sun ahead already seemed to be getting very low, although there would still be a couple of hours before sunset. Through the haze on the starboard side, we were converging with an inhospitable-looking rugged black mass of land. As we got nearer, we saw a glacier coming down almost to the sea. Norman said it was called Mýrdalsjökull (jökull meaning glacier), but this was only a small one. Soon after, we were passing over a group of barren-looking rocky islands, which Norman pointed out were called Vestmannaeyjar and 'Don't forget they are there in bad visibility'. The coastline began to recede and get flatter, but was still dark and inhospitable, etched by white breakers catching the weak sunlight through the haze. The coastline began to converge with us again as we headed for Reykjanes, the extreme southern tip of the peninsular. It still looked very barren—not a tree or living thing in sight—just a dark, slightly pink, rock. Norman told Fred he could pack up now as we turned over Reykjanes to fly north up the coastline to the northern tip of the peninsula, where Norman pointed out a lighthouse called Sangerdi and said that it would be the point from which we would set course on most of our trips. I noticed a nearby airfield, which Norman said was the new American staging post called Keflavík, or Meeks Field as the Americans called it, but we did not use that. That was interesting as I had heard about this at Ferry Command.

Disconnecting 'George', we turned 90 degrees to starboard, over the water again, and into Faxa Bay. We made sure that Fred had come up from the nose, as we did not want him down there when we put the nose wheel down, and that the ground crew bods were all up on the flight deck. With the low sun behind us, and only a few broken fluffy cumulus clouds in the sky, it really looked nice as we flew up the bay; even the sea looked blue on that nice late autumn afternoon. The end of the bay was ringed with snow-capped mountains under broken white clouds. There were some flat islands in the bay and a promontory on which white buildings stood out in the late sunlight.

Norman pointed ahead and said, 'That's it—take her over the top at 750 feet. Altimeter setting is 998, then I'll have her'. The three concrete runways were clearly visible now—two of them looked very short, right on the edge of town, with lots of little white houses with blue, red, and green roofs throwing long shadows in the late sunlight.

Preliminary landing checks done, Norman took over and I called 'Arctic Fox from Snowcat V Victor, request landing instructions' as we did a circuit around the town and back over the water. I noticed a big building like a cathedral standing on its own on a grassy mound, a lake in the middle of the town, the harbour, and rows and rows of little white houses with coloured roofs; it all looked so clean and tidy. We were soon down and parked by the flight Nissen hut with ground crew around eager to collect the mail we had brought for them. There was one more Lib nearby and one was out on a trip, meaning there were to be three up here on detachment.

Norman pointed out that we were seeing Iceland on one of its good days: 'Don't expect it to be always like this'. On the way to debriefing, I remarked that I thought Reykjavík meant 'Smoky Bay' but I had not seen a whiff of smoke over the town, and surely folks must have their fires on as it was only a few degrees above freezing. He enlightened me, 'It got its name from the steam "smoking" from the hot springs all around the town and near those hills at the end of the bay but now all the springs have been harnessed and instead of going to waste, the hot water is piped away and supplies domestic hot water and water for central heating which is just as well as they have no coal here or trees to cut down.'

Norman and Les went off to their Mess while the rest of us were introduced to our new home—a Nissen hut with timber ends, two windows in each end, one window in the side, and a big pipe stove in the middle of the concrete floor. The end nearest the door had two bits partitioned off, one on each side, making a little passage to an inner door. One of these partitions was a kitchen with a cold-water tap, the other was the coke store. We had electric light, which was just as well as it was now dark and we were told that when it gets to December, there were only two hours between sunrise and sunset. A cheerful 'erk' delivered some mattresses, blankets, and sheets, explaining that they did not leave them in empty huts because they would get damp. We chose our beds and soon got the fire going, then headed to the Mess; it was not bad, a bit basic—just two big Nissen huts. The meal was okay but the orderly pointed out we did not get eggs every day—that was only when setting off or returned from a trip; it was usually corned beef fritters. The bar was a bit limited as canned beer was on ration, but they had plenty of shorts, especially Canadian Club whiskey. There was also a dart board, table tennis, and big roaring pipe stoves.

We were a bit late getting back to the hut as we had met some very congenial lads. It was a bit frosty outside but the old pipe stove had got the hut nice and warm. Within a few days, the hut was a transformation: pictures pinned to the fibreboard lining; our Irvin trousers when unzipped and laid on the floor made cosy bedside rugs; we had scrounged or knocked-up bedside furniture; Freddie fixed up some bedside lights; we had a kettle, teapot, and mugs for the morning cup of tea; a stock of glasses; a bucket and enamel bowl for doing the laundry; and table and chairs and various odds and ends. It was really quite cosy.

The day after our arrival, we had a chat with the Station Commander, who pointed out that strictly speaking, we were an 'occupying force' in Iceland. A number of Germans had settled in Iceland during the years before the war as they too realised the important strategic position of the island in the event of war as a base from which to attack Atlantic convoys. Some Icelanders had become friendly with these Germans and were not very pleased with us when we took the Germans away for internment. So, we must be diplomatic and polite to the Icelanders but we should not expect them to go out of their way to be friendly. Most of them spoke English and would be fully aware of what you said but they may not let on that that they understand. We were not to talk about anything we were doing as you never knew who may be listening. Also, we were to always be on our best behaviour in town and respect their feelings. They were a very small country: only about 130,000 people. The shops were well stocked—the Americans saw to that. They had luxury goods like nylons, make-up, furs, jewellery, and leather goods, which would make the girls back home green with envy, but we must not upset their small economy by flooding it with paper money. The Station Commander said:

> We therefore want you to have most of your pay paid to someone, or an account, in the UK, so please see the Accounts Officer to arrange this. It is no use collecting money here, you will not be able to change Kroner into pounds before you go back, or change it in the UK. Officially, you are only here on detachment but when more VLR Libs become available to take over the UK end, we want the whole squadron up here to look after the middle section of the convoy routes. At the moment, with only three of you here, we have to work out where the risk seems greatest and deploy you there—we can't cover all the convoys or fly speculative searches which we hope to do eventually. By the way, there is a cinema in town that shows American and English films with subtitles in Icelandic. You have to book a seat and if you try to book during the day, they would always say it is full, but if you go a few minutes before the performance, you will probably get in.

Our next call was on the Met Officer, a right cheerful Charlie. He gave us what sounded to be a stock talk. In spite of its name, Iceland is only 12 per cent glaciers; in the Reykjavík area, long periods of severe frosts are not common due to the warming influence of the sea; winters are by no means as cold as in some parts of Canada, very much more stormy and humid, like a very bad English winter of rain, snow, slush, and high winds; I thought I better get some wellies. He went on, explaining that one branch of the Gulf Stream would strike the south coast, then flow clockwise around the island to meet the Polar current; this would keep icebergs and drift ice away from Iceland and wash them down the east coast of Greenland. In the air, masses of warm humid air from the southwest and cold air from the north are constantly colliding, blocking one another and merging giving frequent weather disturbances along the 'fronts'. These masses of such dissimilar air collide so rapidly and violently that they do not allow time for the 'front' to gradually build up as they do in the temperate latitudes with the usual sequence of cloud formations; they just crash into each other so masses of cloud form almost instantly and the wind goes wild. Low-pressure systems pass over Iceland in an endless succession, with unpredictable patterns, so, although the winter will be relatively mild, it will be stormy, humid and subject to sudden change. The locals had a saying: 'if you don't like the weather, just hang on a moment'. In Reykjavík, you could expect the temperature to drop to minus 12 degrees, but the next day, it could be plus 8 degrees and raining. In midwinter, we would get a few days with clear sky but on 75 per cent of days, there would be precipitation of some kind: rain or snow. There would virtually always be strong winds, very changeable in direction. He showed us the data on which he had to work: reports from US stations in Greenland, from RAF and Naval Units round the coast of Iceland, a report from a daily (weather permitting) Met Flight by a Hudson from Kaladarnes (another airfield on Iceland), reports from the Canadian coast, from the UK, and incoming aircraft, but none of these could fill in the picture here, especially when trying to forecast landing conditions several hours ahead. That was why you would invariably have to keep enough fuel to reach Scotland or Northern Ireland because the only other airfield on the island that could take a Lib was Meeks Field and it was so near to us that if we were 'zig', they will be 'zig' too. Finally, there is a lot of Aurora Borealis—Northern Lights activity around here-which was quite unpredictable; it could put your wireless right out, bugger up the radio compass, and also affect the magnetic compass, especially if up north and the needle is already sluggish do to increase dip. It looked pretty, but it was a damn nuisance.

The most interesting visit was to the joint Naval/RAF operations room. The main joint operations centre for the North Atlantic, Arctic, and Western approaches was in Liverpool and this was a sort of branch office for naval and air ops from Iceland. The naval chaps were most friendly and even started off by telling us that in their eyes, one VLR Liberator with trained crew was the equivalent to one escort vessel, especially while there were so few of us, and that during close escort work, we would be an integral part of the escort, working under instructions of the senior naval officer (SNO).

We had a brief rundown on the activity during the last few months: in January 1942, the U-boats had moved close to the American and Canadian coasts for easy pickings as ships were sailing singly and chattering freely on the R /T; they sank seventeen ships. In February, they moved south as far as the Caribbean using re-fuelling boats, operating off Florida, and even bombarded fuel tanks on the shore. Sinkings continued in these areas until June, when proper convoys and American escorts were organised. That month, the U-boats moved back into the North Atlantic, which had been relatively free for a while, catching convoys in the Great Circle route, soon sinking eleven ships plus a Corvette. In July, a slow convoy to the UK had had a very rough time, losing eleven ships and one badly damaged destroyer for the loss of two U-boats. Only last month, September, an outward convoy to Canada lost seven ships plus a destroyer, with another four ships badly damaged. The U-boats were attacking in packs. When one U-boat spotted a convoy, it made a report to its base; other U-boats were then called up while the first continued to shadow. When at least six U-boats had gathered, they attacked together. Fortunately, their wireless transmissions could enable us to know that they were about, but so far, it was difficult to get a fix on them. The officer then explained the symbols on the big wall map. One symbol, marked 'SC104', denoted a convoy nearing our area on its way from Halifax to the Clyde. He explained that convoys are made up of 'slow' ships and 'fast' ships. The slow convoys are 7 to 9.5 knots, the fast convoys, 10 to 14.5 knots. The slow ones are the worst because, not only are they slow, but they often include many old coal-burning ships that cannot avoid making smoke; too much smoke, especially if it is calm and visibility is good, can be seen for miles and hangs around for ages. The fast convoys to the UK were given the pre-fix 'HX', the slow ones 'SC', while those going west were coded 'ON' if fast or 'ONS' if slow. Ships of 17 knots or over often proceeded on their own unless they were troop ships; although, very fast ones, like the 'Queen', would go alone, even when carrying troops.

Then we got to the crunch. The position was that during the last six months, the shipping losses overall had been very high. U-boats were being built faster than they were being sunk and ships were being sunk faster than they could be replaced. We also knew that the Germans were building more supply U-boats so that those on patrol could stay at sea longer. We also knew that they were concentrating on the North Atlantic convoys once again and to make matters worse, some of our escort ships had been withdrawn to cover operations planned in North Africa. We also gathered from intelligence from the bay area that the U-boats seemed to have a means of detecting our ASV. We had got to get these convoys through because without the supplies from America, we could not carry on the war—it was as simple as that; if the Germans could stop the ships getting through, it was all up. The battle out there was the most important of the war; it had to be won.

After hearing about the atrocious weather we could expect and the grim state of the U-boats situation, Freddie and I decided to have a look at the town in the evening. We found the main street, called Laugavegur, with interesting shops, bright lights, lots and lots of bookshops, and some cafes. We ventured into a cafe for a coffee and a huge piece of cream cake; they were not in a hurry to serve us but the waitress came eventually and obviously knew more English than was letting on. We caused a bit of a commotion when we left, which we gathered was because we left a tip and they do not accept tips in Iceland as it indicated you had immoral intentions. On leaving the café, we found it was snowing slightly—not a lot, but a thin white covering, except on the pavements, which we thought was odd and later learned that the pipes carrying the hot water are under the pavements, which was thought was a very clever idea. It looked quite pretty, especially around the lake, with lots of coloured lights reflecting on the water and the snow gently coming down. On our return, we learned that we were scheduled for a trip the following day and may be called about 5:30 a.m., so we got off to bed.

At the briefing, we learned that SC104 had run into trouble and lost three ships. She was not yet really in our area; we could reach her okay, but would not be able to stay with her, so our brief was to do a search in a certain area ahead of the convoy unless we received other instructions or were called in by the SNO. The convoy had obviously broken radio silence with having U-boats in contact, so we could break radio silence too if we made a sighting.

It was not snowing when we woke up. Take-off was planned for 10.15 a.m. and I was delighted to see the careful attention that Freddie and the ground crew paid to sweeping the snow off the wings and tail-plane, and plastering de-icing paste on vulnerable parts, such as the ASV aerials. The trip was most uneventful: there were no sightings; the weather was not bad (a bit mixed); and the sea looked a bit rough, which made me thankful I was in the Air Force and not in the Navy—at least we got back to a motionless bed. I was pleased with the way Norman organised things; he made out a roster, which we stuck up by the throttle quadrant, divided into hours against which he wrote, 'Norman' or 'Jack', so we shared the time in the left-hand seat; on the way out and back, Freddie took turns in the right-hand seat. Les looked after the WOP/AG's roster but all the time and especially in the search area, we were all diligently and methodically searching our allotted sectors. As our Met Officer friend had not been able to give us any assurance of landing conditions, we had only planned on a thirteen-hour trip, which gave us roughly four hours out, four hours back in, and five hours in the area. It was dark all the way back but a pleasant change from staring at the sea, which can be quite hypnotic after a while. It was just a matter of watching the weather for icing, flying the odd dog-leg, and dropping flares for Fred to calculate drift and wind and doing what he says, plus playing about with the radio to see if we could pick up any odd bearings and moaning about the coffee being cold. We decided that we must try to get a Lib I next time.

Eventually, Ron who was looking out on the ASV, told us he had land ahead. Soon, we had the beacon flashing 'G' in red at Grindavík on the starboard and the red 'KF' for Keflavík, so we took out 'George' so Norman could get the 'feel' of her as we flew into Reykjavík, whose red 'RK' was flashing out ahead. The town looked bonny with all its lights on, even though it was raining; the snow had gone. It was about 11 p.m., but it was nearly 3 a.m. before we got to bed, what with debriefing, putting stuff away, and having a meal, but we had forgotten to arrange for someone to light our stove so the hut was bloody cold.

The next day, we learned from the ops room that SC104 had lost four more ships during the night. We all felt really bad about that and would have gone off straight away again if we thought there was anything we could do, but all those attacks seemed to be at night, when we could not see them; we ought to have had those Leigh Lights like Peter's lot had, but how the hell would you judge 50 feet out there in the dark, where you had no idea of the barometric pressure and altimeter setting?

By the end of October, we had done another three trips and fitted in a couple of practice dropping sessions when an aircraft was available during daylight and a Navy launch on hand to tow a target in Faxa Bay. It was usual to combine dropping practise with an air test of an aircraft that had just been serviced in order to save on aircraft hours. The poor ground staff had to work in terrible conditions; as there was no hanger big enough to take a Lib, all work had to be done in the open and if it was not raining or lightly snowing, it was probably blowing a gale and always pitch dark by 5 p.m. There were no facilities for major servicing so flight schedules had to be planned so that an aircraft would land back in Northern Ireland when a major inspection became due; the crew would then bring another aircraft back to Iceland. It was amazing, however, what the ground staff could do under a tarpaulin rigged up on scaffolding with the aid of lights from a portable generator. Freddie and I often wandered down to the flight to have a chat with the lads and brew a pot of tea to keep them going. Old Flight Sergeant Dann, in charge of servicing, was a grand bloke; he seemed to be permanently on duty, day and night, and we always bought him a drink on his rare visits to the Mess.

Most of my spare time, however, I spent in either the briefing or the ops rooms, compiling my 'little brown book' and remembering what O. P. had told me. I condensed gen on lighthouses and light beacons; radio beacons and ranges; broadcasting stations; ASV beacons; airfield data, landing aids, and call-signs; and any other bits of useful information from Eastern Canada clockwise through Newfoundland, Labrador, Greenland, Iceland, the Faeroes, Scotland, Ireland, England, and right down to Gibraltar, even including the German Loran system, which the Focke-Wulf Condors used on their Atlantic patrols. I included radio frequencies, communication procedures, and call-signs; identification procedures; convoy procedure notes; and little sketches to help identify British, American and German ships. The ops officer was quite happy about my little book, as long as I promised to keep it in the weighted Nav bag when out on a trip and not actually being used as he did not want it to be found by the 'opposition' on a body they fished out of the sea. With useful gen about the Lib also in my little book, I felt prepared to go anywhere as long as I had that book at hand. I also scrounged a small-scale map, some Perspex, and chinagraph pencils from ops, some bulldog clips and plywood and made up O. P.'s handy map. Now, I really felt well-equipped.

On the last of those October trips, I saw, for the first time, a convoy in weather good enough to see a whole convoy at once; it was quite an impressive sight. We went to meet a fast convoy, HX212, way out at 40 degrees west, about as far west as it was practical for us to go to spend a worthwhile time with her but since getting out of range of Canadian aircraft, she had lost seven ships during the night and she was still only about a third of the way across. Ops told us that the escorts had not been able to make contact with any U-boats on the ASDICs due to the heavy sea and the U-boats could still be in contact with the convoy. We took off in the early hours, to make contact at first light, feeling that this time, we had a good chance of getting a U-boat or maybe even two. We took extra care with the navigation, not wanting to let the squadron down by not finding a convoy. Every forty-five minutes, we did dog-legs and dropped flame floats so that Fred could take drifts and recalculate the wind. For a couple of hours, we were under some very low cloud but did not want to risk getting into cloud if it could be avoided because once in cloud, it was dodgy coming down if the cloud base was low and you had no accurate altimeter setting. If you knew the convoy had broken radio silence, you could then ask them for the cloud base and pressure setting, but if they had gone into radio silence again after the previous attacks, they would not be very amused if an aircraft starts chattering away and alerts any stalking U-boats. Now and again, we chucked out a flame float as by looking back at it from the rear turret or through the drift meter, you could get an idea of height—at least whether you were getting dangerously low. An hour before first light, we notice odd stars through broken cloud, then soon, a few more stars; as it was getting smoother, Fred got some star shots. Freddie checked up that none of us were smoking (we were each issued with a package of Martin cigarettes before setting off) before he went into the bomb bay to pump up some fuel from the overload tanks. Norman and I decided to have a coffee and a sandwich and Fred gave us a slight alteration of course, telling us that we should be at the datum point in twenty minutes. Lee was on the ASV. Norman asked him to use it only for short spells to see if he could pick up the convoy but not to keep it on in case the U-boats could actually pick up the transmissions as we may catch one on the surface at first light if they did not know we were around.

We listened out on the convoy voice frequency but all was quiet; with about ten minutes to go, Les reported, 'Skipper, convoy about twelve miles on port side'.

Norman called Fred, saying, 'Good show Fred, we'll hang on at eight miles till first light, then close and identify'. At first light, we could see the sea was almost flat calm; the white bow waves and wakes became discernible as little fluorescent flecks. As the light improved, we could identify an escort vessel on the flank of the convoy, so, with the Aldis lamp, we flashed, 'Hello Turret, this is London' (our code words for this convoy).

Shortly after came the reply, 'Pleased to see you. Wait.' Then, a couple of minutes later, 'Show to escort at head of CV'. We knew this meant that the senior naval officer was on the escort at the head of the convoy so we moved nearer the head, still keeping a safe distance and repeated our signal to the destroyer ahead of the convoy. The Navy signalling was so easy to read—bright, clear and crisp with a perfect rhythm stabbing out into the pre-dawn twilight. 'Glad to have you with us London. Okay to close and let the boys see you.' He then went on asking us to sweep a certain sector to a depth of 50 miles. On the way in, we asked if there were any more losses; the reply was 'Negative'. As we closed and flew around the convoy, the sun was rising. The convoy seemed to extend over miles and miles of sea; it was not very evenly spaced out as it must be difficult to keep accurate station without lights during the dark, but the sight of all these ships was remarkable—tankers in the middle; some of the new Liberty ships, many look really old with thin, tall funnels; and a few quite big cargo liners, but all looked well-loaded down and many had crates and equipment lashed to the decks. As we flew down the lines at about 500 feet, we could see chaps waving at us and it brought a lump to my throat as I remembered my feelings on the way across the Atlantic when the site of an aircraft brought some feeling of security. We knew that we must not let them down but there was damn all we could do unless the U-boats showed themselves on the surface.

We set off to sweep our sector, cutting the revs and boost right down to give us maximum endurance and reduced the airspeed to 125 knots, with all stations manned so that every bit of the sea was being scanned. A few false alarms turned out to be an isolated whitecap. At the extreme edge of the sweep, we sent our 'convoy met' signal to base in SYKO (code), the position given as a bearing and distance from a prearranged datum point. We did not want to transmit from too near the convoy just in case some U-boats got a quick bearing on us. The fact that the convoy had not suffered any more losses during the night and they were maintaining radio silence made it seem that they may have driven the U-boats off, but it seemed a bit odd if they had cleared off. On our return, we were sent on a sweep behind the convoy; perhaps the SNO's idea was to keep any following U-boats down to prevent them from catching up. When we returned the second time, the ships had all got themselves back into immaculate straight lines and evenly spaced, with a destroyer and a Corvette at the head, one of the old First World War American four-funnel flush deck destroyers and a Corvette on one flank, a Corvette and a trawler on the other flank, and a trawler at the rear; it all looked very impressive and seemed to cover a hell of an area.

It really was unusually calm weather for the North Atlantic at that time of the year. After another two uneventful sweeps, we had to leave. By cutting right down on the power, we had been able to stay with the convoy for nearly six hours but had to leave them with a few hours daylight left. Before leaving, we had to obtain their position, course, and speed for debriefing but Norman always told them what we made their position and asked them to confirm; he said 'we don't want those Navy types to think the Air Force don't know where they are, not like the Americans'. When they flashed the gen back to us, their position was pretty close to ours. So, we wished each other 'Good luck', opened up to give us maximum range cruising, and settled down at the 137 knots for the ride home.

As we flew north-east, it soon got dark. We were soon in rain, then clouds, so we watched the outside temperature carefully for icing, took turns to have a walk around to stretch our legs, ate the rest of the sandwiches, and drank the cold coffee. 'Why can't we get the Lib Is up to Iceland so that we can have some warm grub and hot coffee, or at least a Thermos flask that will keep hot longer?' I lamented. I fiddled around with the command radio and picked up a BBC programme, but it soon got very crackly and Ron, who was on the radio, said he was picking up a lot of static—possibly the Aurora was 'having a go'. In case it got any worse, Norman asked Ron to try to get a landing forecast for Reykjavík because if it should be 'out', we would like to know about an hour before our ETA so that we could comfortably get to Benbecula or Northern Ireland.

We got a report, not a forecast, of rain and low cloud but the wind sounded okay; that Met chap would never commit himself more than about five minutes ahead, but at least we knew that if he suspected it would be 'out', he would have said so. The static continued to build up and a glow appeared on the propeller tips, just like a glowing ring changing from blue to yellow then blue; it was static being discharged, Norman had had this before and said it was quite harmless; it was quite pretty, but a bit eerie. This all faded away after a while. We cheated a bit towards the end as I tuned into the American range at Keflavík and found it was on the air, so, I persuaded Norman to let me keep my hand in at range flying. When settled on the beam, I told Fred what the drift was so that he could keep his log going. We were soon over the red flashing light at Keflavík, with the rain lashing across the windscreen like miniature rivers. After another few minutes, we were back home; those poor chaps on those boats would be out there for maybe another week yet.

We found out that another crew had come up to Iceland, making four of us. We also learned that we would be staying up here and the rest of the squadron would be coming up as soon as another Lib squadron became operational to take over the Northern Ireland end of the job.

20

'Lows' over Iceland

There was great celebration in the Mess at the beginning of November as one of our crews got a U-boat on the 2nd. From the photographs, there seemed to be no doubt that it would eventually be classified as a 'kill'—bodies, wreckage, and oil were floating on the surface, but it apparently always took some time for a 'kill' to be confirmed; until then, it went down as a 'possible' or a 'probable'. This U-boat was around a slow convoy heading for the UK: SC107. Canadian aircraft had already got two U-boats while the convoy was still within their range, but then in two nights, she had lost fifteen ships. Our crew met her about where we had met our convoy a few days previously so the losses all took place in the 'air gap' and this gave us all encouragement as it did look as if our cover was doing some good.

We got away on another close escort on the 5th to a fast convoy: HX213 to the UK. We never saw the whole of this convoy at one time as the weather was too bad—low cloud, rain, and a very choppy sea. We had to fly tight 'figures of eight' near the SNO's ship, when we eventually located him, in order to keep him in view while we signalled to each other. He wanted us to spend all of our time doing a 'moving square search' some distance from the convoy so he must have had some idea that there was something there. We had to fly at lower than 500 feet with only half a mile between legs because of the poor visibility, which meant hand-flying all the time, which was damned tiring, especially as it was a bit bumpy and so much sea clutter that the ASV was not much use.

When we awoke late the following day, we heard howling gale-force winds and opened the hut door to find driving snow. We learned that a crew had managed to get off in the morning to go to HX213 but they had been diverted to Ballykelly. Later that night, Freddie and I were called out, along with Norman, to go to our aircraft to 'stop it blowing away'; this became quite a regular occurrence. The aircraft was thumping about, bumping on a pile of sandbags that the ground crew had placed under the belly in place of the tail strut and the four props were wind-milling in the wind. It was bad enough struggling to the aircraft from the truck; fortunately, it had almost stopped snowing but the wind was really howling. Our job was to prevent the aircraft blowing into something and to avoid strain on the undercarriage. An aircraft is not very 'at-home' on the ground in these conditions, especially when the nose-wheel can be damaged by turning 'on the spot'. Fortunately, there was a good expanse of clear ground around us. We decided that the first thing to do was to start two engines and get her facing into wind; it was a good job we had Freddie with us as neither Norman nor I were very certain how the starter gear may be affected with the props already wind-milling. One of them fired without using the starter but we needed the starter for the other. Then, what about the sandbags under the belly? Freddie came in for all the dirty work; he and some ground crew had to shift the top ones in case we hit them with the tail fin. It was a hell of a job to move her straight to start with, to ease the nose-wheel, as she wanted to shuttlecock into the wind. Eventually, we got her moving with a lot of engine on one side, then she whipped around into wind. Freddie got out and struggled to put sandbags behind the wheels and returned looking absolutely buggered, but we had to keep the engines running to hold her and keep the tail up. Four times we had to move her as the wind swung. By 9 a.m., the wind eased with the dawn and she was safe to leave. What a frightening night—more frightening and more tiring, than being in the air. For the next week, no one was able to take-off—just high winds, snow, rain, slush, more snow, and low driving clouds.

We heard on the wireless that Allied Forces had landed in North Africa so realised that that would be where the escort vessels would have gone, which the intelligence officer told us had been withdrawn from our convoy routes; we hoped they would be back soon. We also learned from the ops people that it was hoped to replace the ASV shortly with the new model, the Mark II. This would still be on the 1.5-m wavelength but had a frequency of 176 instead of 214, giving a greater range of 12 miles on forward aerials and 20 miles on beam aerials. The big advantage would be that the aerials would be smaller—no big mast aerials on top of the fuselage and this would improve our fuel consumption. The screen would also be clearer with less clutter. We learned that there was a Mark III ASV with a wavelength of only 10 cm with a circular scanner, which had a range of 40 miles all around but there was a big argument going on in high places as to who could have the sets, which were in short supply. Bomber Command was getting most of them and the few allocated to Coastal were to go to the Leigh Light Wellington squadrons. We hoped to get them eventually.

After several more days of grim wet weather, sometimes freezing and snowing, sometimes all slushy and raining, writing letters and hanging around the Mess, but watching the drink in case we had to look after an aircraft if the wind strengthened, we got off on a sweep ahead of a slow west-bound convoy. It was 15 November. We made sure we had our 'diversion kit' with us—shaving tackle plus plenty of fags and some nylons, as we could get these easily and they would be good currency in the UK. The ops officer said we were to do a sweep ahead of the convoy because the weather out there was such that we had little chance of making contact with it. It was quite a performance getting off as the wind was gusting around our take-off limits. We waited about an hour at the end of the runway; control kept telling us when the wind speed and direction looked to be coming into limits. We had to keep 'clearing' the engines, then they gave us the okay at 45 knots, 15 degrees off runway and off we went, hoping to God it didn't alter before we became unstuck. It was a bloody miserable trip, but at least it was good practise for estimating the wind speed and direction from the surface of the sea. I would pick a whitecap a little way ahead and watch how it seemed to drift either towards us or away from us, then pick another one or two and soon, I could judge drift pretty accurately and tell Fred if I noticed it had changed. From the size and length of the 'wind-lanes', I could get a pretty good estimation of the wind speed and once again, drew Fred's attention to any change. Once again, we had no luck; we even managed to get back into Reykjavík when I think we were all hoping for a day or two somewhere in the UK. At debriefing, we were told that intelligence reported that many of the U-boats from our area had been redeployed off Morocco following the Allied landings in North Africa. We often wondered how intelligence got some of their information, but it was not up to us to ask.

Between trips, we had lots of freedom as with being away from the squadron on detachment, we were not involved in any squadron duties. We had a grand relationship with the station personnel, all mucking in to get things done, and the station commander left us very much alone. Our hut was now really cosy; we had got the pipe stove really sorted out so that it would stay on all night. Sometimes, it got a bit steamy if a few of us decided to do our laundry one after the other, boiling our things in Persil in a bowl on top of the stove, hanging them around the stove to dry, starching our collars, and then ironing, but we did not do that too often. I received a big batch of mail, forwarded by the Air Ministry, mostly written during the time I was in Ferry Command and nobody knew where I was. It had been forwarded all over the place; in fact, some of it seemed to have crossed the Atlantic four times. Some made amusing reading now that I was married. I had a good session writing to Peggy, Mother, the Pearsons, St John, and Harry (my instructor in Canada). With the censorship regulations, there was not much I could tell them, only things such as follows:

> Things are very expensive here ... Freddie and I had a glass of milk and a piece of cake in Reykjavík, which cost us 2 Kronur 25 aurar, the equivalent of one shilling and eight pence ... there is a daily paper called the *Daily Post* written in English, but it is only a single sheet and doesn't tell you much about what is going on outside Iceland ... no trees here and hardly any dogs but plenty of cats and rats ... the days are getting very short now, only five hours of weak daylight and in another month there will be only be a couple of hours of twilight around midday ... we have sessions on the Ultra Violet lamp to make up for the lack of sunshine, starting with three minutes each side increasing by one minute each time, I am now on nine minutes ... we have made a Badminton court in one of the buildings and got some equipment so that we can get some regular exercise ... the other lads on the crew are a grand lot.

Suddenly, the weather improved: rain had washed the slush away; the wind had dried everything up; the clouds had disappeared; and the sun shone, although low in the sky, but it was much colder. With little warning, we set off on a search in the Denmark Strait, between Iceland and Greenland. Intelligence seemed to think that something would be coming down through this Strait into the Atlantic.

There was not a lot of daylight left when we set off, but the sea was calm, so, in addition to two fully trained homing pigeons, we took two that were 'under training'. The idea was to release them about fifty miles after take-off while there would still be enough daylight left for them to get back; also, you could only let them go if the sea was calm, otherwise they may fly into the waves. The poor little things were in their yellow tins with a round lid at one end and a little hole in the lid so that they could look out. After forty-five minutes, we reduced airspeed, lowered the flaps, and reduced speed as low as we dare, while Freddie took them, one at a time, from their tins. We opened the bomb bay doors about a foot then Freddie knelt on the catwalk, lowered them outside as far as his arm would reach, facing them into the wind, and let them go.

For just on fourteen hours, we flew a creeping patrol across the Denmark Strait. It was dark for practically the whole time so we used the ASV, not knowing whether we were looking for a U-boat or a surface vessel; all we knew was that intelligence had picked up some radio signal, which they thought came from that area. We found nothing but at least we could see some stars most of the time, although, for a couple of hours or so, they were blotted out by a most magnificent display of the Aurora Borealis—vivid bands of light changing, rapidly, almost instantly, from red to yellow, to green to magenta and back again, just like an enormous curtain. The brilliance varied as rapidly as the colours changed; sometimes, for a few seconds, it seemed as light as day. It was a most spectacular and impressive sight, but a bloody nuisance as a radio was completely blotted out by static and as the colours intensified and then died down, the crackles on the radio increased in sympathy. After a while, we also had a little display of St. Elmo's fire, the ring of rapidly changing colours around the prop tips blue and green. This seemed a bit odd as this was caused by a static charge usually picked up when near highly charged storm clouds but we could not see any storm clouds, so, could it have been something to do with the Aurora? The Aurora plus the glow round the prop tips and the instruments glowing green under the resin lights was like being in some sort of fairyland. For the last few hours, all these outside effects had disappeared, including the stars, when the clouds had returned. We were pleased to learn on our return that our little pigeons had made it okay.

Some days later, it transpired that one of our crews had got themselves stuck in the Hebrides with an unserviceable aircraft so we came in for another trip before we had had our normal quota of rest. This was to meet a fast westbound convoy: HX216. It was now nearly the end of November. We calculated that, in the area of the convoy, there would be about six hours of daylight; we ought to be able to spend about five hours with her and planned to meet her at 57 40N, 36 33W, one hour after first light, and stay until around about sunset. At her position, first light would be at about 10 a.m. Icelandic time, so to be there at 11 a.m., we got away at 6 a.m. There was a freezing wind with occasional light snow flurries, so while Norman, Fred, Les, and I were being briefed in the ops room and Ron and Harry were seeing to the rations, Freddie and the ground crew were walking about on the wings, sweeping the snow off and applying de-icing fluid. I was always afraid that poor old Freddie slipped off and hurt himself. The lads in the Control Tower kept a light shining on the windsock as we taxied out, but the goose-neck flares with the black smoke billowing from them gave us a good idea of the surface wind. It was often a bit tricky getting off with a fully loaded aircraft in a bit of a crosswind as there was only one runway long enough for us. Once airborne, we soon settled into the old routine, one hour for Norman, one hour for Jack. It was quite a nice night (or early morning); shortly after setting course from Sangerdi, all cloud had disappeared and Fred had the whole array of heavenly bodies from which to select his star shots. We dropped the odd flame float so Fred could check on the drift, kept resetting the turbos, kept resetting the trim, and managed to pick up some American Forces radio playing pleasant music. Harry said he could hear Iceland, Liverpool, Plymouth, and even Dorval and Gibraltar coming through 'clear as a bell' on the radio. As I went down to the nose for a while to see Fred and let Freddie have the use of my seat, it looked as if we were in for an easy trip. Les and Ron were curled up together on the floor having a kip.

After some three hours, Fred asked us to fly another dog-leg as the drift seemed to be increasing rapidly. A few minutes later, he asked us to fly another dog-leg just to check and then gave us a big alteration of course to port as we had a lot of starboard drift and he reckoned the wind speed was about 40 knots almost dead on our port side. There were still some stars and a fix confirmed we were a bit to the north of track. Fred corrected for this, then another dog-leg gave a wind of nearly 50 knots, still almost at right angles to our track, giving us even more starboard drift. I doodled on the Perspex on my little chart (good old O. P.) and reckoned we must be flying right into the middle of a low-pressure area; Norman obviously thought the same as he said we had better wind the altimeters down 20 mbar to make sure we did not get too low. The stars were all gone now—must be a layer of cloud. Another dog-leg only produced two drifts instead of three, even though we chucked out two flame floats on each leg so we concluded the sea must be cutting up rough and putting them out. However, on these two drifts, Fred made the wind 60 knots and still from the same direction, so we were heading slap bang into the middle of a deep low. We over corrected on the assumption that the wind was going to continue increasing. Les had a look on the ASV and said there was a hell of a lot of sea clutter—almost halfway up the screen—so the sea must have been getting pretty rough.

Suddenly, we were lashed by heavy rain squalls, which rattled on the windshield like pellets and our first thought was, 'Christ, we've hit the sea'. Norman and I, as one, both wound our altimeters down another 10 mbar.

It was getting bloody bumpy, so we both fastened our harnesses. 'It should get light soon.' I thought. What a sight it was—a vivid pink light from almost behind us revealed angry, dark grey clouds ahead, which seemed to come right down to the sea. The sea looked jet black with great long white trails of spume being whipped off the top of bloody great rollers. We were supposed to be at 1,000 feet, but we established we were lower, although it was impossible to be sure as I had certainly never seen the sea like this before; however, we wound our altimeters down a bit lower still to make them read 500 feet. The spume showed that the wind was still at about right angles to our intended track; the drift seemed to be about 30 degrees but to estimate the speed was impossible—it was a hell of a lot. Fred reckoned it was between 75 and 80 knots. Looking at that sea, it seemed impossible that any ship could stay alive in it. This featureless, dark grey cloud mass was getting nearer. We came down to what we estimated was about 300 feet in the hope of getting under it as it looked as if it came down to the sea in 'pillars' and there were gaps between. It was rough down there. We had to take 'George' out as it was too rough for the automatic pilot. Shortly after, we had to increase speed as she was too difficult to handle in these conditions at economical cruising power; this gave Freddie more work to do, keeping check of the boost and revs to calculate fuel consumption. Freddie was already looking pretty sick. We did not ask anybody to go in the rear turret as it would have been murder back there with all this bumping and wagging around. As Fred announced our arrival at the supposed meeting point, we were bouncing about at an estimated 400 feet just under the cloud base, with visibility varying between nil and about half a mile. Now and again, we would be lashed by a rain squall and, all the time, this heaving foaming sea below. Norman reduced our flying stints to ten minutes each as it was damn tiring hand-flying her in these conditions, but we were both there all the time as now and again, it needed us both heaving or pushing on the wheel together. I had doodled some more isobars on my Perspex and reckoned that we were still heading for the eye of this low, but if this was an occluded front we were going through, it should be spiralling out from the centre of the low and, with a bit of luck, we may soon get behind it. Yet where was the convoy?

We realised that, in these conditions, we could be of very little use to the convoy even if we found it, so we were probably wasting our time, but as conditions might have improved, we did not want to go down as having failed to meet a convoy, but we wondered where to look. We decided that, in these conditions, she was more likely to be behind schedule than ahead of it, unless they had been able to forecast this dirty great low and sail south of it to get the following wind and sea. Norman, Freddie, and I consulted over the intercom and we decided to commence a line ahead search towards the west, but with the legs at a 45-degree angle across the convoy course on the basis that if she were south of course, she would be ahead of where she would be if she were north of course—that was all, of course, depending on us being where we thought we were. For some two and a half hours, we flew parallel legs across what we reckoned would be the convoy's course; at one stage, the leg in one direction was only taking half the time of the leg in the opposite direction because of the terrific wind. Most of the time, we seemed to be in this damned front, just keeping below the cloud except when we had to go through patches, which came right down to the sea. At times, we felt we were dropping as if in a lift; the engine sounded to speed up as if the props were flailing around trying to find some air to bite on, then with a big thump, we stopped falling and the wings would shudder; one second, you could see the wings tips above the engine nacelles, the next second, you could not. I hoped to goodness these Liberators were strong and not suffering from corrosion with all the sea air they were subjected to. When I licked my lips, they tasted of salt, or was it just imagination? With these sudden drops and the thumps at the bottom, it was not long before both Norman and I were sick. It was a sickening feeling dropping towards the sea; in all probability, it was only a few feet but each time, your stomach came into your mouth, probably with fear of dropping into the foaming sea, then the sudden stop seemed to jerk the sick out of your mouth like the shot from a gun and it would be on the wheel, running down the instrument panel, and all down your flying jacket. What a sticky mess we both were, but we would smile at each other while trying to clean up a bit with bits of paper. Trouble was that we had not eaten since before take-off and we were shortly feeling sick with nothing to be sick with and that was worse. Poor Freddie was absolutely prone on the floor of the flight deck. Les was glued to the ASV but did not have a lot of hope in spotting anything through all the clutter and we could not see far in the murk.

After two hours of searching, there was still no sign of the convoy, so, reluctantly, Norman asked Ron to send the 'not met' signal in SYKO, giving the visibility as half a mile, but still searching. It would have been easy for us to climb out of all this muck and go home, but Norman was not like that, and none of us would want to give up while there was still some chance of finding the convoy because even if we could not do much good, it would at least be good for morale if we could find them. Another half hour or so passed, then Les excitedly announced that he thought there was something on the port side, about twelve miles away; it kept disappearing but he felt confident it was a ship because when it reappeared it was in the same place. We switch onto the homing ASV aerials and turn to port; it took Les a little while to find the blip on the forward aerials and when he did, it was a bit of guesswork as to when the blip was the same size at each side to tell when it was straight ahead. As this blip was about to disappear into all the clutter lower down the screen, Les said he had spotted another one a bit further away.

We peered out into the murk, ready to fire off the 'colours of the day' as soon as we spotted anything because the last thing you wanted was for some trigger-happy Naval guy to shoot us down. Listening out on the short-range convoy R/T frequency, we faintly heard someone talking—two escorts talking to each other; they must have broken radio silence because the weather was so bad that they could not speak to each other any other way and there could be no danger from U-boats in a sea like this. As soon as the talking stopped, we called them and advised that we were about three miles from the ship, but we did not know which one. We requested surface pressure reading and asked if they had any instructions. They expressed surprise at seeing us today, gave us the pressure as 940 mbar (gosh that's low), and said that any help in rounding up the convoy would be appreciated as they were all spread around due to the weather. The Navy were always so polite in their messages and this time, they did not seem to worry about being brief. We explained that we did not really know where we were in relation to the bulk of the convoy; they thought we sounded pretty close and then we saw a ship. Jesus Christ how a ship could stay afloat in that sea seemed a miracle. She was a medium-size cargo vessel; one minute, her bow seemed to be right out of the water as she toppled off the top of a huge wave, then went plunging down into a trough, almost disappearing from sight in a mass of spray, somehow to climb up the next wave and leave her screws in the air as she slid down into the next trough. We did a tight-ish turn around the ship, Norman and I both on the controls. We realised that we ought to send a 'convoy' signal to cancel the previous one, so we got this off, but what could we do? We seemed to be getting away from the ship we were talking to so turned about and soon picked them up again. We warned them they looked to have about 200 miles of this sort of weather in front of them, telling them what we had come through, and, being a bit cheeky perhaps, even suggested they may make better way if they kept a bit south. We spotted another ship, then another very close to it, almost too close for safety. By this time, Fred was just keeping an 'air plot'—a plot of heading flown and for how long; as it was not practical to work out actual tracks as we flew lots of short legs, we would apply a 'wind' at the end of the air plot to get our actual position.

We came into a little area of better visibility and saw three or four more ships, one of which was an escort vessel—that was just a bit of luck. The escort vessel was a Corvette—a sturdy little vessel based on the design of a whale catcher—but what in the world it must have been like on that boat, I shuddered to think as it was riding these waves just like a cork going up and down, this way and that way; you could just not imagine any human being able to survive being on that boat for any length of time, never mind days on end. This was not the boat we were talking to, but now we had the position of one known boat, we could at least look around back down the convoy's route and give them some idea how far they were spread out, using ASV for those ships far ahead away to avoid the clutter.

Freddie had managed to calculate the fuel situation based on the extra power we had been using due to the rough conditions and it was clear that we would have to leave an hour earlier than we intended in order to have a prudent reserve for possible diversion. Before we had to leave, we were able to tell the escort that as far as we could tell, the convoy was scattered over nearly 100 miles and that the ones right at the rear were in comparatively good weather, so were likely to catch up a bit, provided this weather kept moving to the north-east. On checking position with the escort, it was confirmed that they were a long way behind schedule—they had not yet reached the point where we should have met them. Poor devils, they looked like having to put up with these conditions for many days yet. So, when it was time to leave, we could not see the escort but wished them all, 'Better weather and Godspeed', slapped on climbing revs and boosted and climbed up away from that tormented sea.

At 5,000 feet, we levelled out (the highest I have been since leaving Ferry Command), still in cloud, but it was much smoother up here. Still in dark clouds, we settled down to cruising revs and boost and let 'George' do the flying; it was just a matter of watching the icing. We took it in turns to stretch our limbs, go for a pee, and clean ourselves up a bit. We realised how cold and hungry we were, so started on the sandwiches but the coffee was barely lukewarm and I thought it was going to make me sick again. Freddie looked like a living ghost—he had been in the bomb bay to make sure all the fuel from the overload tanks had been transferred to the main wing tanks and was now recalculating the fuel we had left. The fuel gauges were a bit of a help but not very accurate. They were long vertical glass tubes that tended to over read by about 40 gallons on the outboard tanks and 20 gallons on the inboard ones, getting even more inaccurate as tanks emptied due to the flexing of these non-flam tanks, which were something like big rubber bags. We preferred to rely on Freddie's calculations. Norman had written out a 'roster' for the flight home. It soon seemed to be dark so we kept shining the Aldis lamp along the leading edge of the wings to keep the icing under control and debated whether to go down a bit as we were flying away from the centre of the low so the altimeter would be reading low; however, if you were going through the 'warm' front, the air could be colder lower down, as would the precipitation be falling as snow or freezing rain, and we certainly did not want to get into freezing rain. However, our minds were made up for us as we seemed to be coming out of cloud and in another half hour, we could see some stars, much to Fred's, and our, relief.

During my next stint, I found I just could not keep myself awake. A couple of times, I woke up with a start, quickly looking at the panel to see that everything was okay, Norman was fast asleep with his head nearly touching his chest and I kept feeling myself going off again. I called Ron, asking him to see if there was any coffee left; it was stone cold. As I could not stop yawning, I asked Ron to hang over me to stop me going to sleep but try as I may, I could not stop dropping off, waking with a start as Ron shook me as he saw my head nodding. We had a devil of a job to wake Norman when his time came and decided that we had both better try to stay awake. It was an absolute nightmare—we were tired when we set off and now, after all those hours of hand-flying plus the cold and no proper food, we just could not stop yawning and nodding off. We tried to keep an eye on each other, giving a shake if we saw the other nodding, but quite a few times, Ron or Harry had to shake us both.

Fred seemed to be managing to keep going and kept giving us alterations of course and amended ETAs from which we realised we must have a good following wind component. Les got a landing forecast from Reykjavík and it sounded okay: a little medium cloud, good visibility, and a 20-knot wind not far off the runway. I took a few bearings on Reykjavík Broadcasting Station with the radio compass, mainly to try to keep me awake. When Les announced that the ASV showed land ahead, I was completely disinterested and it was quite a while before either Norman or I decided it was time to start losing a bit of height, Les had already got us a QNH for Reykjavík (and altimeter setting). As we flew by the red flashing beacon at Grindavík heading for the red flashing 'KF' at Keflavík, it dawned on us that we had better get ourselves pulled together for landing. We had some cold water in a flask and Ron brought us a mug full each to splash around our eyes to try to wake ourselves up. Norman took out 'George' to hand-fly up the bay to Reykjavík and told us to keep talking to keep him awake. It was a good job that the pre-landing and landing procedures were now almost automatic to us by now; nevertheless, I tried to call everything out very deliberately and to keep his attention and with a bigger bump than usual, we were soon running along the runway at Reykjavík. Norman did a damn good job in quite a fresh cross-wind.

Back at the debriefing, all we wanted was mugs of hot tea. Fred sat down while the debriefing officer was talking to Norman and I; the next minute, he was leaning forward on the table, fast asleep. We apologised to the ground crew for the cleaning up to do in the aircraft. The truck took us to the hut to dump our kit, where Harry volunteered to get the stove going while the rest of us went to the Mess for a meal. All we could talk about was those poor buggers on those ships. We were back on dry land, soon going to be in a cosy bed, but they would still be out there, pitching and tossing and rolling about, with water swirling around on the deck and condensation dripping on them in smelling Mess decks—how do they ever get any sleep when there is always the prospect of the ship been ripped apart by a torpedo and leaving them in that cold, roaring sea? They did not just have to put up with it for one trip, but for trip after trip—if only the folks at home knew what these blokes, both Navy and Merchant Navy were going through to get stuff to the UK and keep the war going. The only blessing was that in weather like that, they were reasonably safe from the U-boat attacks. After our meal, we dived into bed without even bothering to undress properly.

'Wake-up, you lazy, unshaven shower. Tea's made'. This was Harry, coming around with mugs of hot steaming tea with a tin of Carnation milk. He had got up, got the stove roaring, and brewed up. 'What time is it?' I asked, 'Four o'clock', 'What, morning or night?' 'Afternoon. You've been in bed almost sixteen hours'.

Fred, Freddie, Ron, and I sat up in bed drinking tea. Freddie still had his flying jacket on. It was nice and warm in the hut but blowing hard outside and we could hear rain lashing against the window. One by one, we went for a pee in a bucket—we were not dashing outside in that—got washed and shaved and went over to the Mess, where we learned that the crew who had gone out today to find that convoy had been diverted to Northern Ireland but the one from the Hebrides had got back, so we were still down to three. With no danger of being called to fly in this weather, we had quite a night in the Mess, often remarking about those poor blokes out on those ships.

We were coming into December. We learned from ops that convoy ONS144 lost five ships and a Corvette after she passed out of our reach, but that HX212 got through to the UK without any further losses apart from the seven she lost before coming into our patch, so it did look as if the U-boats may be keeping away from the areas covered by us and the Libs from Northern Ireland. The trouble was that they were going somewhere else. We knew we must get some Libs operating from Newfoundland to fill the 'gap'. On the news, we heard that the Germans had entered Toulon and the French Fleet had been scuttled; we did not seem to be winning yet, but those chaps on those ships were doing their best.

21

Atrocious Weather

As we moved into December 1942, the convoys were still experiencing atrocious weather, scattered over miles of ocean in storm force winds with practically no visibility and days behind schedule. There was nothing we could do for them even if we could have taken off in the strong winds and intermittent sleet or snow showers we were getting because had we been able to get to them, it would only be a case of a fleeting glimpse of one ship at a time. Fortunately, the U-boats were unable to do anything in this weather either. We would keep popping along to the ops room to see what news they had. Freddie and I would go to the flight to keep the ground lads company, but there was nothing much to do. It was dark most of the time, with only a couple of hours of grey twilight in the middle of the day; sometimes, we had to move aircraft around as the wind changed and a couple of times, we spent a few hours in an aircraft when the wind was particularly strong.

Freddie and I had a trip into town; it seemed odd looking in brightly lit shop windows in the pitch dark at 2 p.m. We bought some Christmas cards, had coffee and cream cake, looked at coloured lights around the lake reflecting off a thin layer of ice, and got back as soon as we could to our cosy warm Nissen hut.

On 5 December, we got away to do a 'sweep' ahead of a convoy in the area that the Met Officer thought would be 'reasonable'. It was a murky, miserable trip, although we were able to see reasonably well under an 800-foot cloud base. The sea was still alarmingly rough, the wind ripping spray in great long grey tails off the top of breaking rollers, but at 800 feet, it was not too bad. After six hours, we were instructed to divert to

Ballykelly. We seem to get from 58 30N, 25 10W to Ballykelly in no time at all; we had such a hell of a wind behind us.

I did not know about the lads at Ballykelly, but having got used to the freedom of being part of a small detachment, none of us took very kindly to becoming involved in the squadron routine, or being in a nice little room for two. Only 'skippers' were allowed in the ops room. We all wanted to get back to the comradeship of our Icelandic Nissen hut as soon as possible.

We did not have long to wait. After a couple of nights, we returned to Reykjavík with eight passengers, some spares, equipment, and mail. We flew direct but it took seven hours due to adverse winds. It soon became dark as we flew northwards; the passengers were huddled in a heap trying to keep warm till eventually, Iceland appeared under a thin white layer of snow. The lights of Reykjavík looked fairy-like, shining on the snow, but, by Jove, it had turned cold and the thin snow crunched under our feet as we left our big, white Lib, which looked magnificent in the lights on the white landscape. Soon, we were enjoying ourselves back in our Mess and our own matey Nissen hut.

A couple of days free passed, then another two days being briefed and re-briefed, standing-by hoping to get away, sometimes even going as far as starting up the aircraft but having to call it off because it was snowing faster than they could clear the runway. We had a few hours of kip fully dressed till eventually, another crew took over. We had a full day's sleep, waking to find that the weather had changed; it was now raining on slush. They had got away and someone decided that we should take an aircraft, due for a major inspection, down to Ballykelly. We had eleven ground crew on board, all delighted to be going back to Ireland, some expecting to get leave, but we were not excited, hoping that there would be another aircraft for us to take back pretty soon. Talking to some of the second pilots at Ballykelly, I was a bit dismayed to find that they seemed to take for granted that they were going to be second pilots throughout the whole of their tour; some did not even appear to want to become 'skippers'. Also, some of their skippers never let them do anything except brace the rudders on take-off and landing, call out airspeeds, and watch 'George'. It seemed to me that after twelve months of only doing that, it would be a deception to call yourself a pilot as you would need a refresher course before becoming a real pilot again. It also transpired that some of the second pilots had not been through all the courses that I had done and none of them had 'checked out' on Libs. That night, I felt quite depressed. I did not want to spend all my time with the squadron as a second pilot; it seemed that I was very lucky in having a skipper like Norman, but he would finish his tour before I did and then, who would I get? I did not want to fly with anyone else; I wanted to be my own skipper. The next morning, I managed to persuade the adjutant to let me see the CO. I told him that we were a very happy crew and I liked flying with Norman, but I did not want to remain a second pilot for the whole of my tour. I pointed out that I had completed a general reconnaissance course, completed an OTU on Hudsons, ferried Hudsons across the Atlantic, checked out on Liberators, and completed ten ops, so, how long would it be before I could be considered as a skipper? I suspected he thought me a bit cheeky, assuring me that he knew all about my record and that was partly the reason why he sent our crew up to Iceland but ten ops were 'nothing'; he said he may think about it when I reached 300 operational hours but he could not make any promises. At least I felt that I had made my point and let him know that I did not want to jog along as a second 'dickie' indefinitely; I was relieved to know that he did know that I had more previous experience than some of the other second pilots.

Later in the day, Norman told us that we could push off on seven days leave. I borrowed a tie, clean collar, and a pair of shoes from Tug, as he was still at Ballykelly, as with being diverted, I only had my battle-dress, flying gear, shaving tackle, some nylons, and plenty of fags; collected my rail warrant; and caught a train to Larne to get on the night boat. I did not mind the lousy long journey in dirty, smoky, blacked-out trains as I was going to have a six days and nights with Peggy. It was a pity I would not be able to stay over Christmas as we had to be back on 23 December.

For the first couple of days, all I wanted to do was sleep; I did not realise how tired I was. Mother seem to be 'full of beans', very fussy about some Canadians who kept coming to see her and dashing off in the blackout to walk to the railway station where she did duties serving at the Forces Canteen. Peggy and I visited Uncle Tommy, Auntie Muriel, and Heather and met some of our friends in Ye Olde Starr. One night, there was a bloke in their who really got on my tits; he was moaning away because he had been woken about 4 a.m. by a plane, presumably returning to Linton, and he had not been able to get to sleep again—no thought for the bods inside it who had possibly been shot up and that is why they were returning after the mainstream. I thought that it was for blokes like this that those chaps in those ships out in the Atlantic were doing without sleep for nights on end, to get stuff over here to keep things going. The leave went far too quickly and soon, I was on my way back to Ireland, but I would not let Peggy come to see me off—I wanted to keep thinking of her at home, not standing on a dismal railway platform. My Christmas card from Iceland arrived the day I left.

Back at Ballykelly, we were completely in the dark as to what was going on both on the squadron and out in the Atlantic. We gathered that the storms had flared up again but no one would tell us anything—such a contrast to Iceland where the ops people were always pleased to see as and have a chat. Christmas passed with a church service in the morning then eating, drinking, and singing in the Mess. I had to buy the old warrant officer a couple of double whiskeys when he bet me I could not name the RAF aircraft with the biggest wing-span; naturally, I said the Lib with 110 feet, then he said that just after the first war, he worked on a Handley Page V/1500, a four-engined biplane with four engines, two pushers, and two pullers, with a span of 126 feet. I learned he did very well out of pulling this trick on the youngsters. We managed to get an aircraft one day for a couple of hours' practice bombing. I looked at the new Mark 2 ASV, which was being fitted in aircraft as the sets became available. The aerials were much smaller, with no need for those four tall masts on top of the fuselage, so that should improve our performance. We also genned up on some modifications to the Lib IIIAs, mainly to the fuel system so that we could carry more fuel; these became known as Modified IIIAs. We learned that the two other Lib squadrons were very shortly to become operational, so, before long, there would be three VLR Lib squadrons—about fifty aircraft altogether. Two of these would be operating from the UK, then the whole of our squadron would move to Iceland. Twelve months ago, there were only nine Libs. It looked as if before long, convoys would get continuous cover from east of about 40 degrees west but there would still be a gap until the Canadians got some Libs operating out of Gander or Goose.

At last, on 3 January, we got away on an op, with the plan being to land back at Reykjavík. It was three weeks since we had flown, apart from a couple of hours practice dropping, and we were all jolly glad to be on our way. The feeling that had grown between us as a crew on those long trips is difficult to describe; perhaps it was comradeship, but as soon as we all got together and away on our own, we all felt to be part of a family. It was not a bad trip; the sea was rough but the weather not too bad. We were getting a bit brassed off at not yet having seen a U-boat, never mind attacking one, when we were recalled to Ballykelly due to weather in Iceland. About an hour before our ETA at Ballykelly, we were diverted to

St Eval, Cornwall, as Ballykelly had gone 'zig'. The weather seemed quite good as we approached St Eval, but they put their Sandra Lights on for us (a cone of searchlights centred over the airfield). They must have thought we would be short of fuel but we had only been up for fourteen hours, so had plenty of fuel left. Several other aircraft were diverted there, so it looked as if Cornwall was about the only area having decent weather. By Jove, they ate well at St Eval; we had some smashing meals.

On 5 January, Norman informed us that we were off on an op. The folks down here had arranged with our group that they could 'pinch' us for a trip out to a convoy that had met a bit of trouble as the range of their aircraft would not permit them to stay with it for any worthwhile time. This sounded as if it could be our chance to bag a U-boat but it was not to be. We soon ran into low cloud, fairly rough seas, met the convoy but could not see the whole of it at once and before long were instructed to return immediately to St Eval. Although conditions were not ideal, at least at this latitude, there was no Aurora to muck things up, no static, no icing, no St Elmo's fire, and no worry of a possible six hours' diversion when arriving back at base. It was almost a pleasure trip and landing was no bother with a SBA (standard beam approach) system to bring you down. We learned later that the convoy had not been attacked so I did not know what all the panic was about.

We spent two more nights at St Eval, enjoying the good food and a night out in nearby Newquay before the weather enabled us to fly back to Ballykelly. The next day, 9 January, we heard that Pete (a very experienced warrant officer pilot), his crew, and five ground-crew passengers had all been killed, taking off from Reykjavík. The aircraft had been completely burned out. It was not clear whether it had caught fire due to the crash or whether it had crashed because of its fire. We all felt bad at this news. We had got to know them all very well; they were a grand bunch of lads and Pete, apart from being very popular, certainly knew his stuff—you had to do to become an aircrew warrant officer. He was a very rare breed. They were bringing the aircraft—'B' for beer—back to Ireland for a major inspection.

The following day, we flew straight back to Iceland. After the funerals, no one mentioned the incident again but there was a dark cloud over the Mess for a few days. We soon got our hut warmed up and rid of the damp. We had been away for about a month. It was nice to be back 'home'. We noticed that there were now a couple of Lib Is on the tarmac and hoped that we could have one for our next trip. There were now six crews up here, including one of the flight commanders, a small squadron leader called Jimmy, with a big handle-bar moustache. We hoped that this did not mean that the 'bullshit' was going to be introduced. We had no need to have worried though; the weather and flying meant that there was no time for bullshit. With the constant cloud cover, it never seemed to get properly light at all now, just a murky sort of grey for an hour around midday. The ops room chaps told us that the weather in the Atlantic had been the worst that any of them could remember, apart from the brief lull towards the end of December. It had been a matter of one severe storm following on the heels of another and there seemed to be plenty more to come. This had, however, denied the U-boats any success at least in this part of the ocean.

On 14 January, we got away in the Lib I for a sweep ahead of a convoy. Ops thought it would be pointless trying to do a close escort in view of the weather. We enjoyed having a Lib I. Freddie had his own seat and desk; we could brew up, make coffee and warm meals; no transferring fuel to bother about; no turbos to keep re-setting; not so many drafts; and a bunk to stretch out on. We had an extra WOP/AG with us, a pilot officer who was supposed to have already done a tour with Bomber Command but the poor fellow was scared stiff about being over the sea, especially when we were below very low cloud and bumping about a bit. He kept asking me where we were; when I indicated to him on the map under my sheet of Perspex, he immediately asked how far we were from land; he then gulped and was sick. Poor fellow—I thought he would rather be getting shot at over land than be over the sea. He kept his Mae West on the whole trip whereas the rest of us usually took them off when we got a fair way from land because in this sort of sea, there would be no point in prolonging the agony. Apart from that, you could really easily catch the lever on the gas bottle or something as you squeezed through the bomb bay and inflate the thing by mistake, wedging you between a couple of uprights. Sometimes, we would keep them on for a bit of extra warmth. He did not stay with the squadron long but he was a nice chap; he just could not bear flying over the sea but I bet, if he went back to Bomber Command, he would have plenty of guts.

It seemed rather a useless trip. It was light for about eight hours at that latitude and we spent the whole of the daylight hours sweeping the area, but, as usual, did not see anything except a grey, storm-tossed sea with patches of grey cloud coming right down to the deck. If we had seen anything, I doubt whether we could have got in an attack and would probably have pranged ourselves had we tried. It was a delight to have freshly made hot tea and coffee, even though sometimes, more of it went up your nose, or down your front, than down your throat. On the way back, when we were able to get up out of the worst of the bumps. Harry produced some singed pieces of Spam on toast and we kept him supplying toast until all the bread had gone. Fred could not see any stars and had not been able to get any accurate drifts as the smoke floats could not be distinguished against the waves and spray. After dark, the flame floats were extinguished so we used the good old American system to find our way home—radial bearings and then the Keflavík range. Norman knew I liked range flying, even though he regarded it as cheating. Low cloud, rain, and a strong wind fortunately almost down the runway meant we had to do a low circuit around the town of Reykjavík. I could faintly pick out the Lutheran cathedral, which stood on a mound near the town centre, we rounded it at about the height of the top of the tower, half the runway flares seem to have blown out, but we were home.

Shortly after, I was to experience the most frightening night of my life. There had been little, or no, movement on the airfield for a few days because of driving winds and snow. All pilots and flight engineers were called to the aircraft as the wind was getting stronger. Having been caught on this job before, we got Ron and Harry to collect some food and drink from the Mess and get it out to us. Norman, Freddie, and I, with full flying kit, tried to take stock of where the other aircraft were in relation to the buildings and other obstructions, climbed in, and shook the snow off our clothes. She was already rocking and bumping about, so we decided to get the tail support away straight away before it did any damage, just as Ron and Harry were struggling up with a box of rations, so they helped Freddie and I, then we told them to get back and keep the hut warm. As soon as Freddie and I got back inside, we started a couple of engines and turned her into wind. We had to keep the engines going to hold her still and keep the tail up. Winding the altimeter to read zero showed that the pressure was down to 944 mbar. The wind was getting stronger, with some gusts that moved us so fiercely that we had to give a big burst on the engines. By now, it was snowing so hard that we could not see anything around us, the wind had swung again, and it was trying to twist us. It was a real struggle to bring her around into wind, having to move her straight ahead a little way first so as not to damage the nose wheel, then she would whip round into wind, just like a weather vane, but the most frightening thing was that it was a complete 'white-out' outside; you could not see a bloody thing, just a wide impenetrable sheet slap bang in front of the windscreen. We knew we had over 50 feet of wing stuck out each side; were we near anything, or was someone likely to bump into us with their props going? To prang an aircraft on the ground would be unforgivable; we would much rather have been in the air. The altimeter showed us to be up in the air. By winding it back to zero, it showed 941 mbar—that was down low and still falling. A pile of snow had blown up through the nose wheel doors and wind was whistling through every crack. We kept speaking to Control and to the other aircraft for company but no one could see anything so we could not warn anyone if we were getting near to each other. The outside pressure was down to 936 mbar, almost as far as the scale would go, but we were not shaking about so much. We realised we were in a snow drift and would not be able to move any more so we cut the engines and just let the snow build up around us. We had been in the aircraft about five hours. There was nothing we could do now but wait and keep warm. We set about the food; it was quieter now as we became sheltered under a blanket of snow. The windscreen was entirely covered by a pile of snow and the catwalk was under about a foot of snow, which had blown in through the gaps in the bomb-doors, but we could get to the back and could see it still snowing through the rear turret, so at least we were okay for air. We could still speak to Control so the top aerials must be out of the drift. It all seemed very quiet and calm now, but still a whiteout through the rear turret, the pressure was rising, up to 940 mbar now. It seemed ages before Control told us that the snowploughs had started out as the snow had eased another hour or so and we could see lights through the side windows, it seemed to have stopped snowing. Eventually, we could pick out the lights of a snowplough heading towards us to be followed by voices outside, then a friendly bang on the side of the fuselage and a voice shouting 'come on, you'll be late for breakfast'.

After a few days hibernation, we were back to rain and piles of melting snow and slush. A convoy escort came up; two of us were to go this time: the flight commander and ourselves. We were to go first in Lib I 'P' (for Peggy); he was to follow four hours later in another Lib I, 'W' (for Willie). For four or five hours, we should both be with the convoy so it must be pretty important. A fast convoy to the UK, which had been routed as far north as practical to try to avoid the worst of the Atlantic storms, this was taking it to within about 75 miles off the tip of Greenland where icebergs had been reported and our job was as much to look out and report icebergs as it was to look out for U-boats. The weather was expected to be pretty grim, with sea fog and low cloud, so it would be a matter of us using the ASV and both of us staying as long as possible, whether it was light or dark. We were glad to have another Lib I. We thought it a bit early in the year for icebergs; we thought they broke off the Greenland glaciers as the weather got warmer and we also thought that if there was sea fog, the conditions must be pretty calm, but how wrong we were.

On the way, we soon figured out we were heading into the middle of yet another intense low—rapidly increasing drift to starboard, low cloud, and driving rain—so we wound the altimeter down to be on the safe side. There were bags of clutter on the ASV, so the sea must be cutting up. We were bouncing about a bit too, so we put on our seat harnesses, increased the revs and boost, and started to hand-fly. As it began to get light, a poor grey light—an apology for dawn—we saw the sea, the same tumultuous sea we had seen before, and the wind whipping the top layer away in white foam and spray. We guessed our height and re-set the altimeters. We could not see very far and were getting a hell of a battering. I asked Norman how high these icebergs were likely to be; he did not know but had heard of them as high as 500 feet. It was the previous trip all over again: the sudden drops ending in an abrupt bump, the revs screaming up as the props seem to be vainly searching for something to bite on, and the tenseness in the pit of your stomach. Thoughts went through your mind such as: 'I hope the tail doesn't come off ... hope those suspension lugs on the D. C.s don't pull out ... as the main wheels retract outwards there must be a hell of a strain on the legs as we thump up and down; those wings are flexing a lot—hope there's no corrosion ... those engines are only held on with a few bolts.'

After going through a particularly rough patch, we noticed the wind had suddenly swung all the way around. We were now drifting to port and although it was still bloody rough, at least the cloud base was lifting and the visibility improving. We used an American radio beacon on the tip of Greenland for a single bearing and at least it gave us a check on our east-west position but did not tell us how we were in the other direction. Fred reckoned we were nearly at the convoy's position and the Good Lord must have been with us because the visibility improved and we saw some ships, tossing and bobbing about like little toys. We fired off the 'colours of the day' two or three times then spotted a brilliant little light blinking at us. We flashed our 'convoy code' back and made towards him. As we closed in, the site was almost unbelievable, a long 'flush deck', four-funnelled destroyer of First World War vintage (one of those the Americans handed over) behaving like a corkscrew on a rollercoaster, pitching and rolling wickedly all at the same time, crashing into and out of the water in clouds of foam and spray. How anyone could survive a trip like they were having only God knows—every man aboard deserved a 'gong'. The Navy were always perfect gentleman, how the devil they manage to keep their light trained on us was a miracle but they signalled, 'Glad to see you. What's it like up there?'

To this, we replied, 'Better than it is down there. Glad to have found you: instructions please'. They gave us a sector to the north-west they wished us to search and told us to use 2 kHz R/T in case of sighting a U-boat or iceberg. This took us back into the worst of the filthy weather. After an hour or two of peering out into the murk, trying to drink tea which Ron and Harry brewed from time to time but very little of it arriving as far as your mouth, being sick a bit and shifting around to give Fred a break from navigating, Les thought he had something on the ASV so it was all back to our normal positions. We lost the blip at about four miles as we honed onto it with the bomb-doors open and pregnant anticipation. Then, we both heaved back on the wheel as, out of the murk appeared two bloody great greyish white spires: an iceberg. We flew a fairly tight circle around it; it was grotesquely fascinating, these two tall rugged spires, perhaps 250 feet high on a big smooth base with waves and spray crashing all around it. Fred was confident the position was 58 3N, 45 12W. We broke radio silence, reported our find and the position to the convoy, then kept on for a brief while in case they could get a fix on us. We returned to the convoy after four hours (about half our anticipated stay with them) found the SNO's Destroyer and checked by lamp that he had received our message. We verified the position of the iceberg as a bearing and distance from his position. We set off on a search in another sector, he told us we now had company, they were in the south-east, we knew that meant that Jimmy had arrived. We were glad to know where he was, we did not want to prang into each other in this murk. So, it was back into the thick of the weather for another four hours. All we could do was search for icebergs, with no earthly chance of doing anything about a U-boat in this weather. The poor aircraft was getting a hell of a bashing, a bloody great advert for the design of the Lib. It was better designed than we were, we kept being sick and now and again, we thought Freddie had gone for good but he kept pleading with us not to tell anybody when we got back because he did not want to be taken off flying; he could trust us and he was too good a flight engineer. We found another iceberg, not quite as big as the first; they must be coming down from the east coast of Greenland. We were not sorry when we returned to the vicinity of the convoy for the last time; it was dark now and we heard them talking on R/T, we wished them a quick 'Good luck and safe sailing', climbed up to try to get out of the rubbish, and set course for home. We listened out until out of R/T range and heard them send Jimmy off into the area of the icebergs.

It was now that the Lib I made all the difference. Norman went for an hour on the bunk; we left him until we were nearly home and then woke him with some hot tea and soup. The rest of us had enjoyed ours already. We even warmed some water to have a wash so we all felt a damn sight better than we did returning from our previous rough trip. Fred could not get a star shot or a drift all the way home, so we did it the American way—bearings on the radio compass and then on the Keflavík range. The RAF types considered this to be cheating, but as some others argued at Ferry Command, both methods of navigation were useful in different circumstances and I felt lucky to have experience of both; what the hell did it matter which you used as long as it got you home.

A week or so after that trip, the squadron received the signal from the AOC (air officer commanding) Iceland; it read:

> A signal has been received from the Air Officer Commanding in Chief, Coastal Command to convey his congratulations to Captains and Crews of 'P' and 'W'—120 on the very excellent flights carried out on 23 January in extremely trying weather conditions.

It was nice to know that the AOC in chief Coastal Command did know what we were doing, although prior to receiving that signal, we had learned that HX224 had lost three ships somewhere along the journey to the UK.

A large slow convoy had left Canada two days after HX224; it was not sailing quite so far north as the previous convoy. On 28 January, we met this slow convoy, SC117, at 56 39N, 32 15W. It was a big convoy, starting off with sixty-three ships plus an escort of twelve warships of varying shapes and sizes; it was the biggest escort we had seen, but it had already run into trouble. The weather around the convoy was much better than our previous trips. The sea still looked pretty rough but nothing like as wicked as before, although there was still a lot of cloud about and we could not see the whole of the convoy at once. We could only count about fifty ships so it looked as if they had had a rough time, or else some of them had been unable to keep up, in which case, they would be sitting ducks. Some other ships looked very old, making lots of black smoke, which was thankfully soon dispersed in the strong-ish wind, and were having a job to keep up with the rest. Almost from the time we reached the convoy we experienced a complete radio blackout. All the WOPs in turn reported nothing but crackles; they could not pick up anything from anywhere. The SNO in a Destroyer had been keeping us pretty close and communicating by lamp for about four hours; when he broke radio silence, although rather distorted, we understood we were to close with him immediately, we found him steaming at his full 36 knots, pitching, rolling, and crashing through the water, heading towards a Corvette on the south flank of the convoy. He told us they had a contact and to keep in company. As the Destroyer and the Corvette closed, we could see splashes in the water as the Corvette fired a salvo of Hedgehogs, but there was no explosion so none of them could have hit, then the Destroyer threw out a pattern of Depth Charges. We circled around, scanning the water, with our bomb doors open, thinking we were in with a good chance but, once again it was not to be. For maybe an hour, the Destroyer and the Corvette sailed around, sometimes crossing in front of each other, the Corvette releasing more Hedgehogs, while we kept a good look for any other U-boats that might have been around and crept in while the two ships were busy looking for this one. Then the two ships returned to the convoy, the SNO telling us to remain in that area. We thought this may be our chance; if the U-boats knew the ships had gone, he may surface and then we could get him. The light was beginning to fail but we felt that something was going to happen. It did; Ron on the radio said he could hear someone calling us but the reception was very bad. Les took over and eventually made out the signal, which, when de-coded, was roughly 'Urgent, repeat our signal TOR (time of origin) 14.05Z, return to Reykjavík immediately, weather. Acknowledge'. They must have been calling us for about four hours. We told the SNO we had been recalled and set course for home, at the same time coding a signal giving our ETA for Reykjavík and requesting landing forecast. It did not seem too bad—a 500-foot cloud base, snow showers, and 20 knot wind. We discussed whether to take about three hours at maximum range cruising to save fuel in the event of landing conditions getting worse, which would leave us with enough fuel to divert to Benbecula, or whether to speed up a bit in the hope of getting home before the weather got worse, but this would not leave us a prudent amount of fuel for diversion. We decided to be prudent and settled down to maximum economical cruising. It was a pity we were in the Lib IIIA as there was no hot food. Soon, the bloody Aurora was buggering up the radio again—just crackles fluctuating from loud to soft and back again, just as if someone was turning the volume up and down all the time—then we started picking up ice; the long ASV aerial on the nose was vibrating as the ice built up on it, then bits would crack off and bash against the windscreen. We had to increase the revs a bit to maintain airspeed, presumably due to drag caused by ice on the dorsal aerials, and just to add interest we had a small display of St Elmo's fire around all four props. We tried slowly operating the rheostat switch for the prop de-icers and this gave a most spectacular display; bits of glowing light flew off the props, making them look like Catherine wheels—presumably because the drops of de-icing fluid, which flew off carried a static charge—quite fascinating but a bit uncanny. We crept into Reykjavík below cloud in falling snow. The smoke from the flares seemed to be blowing diagonally across the runway but Norman pulled off yet another immaculate landing. I would not have liked to have gone into Reykjavík that night unless both of us had got to know the place pretty well.

Eventually, we learned that that convoy had lost thirteen of its sixty-three ships and it was hoped that three or maybe four U-boats had been sunk. U-boats were certainly back after the severe storms.

22

Introduction to the Arctic

February saw the days getting noticeably longer—about eight minutes more daylight each day. Although it was dark by 2.30 p.m., each day was a little longer and we were looking forward to the time when we would be getting twenty-two hours of daylight instead of only two.

February also brought us one fantastic day—a cold breeze from the north, without a cloud in the sky, and pencil-sharp visibility. Looking to the north-west, across the deep blue water of Faxa Bay, the white glacier of Snæfellsjökull looked to be only a few miles away, yet it was at least seventy. This glacier, surrounding an extinct volcano, was featured in Jules Verne's book, *Journey to the Centre of the Earth*; it was here that the entrance to the centre of the Earth could be found. We had never been able to see this far from Reykjavík before. I reckoned that everyone in the station was out that day, admiring the scene of the faraway glacier, the snow on the hills encircling the bay, and the site of the sun low in the south. We did not notice the cold but all too soon, the long shadows got even longer and we were back in the darkness. A Lib, which had been up in the air test, flew overhead at 1,000 feet. They were still in daylight, looking just like a big white bird against a black backcloth, most unusual. The crew told us that they had stayed up well after the air test was completed as the visibility was so amazing and that when they returned, it was perfect daylight in the aircraft, but the ground below was in darkness so they had to wait for the flare path to be lit.

February also saw Norman promoted to flying officer, I became a flight sergeant, and, incidentally, Jack Slessor became commander in chief of Coastal Command. It also saw our first trip into the Arctic with a Russian convoy.

We were warned a couple of days beforehand that we were earmarked for a Russian convoy job so spent a lot of time in the ops room, getting genned-up. The first convoy to Russia sailed to Archangel in September 1941 but when winter set in, the White Sea froze over so they went to Murmansk in the Kola inlet. Up to March 1942, 110 ships had sailed and only one was lost, although conditions were most uncomfortable, with ice building up on the ships and almost continual darkness. The cargo was mainly planes, tanks, Bren gun carriers, tools, and food, which both Roosevelt and Churchill were adamant must get to Russia to enable them to continue the fight against the Germans on the Eastern front, even though we could well have done with all this stuff ourselves. In March 1942, the convoys still had to pass within 250 miles of the North Cape and the Germans, realising the importance of these convoys, moved ships, U-boats, and aircraft into the Trondheim area. That month, we lost five ships, two by U-boats and three by aircraft. The next convoy lost five of twenty-four ships and on the return, the cruiser *Edinburgh* was torpedoed. By May, the ice was giving so convoys were able to sail more to the north to increase their distance from the German bases but convoy PQ16 of thirty-five ships still lost seven ships, one by U-boat and six by aircraft. The real calamity came in June when convoy PQ17, which was heavily escorted and had heavy forces standing off, was ordered to 'scatter' because it was thought that the *Tirpitz* was about to attack. The scattered ships were cut to ribbons, twenty-three out of thirty-four being lost. The next convoy, PQ18 in early September 1942, was escorted by an escort aircraft carrier, three anti-aircraft vessels, twenty destroyers, a battleship, and four cruisers—a hell of an escort—but out of forty-six ships, it lost thirteen to U-boats or aircraft.

No more convoys were sent until mid-December, when the continual darkness would make it impossible for a large convoy to keep together, so it sailed in two parts, a week apart. The first part got through to the Kola inlet without loss but the second part had a rough time; a gale six days out caused five ships and two escorts to lose touch. They were spotted and on 30–31 December, there was a big battle with the German cruisers *Hipper* and *Lutzow* and their escorts. Two of our escorts and one German escort were sunk and the *Hipper* was damaged. After a break, mainly due to the atrocious weather, another convoy was on its way and as there was now a bit of daylight up north, we were going to cover it as far as possible. This meant looking for, and attacking, U-boats, looking for surface vessels, and also aircraft. We were to be given an extra WOP/AG so that we could keep all stations manned all the time and have an extra pair of eyes to watch the sky as well as the sea.

We genned ourselves up on the types of aircraft we were likely to meet: Blohm & Voss BV 138 flying-boats, Focke-Wulf Fw 200 Condor, Junkers Ju 88 and Ju290. They all seemed to outgun us, the first two having 20-mm cannon; also, the Junkers would outdo us for speed. If we got a Lib I, the forward-firing fixed cannon would not be much use against aircraft.

We got Lib I AM919, dear old 'P' for Peggy—my favourite. As usual, Freddie made sure she was free of frost and ice, and with plenty of de-icing paste on the ASV aerials. We got away at 5 a.m. with fuel for eighteen hours at economical cruising. We reckoned on four and a half hours out, the same back, with five hours with the convoy and four hours in hand for possible diversion to Scotland. It was dark as we rounded the southern tip of Iceland. We were not allowed to overfly the interior of Iceland so flew along the south-east coast from where, even in the dark, we could faintly see the outline of the Vatnajökull, the largest glacier in Europe (Greenland not being in Europe) and the third largest ice mass in the world. We set course for the convoy, getting a bearing on the bacon, which transmitted for five minutes every half hour, belting out its call-sign 'MHM'. There were no stars to be seen, but no 'weather' either, so we decided to have a brew.

Some hours later, the stars appeared so I gave Fred a shout so he could get some shots in case they disappeared again and thank goodness there was no Aurora to blot them out. Spotting Ursa Major (the Plough) and following the line through Dubhe to find the Pole Star, I had to look almost straight up through the Perspex in the top of the flight deck. It then sunk in how far north we were getting, about 68 degrees north and we still had to go to 70 something. Soon, we would be nearer to the North Pole than we were to London and Jesus, it was getting cold. The nearest bit of land was a rocky island called Jan Mayen; there was no chance of putting down on that. We became aware that the sea below was white; it was drift ice. Les reported that there was no sea clutter on the ASV but nothing on the radio either, not even static, just complete silence. It was all a bit eerie so we just decided on another brew up. Then, we decided that we had better get the guns loaded and tested and the D. C.s armed, also the correct 'colours of the day' loaded into the Very pistol because you could not blame the Navy if they were a bit trigger-happy out here if they spotted an unidentified aircraft. Norman and I re-capped on the ships in the escort, the SNO was in a County-class cruiser: three funnels, the middle one slightly thicker than the others, one mast forward just behind the bridge, other mast halfway between aft funnel and stern, eight 8-inch guns in four turrets, two forward and two aft, and no doubt lots of light AA guns as well, 32 knots maximum speed.

The compass was now starting to do funny things. Fred gave us a slight alteration of course and although we turned on the gyro, the compass just came around with us, still showing the old heading. We tapped it, tapped it still harder, then the needle would jump and stay put, staying anywhere it fancied. Fred found that his compass was the same. We realised the increased angle of dip was causing the needle to either stick on its pivot or scrape on the glass so it was unable to take up its proper heading. We decided to try to use the hand-held bearing compass; by holding it at an angle we could get the needle to swing but it was bloody difficult to read it accurately. While we were buggering about with the compasses, we were also startled by a noise just like a high revving two stroke motorbike without an exhaust which sounded to be just outside the port flight deck window.

In a flash, Freddie came on the intercom, 'Cut and feather No. 2, Skipper, quick'. By the urgency in Freddie's voice, we did not argue. Norman pulled back the boost, I hit the feathering button, turned off the switches and set the Fire Extinguisher to 'No. 2', Norman cut off the fuel. It was all done in a matter of seconds. Norman opened up No. 1 a bit and then asked Freddie what all that was about. Good old Freddie, worth his weight in gold as a flight engineer, knew instantly. One of the cylinders had disintegrated; the piston would have been thrashing up and down in fresh (bloody cold) air and we had been able to stop the engine before con rods and pistons went flying around, smashing up the engine, causing a fire, or maybe even some bits flying into the flight deck. Norman, cheerful as usual, said, 'Good show, Freddie, what revs and boost do you now want on No 1?' Funny thing, not one of us seemed to think anything of carrying on with three engines, as long as one of the others did not think of doing an encore.

Later on, I must admit I did wonder whether the cylinder had cracked because of the cold; if so, some of the others may go too but we were too far from home now for it to really matter. The next job was to check on what we had 'lost' with not having No 2. There was a pneumatic pump on each of the two port engines. Each pump could be used either as a vacuum pump for the flying instruments (directional gyro, artificial horizon, and turn and bank) or as a pressure pump for the de-icing boots on the wings and tail but one pump could not do the vacuum and pressure jobs together. A change-over cock fortunately allowed either pumps to be used for either purpose, but not both at once. It was imperative to keep the flight instruments working, especially as the compass was useless but if we wanted to use the de-icers we would have to turn the cock over and then back again before the gyros started slowing down. The pump on No. 1 was up to scratch, giving five inches of mercury on vacuum and 10 lb per square inch on pressure. Then we realised that we required pneumatic pressure to cock the cannons, so we got them cocked and went back onto vacuum, hoping that we would not have to use the de-icers very much.

We were nearing 71 30N, 00 10W and getting near to the convoy. It was getting faintly light, a funny sort of light, broken grey clouds—more cloud than breaks—with a flat base at about 1,500 feet, ahead looked very black but what was it? It looked more like haze than cloud; it did not seem to be getting any nearer and below broken drift ice in all directions; surely a convoy would not be sailing through this. It was so dashed cold that we had to keep our masks on, otherwise our breath froze on the inside of the screen and the cold air felt almost solid, as if it were pressing on your body. Our moustaches were frozen so they felt like needles pricking into your lip. As it was getting lighter, we got the lads to man all the positions, Les was keeping a close watch on the ASV, and we turned the IFF (Identification Friend or Foe) on as we did not want to be greeted by a ship we could not see by a burst of AA fire. It was all getting a bit tense.

Soon, we left the drift ice on our port. It just seemed to end in an abrupt line and there was a moderately choppy sea below. At the datum point, there was no sign of the convoy so we commenced a square search. It had not got much lighter and there still seemed to be that peculiar haze in the distance. After an hour and a quarter, Les spotted something on the ASV; we approached carefully. As we did so, Les reported that there was more than one blip but we could not see anything yet. I thought at least they would know that we were coming as Iceland would have broadcast to them, even if they were keeping radio silence and it struck me that maybe they had not been able to receive anything either as we could not.

As soon as the image of a white-looking ship came into view, we fired off the 'colours of the day', turning away and firing off the colours several more times in quick succession, also signalling with the lamp. Still keeping our distance, we saw another ship, then another, and one was signalling to us it was unmistakably a County Class Cruiser. We identified ourselves and were told to wait. Then, he called us in and what a sight. The ships look like pieces of iced Christmas cake as the decks and the superstructures seemed to be encrusted in ice—what those Navy blokes had to put up with, freezing, ice covered decks and smelly wet Mess decks dripping with condensation, some of them shut away in the bowels of the ship or enclosed in gun turret with no chance of survival if a torpedo tore the ship apart. We were sent to search ahead and to the south-east of the convoy.

Conditions were really not at all bad for us, only having a few snow showers; it was just the bloody cold, but our thoughts for those blokes below kept any of us from moaning. It would have been nicer if No. 2 prop had been turning rather than just stuck there, standing still. The light began to go just about 2 p.m. so we returned to the convoy while we could still see it, told the SNO we would be leaving at 2.30 p.m., got his position from him, for which we were thankful in view of our compass being up the pole, and wished him a safe journey; he thanked us for coming. I had a great admiration for the Navy. Surely someone could work out another way to get the stuff to Russia without having to come all this way around or make the ruddy Russians come for it themselves.

We left the convoy. Another four and three-quarter hours would see us home and in front of that stove in the Mess with a few tots of Canadian Club to warm us up. The WOPs had had no joy on the radio for virtually the whole trip. We got brewed up and set about the sandwiches while Harry got cracking making toast and heating up sausage and beans. We also had some tins of pears but they were so dashed cold we had to warm them up in a pan before we could bear them in our mouths. I had never been so damned cold, shivering and goose pimples inside all the vests, shirts, long Johns, pullovers, battle dress and Irvin jacket and trousers. Norman and I took turns to stand up and move about to get warm, but it did not make much difference.

With an hour gone, Ron reported that the crackles were starting on the radio, getting worse and worse until he said they were the worst he had heard. We knew what that was: the blessed Aurora. Shortly after, the clouds disappeared and there was the biggest, brightest, and most spectacular Aurora that any of us had ever seen. The previous ones had been in vertical streaks like a curtain but this was quite different. It was just like being under an enormous bell tent, the walls of vivid vertical streaks of green, yellow, and red, all coming to a point at the top. The colours were rapidly changing, quickly rotating in one direction, stopping, and then rotating back again. This all seemed to be high above us so we were out of the cloud, but it was blocking out the stars, so as long as this lasted, it was a matter of having to rely on dead reckoning navigation as there would be no star shots and no radial bearings. Fortunately, it did not seem to muck up the ASV so we would be able to pick up the land mass when we got near Iceland. The compass was also beginning to get a bit more reliable; when we flew a dog-leg so that Fred could take drifts on flame floats, the needle did make a lazy effort to take up the right heading, even though it still needed a little tap of encouragement; the angle of dip was decreasing.

I was sure that I was not the only one keeping an extra special eye on the engine instruments for No. 1 engine; we certainly did not want to lose another engine on that side. Neither Norman nor Freddie mentioned it but I knew what they were thinking. Freddie shifted some more fuel having calculated how much would be required in each tank in view of No. 1 having to work a bit harder than either Nos 3 or 4. Harry cursed over the intercom that we seemed to have run out of water, then came on again to say the drinking water in the insulated containers had frozen but he got the top off and was going to chip some ice out so we could have some tea – that brought cheers all round. The Aurora was still in all its glory but shortly we entered cloud and had to keep using the prop and wing de-icers; to use the latter, we had to flip over the pneumatic pump from vacuum to pressure, wait until the pressure registered 9 lb psi, use the de-icers then, as soon as the ice cracked off, change the cock back to vacuum as quickly as we could before the instrument gyros toppled. We soon got it off to a fine art. Next, Harry announced that one of our little pigeons had died; maybe they did not like the cold, so he had taken the other one out of its yellow tin and stuffed it down the front of his flying jacket and given it a sip of his tea. This damn cloud and icing continued but the compasses were now performing properly when after about three and a half hours, Ron thought the ASV was showing land on the starboard side. Les had a look and agreed with him; it must be Iceland, it could not be anywhere else, but what part of Iceland? The radio was still crackling away. There was nothing showing on the forward aerials so we decided to maintain course and see what happened to the blip on the starboard aerials. Lib Is stay pretty constant at about eight miles. After an occasional flip over to the forward aerials to make sure there is nothing ahead, we decided this was bloody marvellous work by Fred; we must have been running parallel with the south-east coast of Iceland. A big increase in the size of the blip must be the big Vatnajökull glacier so we kept this heading and when the land started to move away, we would be rounding the most southerly tip at Vik, after passing the Vestmannaeyjar Islands, which we would pick up on the forward aerials, we will let down a bit and follow the coast on the ASV till we can pick up Reykjavík and get and altimeter setting. Another half an hour and we should be home.

On rounding the southern tip, we did pick up Reykjavík. Les told us he has got them and they are calling us. Moments later, Les came on the intercom: 'Skip. We have to divert to Benbecula, Reykjavík is 200 feet cloud base, 50 yards visibility'. We immediately turned south and asked Fred for a course. It was now 6.30 p.m. and we had been airborne thirteen and a half hours. It would take about four hours to Benbecula so that would make it seventeen and a half hours, leaving about half-an-hour's fuel in hand. We had a discussion with Freddie about the most economical revs and boost for maximum range at our present weight with three engines and managed to cut the boost a little without losing appreciable airspeed, so we went for four hours to Benbecula instead of under half an hour to Reykjavík.

At least it got less cold and we got out of the icing. We studied our notes on the map of the Hebrides as none of us had been there before, Ron managed to make another mug of tea for each of us as Harry was busy nursing his pigeon and the spare bod we had with us did not seem to be mucking in very much; I thought he got frozen stiff with being in the rear gun most of the trip as Les did not seem to trust him on the radio or ASV. After what seemed an eternity, we picked up the Outer Hebrides on the ASV. The crackles on the radio had all gone now but we were still in cloud. A bearing from MBG (the radio beacon on the Butt of Lewis) tied in nicely and confirmed that we would soon be tracking due south, parallel to the shore of North and South Uist, Benbecula being a small island between the two. At this point, we called Benbecula and this was when the fun began.

First, they told us we could not land due to a 150-foot cloud base and falling. We told them that we had to land as we only had half an hour fuel left; actually, at that time, we had a little more. We requested QDMs (magnetic courses to steer to reach the airfield) and for a BABBS landing (blind approach beacon system, which was a talk down by a controller in a truck near the end of the runway using a radar screen) because we knew they had no SBA (standard beam approach) landing aid. They told us that the BABBS was on thirty minutes notice to get the crew out so, Norman, quite rightly, got a bit cross with them and asked why they had not got it set up already when they knew we were coming and kept on transmitting for them to get bearings on us for the QDMs.

When the first bearings arrived, they were pre-fixed by 'Q' something else, not QDM. We had to look this up in the 'Q' code book to find it meant that it was a magnetic course to the station but must not be flown due to an obstruction in the path. So, we kept on flying south, seemingly for ages, still in cloud, until the bearings given were pre-fixed QDM. As we approached, we kept asking if the BABBS was ready, to be told 'negative'. Then, we were asked if we had any D. C.s aboard; when we told them we had, we were told to maintain 2,000 feet (we were already at 1,500), turn on to a reciprocal course for five minutes, and drop our D. C.s. This seemed a terrible waste and no one had bothered about landing us with these on before; we suspected it was an excuse to give them time to get the BABBS set up. As we returned, following their QDMs, we were asked to turn on to another course for thirty seconds; we realised that this meant they had got the BABBS going and the turn was for them to identify us as the right blip on the screen, so we thought, 'Here we go' and started our pre-landing procedure. Here, we made our big goof.

Looking behind us, Norman and I counted five bods on the flight deck so thought everybody was there, ready for landing, but we had forgotten we had a spare bod with us. The controller was giving us slight alterations in course and the height to fly and rate of descent while Norman asked me for 'Wheels down'. The red lights came on to show the wheels going down, but the green light did not come on to show the nose wheel as down and locked. Freddie then went down for the usual visual check and came back to report that Fred's leg was trapped under the nose wheel door; the wheel had come halfway down and jammed against the door. He said Fred was okay but he would have to saw through the stays on the nose door to free both Fred and the nose wheel, unless it would free if we selected 'Up'. We called the airfield to tell them we had undercarriage trouble and would abort the approach. Freddie popped back to tell us the wheel had not come up, so he disappeared with his hacksaw to cut through the stays. We left Freddie in peace to get on with his job as he did not want anybody bothering him; there would not be room for anyone else down there anyway. The bods on the ground got in a hell of a state; they gave us a holding pattern and kept a watch on us with the BABBS to make sure we did not get near the high ground, which was all we wanted, but some bod kept coming on, wanting to know exactly what we were doing. Norman tried to explain, but with not knowing Libs, they did not realise that the nose wheel door opened inwards, each side being like two flaps hinged together. The hinged part lifted up and then the two pieces lay flat, one on top of the other at the side of the opening so that the wheel could come down. Fred had almost crawled past the nose-wheel when the door started opening, trapping his training foot under the door so that it could not lay flat; thus, as the wheels started to come down, it jammed against the door, which was not clear of the hole. It only caught his heel, but it was enough to prevent him pulling it out or getting out of his boot. The ground bods obviously did not follow what was going on and when Norman told them that the engineer was sawing the stays off, some silly bugger must have thought he was sawing Fred's foot off because the MO came on and started telling us where to inject morphine. Norman politely told them we were not cutting the navigator's leg off and would they kindly shut up and leave us clear to listen to the BABBS operator. However, even then, they carried on about having instructed all blackouts to be removed and lights switched on to which Norman told them that all we wanted was runway lights and for them to clear the air. We would advise when ready to commence final approach.

It was not long before both Fred and Freddie appeared on the flight deck. Freddie looked buggered but Fred was perfectly all right and reported no damage done. So, we selected undercarriage 'up' and then 'down' again; the indicators looked okay so Freddie carried out the usual visual checks to be sure—top brace on the nose wheeled straight and, with the aid of his torch through the rear side windows, checked that the yellow indicator tabs on the hinged struts on the main wheels were showing. We told the BABB's operator we were ready for final approach. Now he was damn good, nice and calm, giving us courses to steer and distance from touchdown, while I gave Norman a read-out of airspeed and height and started putting down some flap.

We were coming in nicely, settled on a steady course, still in cloud. Norman asked for full flap a bit sooner than usual. As we knew there can be no overshoot in these circumstances, we had to get in. Then, just after the flaps were fully down, Freddie pointed out the hydraulic pressure was zero. He cut in on the intercom, 'Jack, watch the flaps don't come up Skip—hydraulic pressure gone, should have enough in the accs. for brakes but don't peddle them too much'.

With no time for any replies, I kept on calling airspeed and height with half an eye on flap indicator and another half through windscreen—150 feet, 125 feet—then faintly through thinning cloud, a higgledy-piggledy mass of dim lights scattered all over the place ahead but where was the bloody runway? After 100 feet, still holding the flap lever down, I looked out properly and in a second or so, spotted a dark strip. I pointed to it and at the same instant, Norman spotted it and with a slight turn, we were nearly over the threshold. He bumped her down a bit fast, I held the throttles back and braced the rudders. We applied two or three touches of brake but did not seem to be slowing up much so, bearing in mind what Freddie had said, Norman applied the brakes a bit harder and held them on.

Suddenly, the nose-wheel seemed to be trying to force its way into the deck. We slew to starboard with a bloody great squeal as the starboard wheel locked solid. A split second later, the port wheel must have locked too as we stopped slewing and with a damn great rock, we thumped down on the tail skid. We came to a stop, gently rocking back on the nose-wheel but we were still on the runway. Our first comments were about the silly buggers who tried to confuse us by having all the hut lights put on, a flare path on its own would have stood out like a beacon in the dark but with all these lights on, some of which were brighter than the flare path. We could only tell where it was by the fact that we spotted a dark unlit strip, which, fortunately, turned out to be runway.

Within moments of stopping, we were surrounded by vehicles and excited bods. The MO came in a blood wagon to collect the casualty; Harry soon told him that the only casualty was a pigeon and he was not going to get his hands on that. It was now 10.40 p.m.; we had been airborne for seventeen hours and forty minutes and we were all getting a bit niggardly at the debriefing. The debriefing officer went on about us not diverting earlier so we asked him if he had ever been up in the Arctic with the Aurora in all its glory because if he had, he would know that you could not get a damn thing on the radio and they could not make out that they did not know what time we would be arriving as one of our WOPs had picked up a signal to them from Group giving our ETA and endurance, yet they had not got the BABBS ready and knew full well we would need it. Also, who had the silly idea of taking down the blackout and putting all the lights on so that we could hardly define the flare path? It was a pity that we made the stupid cock-up with the nose wheel, particularly as we felt they had a silly grudge against Liberators; they had a squadron of Coastal Fortresses and sarcastically commented about us being 'VLR' when they were classed as 'LR'. Before leaving debriefing, Norman insisted on seeing the BABBS operator, to congratulate him on a very good 'talk-down'; he turned out to be a LAC (leading aircraftman, a trade classification until 1 January 1951).

After a good night's sleep, we awoke to find our surviving pigeon flying around in the hut. Harry was self-appointed pigeon minder. He loved his pigeons and was going to look after it until we returned home. It was just after noon. Harry informed us that before we went to their Mess, we must join him in burying our dead pigeon, so, putting the other one back in its tin so that it would not fly out of the door, we seriously trooped out, taking the fire shovel to bury the little chap with due dignity, marking the spot with a pile of stones. Then, looking around, we took in the view. The clouds had cleared. We were quite near the beach; to the north-east, the 1,138-foot high Eaval looked much closer than the 7 miles it was supposed to be and about 15 miles to the south were some very high peaks, about 2,000 feet high, not the place to be buggering about in low cloud. There was quite a nasty little bump, about 2 miles away to the east. It was pretty wild country and we decided we preferred Reykjavík.

After lunch, we went to have a look at 'P' for Peggy, although the folks here would call her 'P' for Peter, which was strictly correct but, she was always 'P' for Peggy in Reykjavík. Old Peggy, she looked buggered. There was a jagged hole in the cowling of No. 2 engine on the outboard side, which we could not see from the cockpit where something must have flown out. There was also a mysterious hole in the port fin and rudder, she was up on jacks with the main wheels off, and a floppy nose-wheel door. Freddie linked up with the ground crews to supervise their activities as none of them had experience of Libs and the Fortresses they worked on had Wright Cyclone engines not our Pratt & Whitney Twin Wasps. We met Norman and Les and before the day was over, it had been arranged that the engineering officer together with a sergeant and corporal would fly up from Ballykelly the following day to see what was what. That night, we found the Mess was full of rumour—it was amazing how rumour gets around. They thought we had been shot up, been on fire, the navigator had lost his leg, and our engines had been cut through lack of fuel while landing. It seemed that someone on the Tannoy had told them to remove the blackouts and put all lights on to make sure we did not crash on the camp. To start with, this was worth quite a few drinks but then we had to tell them the truth, especially when they saw Fred running around on two legs and we took the mickey out of them for getting in such a panic.

The engineering officer and his team duly arrived and decided what spares were required. These, along with a replacement engine, were flown in a Dakota and after seven days, we were jolly thankful to be getting away, even though it was only to be to Ballykelly to get some jobs finished off.

However, 'P' for Peggy did not want to go. As we did our final pre-take-off check, a pillar of smoke arose from the control pedestal as I exercised the prop pitches and they all stuck in fine pitch; it was a good job the electrics burned out then and not just after take-off. So, it was two more days before we boarded her again, together with the ground crew lads for a gentle one-hour-and-forty-minute cruise to Ballykelly, all but ten minutes being in cloud. For the next six days, we seemed to be flying backwards and forwards between Ballykelly and Aldergrove as one of the new squadrons was moving into Ballykelly and the rest of our squadron was getting ready to join us in Iceland. Some of our servicing was being done at Aldergrove and the new tab ASV was being fitted. The old ASV could be picked by U-boats 60 miles away so had time to dive before the aircraft would see them. The new ones worked with a shorter 10-cm wavelength and could not be detected. We learned there were to be a couple of changes on our crew: Les and Harry were to come off for a rest and two most colourful characters joined up—two more Yorkshiremen, so we were five out of seven. 'Ginger', a very colourful lad from Sheffield, had a ruddy complexion like a rising sun, topped with a mass of curly ginger hair. He was medium height, stocky, and had a broad smile and a 'down-to-earth' personality. He had been the Bull's No. 1 WOP/ASV operator and led The Bull onto many U-boats in the early days when they were not picking up the old ASV and they were operating far out, where the U-boats did not expect to find aircraft. The Bull had now completed his tour and was leaving the squadron, so his crew had to be split up, or else gone on rest, so we would be getting a new CO. The other lad, Joe from Hull, was a complete contrast. New to the squadron, with straight jet-black hair plastered down, a thin pencil line Clark Gable-type moustache, he had a big round face but was not very happy looking. Ginger took over from Les as No. 1 and Joe became No. 3.

We managed to get a couple of dropping exercises fitted in as we had not been able to do any for a long time. This also enabled us to get to know Ginger and Joe. Ginger was a great bloke, full of fun and an expert at his job; he thought the new Mk 2 ASV was a piece of cake compared with the old stuff and was picking up the smallest of things with ease, even though we could not pick them out when he let us have a look. Joe was a bit quiet and although we tried our best to make him feel at home, he seemed very aloof. I met a flight lieutenant who was going to be our flight commander when we all got together in Iceland, so I had a 'bash' at him about getting a crew of my own. He looked at my file; my competence card from Ferry Command was not there, so the other flight commander must have chucked it out. However, I assured him that he would be able to see from my logbook, which was in Iceland, that I had checked out on Libs and had now done over twenty ops. I pointed out that if I went on doing nothing but second pilot work, I would be losing my touch. He seemed reasonably sympathetic and to my delight, the next day, he asked me to fly over to Ballykelly with him. For the return flight, he let me start off in the left-hand seat and to do the lot while he acted as second pilot; we went on a bit of a detour to fit in a few climbs, descents, turns, and a mock dropping run over Lough Neagh. The landing went okay and I began to think that I may be getting somewhere; he seemed a nice guy.

By 19 February, 'P' for Peggy was flying again, with a new engine and all patched up, so we took her for an airframe and engine test, swung the compass, and decided she was already to go again. On 23 February, we were off to find a convoy, ONAS167, further south at 47 31N, 29 27W. We were given two extra crew, partly for operational training and partly to keep an extra look out for long-range aircraft from Brest. At 47 40N, 28 45W, we found an abandoned merchant—a very slight list but otherwise it seemed okay. We circled around but we saw no sign of life so rattled a few rounds of gunfire along its sides to see if this would bring anyone in sight but it seemed entirely deserted. We took some photos (with our German Leica camera) and pressed on. It must have been abandoned during the night, perhaps because it had been hit and its steering damaged or maybe its engines broke down. It looked, however, as if the convoy may have been in trouble.

At the appointed meeting point, there was no sign of the convoy so we commenced a 'moving square search'. After four hours searching, we eventually found it, miles off its intended position; this was confirmed when they gave us their position. Radio silence was being maintained but they gave us their new course; it had been altered because they had been attacked during the night. We reported the ship we had seen and went off to search ahead but soon we were recalled to Aldergrove due to weather so had to leave just before dark. Nearly back at Aldergrove, we were told to divert to St Eval due to fog affecting nearly all the country. This was going to run us a bit fine so we kept the navigation lights off and cut over the Irish Free State, making a beeline for St Eval. We were in a Modified IIIA in which the fuel gauges bobbed up and down like a yo-yo due to the flexibility of the self-sealing tanks. As we were crossing the Bristol Channel, the level kept bobbing right out of sight at the bottom of the long glass tubes and at the best of times, they were supposed to over read by 36 gallons each tank but we felt that as long as there was some to bob up at all, there must be a bit left. Freddie maintained his confidence in his calculations, saying that we were okay. No one said very much but it was funny how everybody decided it was getting cold and put on their Mae West for a bit of warmth. I saw a light, which must have been on a boat but for a moment took it for a star and felt we must have gone into a steep turn, but I soon got my orientation back. St Eval control were great, such a contrast to Benbecula; they had their Sandra Lights on so we could head straight for the airfield and gave us landing conditions without being asked: runway QDM 261, SBA on, frequency 36.4, cleared to land. We did not need the SBA and landed after sixteen hours and forty-five minutes. Freddie's calculations were correct. Once again, full marks to the top flight engineer.

Before leaving St Eval on 25 February for a cruise up to Aldergrove, we learned that the convoy had been attacked. It all seemed so frustrating as we had not seen a bloody U-boat, yet alone attacked one, and now the weather had eased up, they were sinking ships again as fast as ever.

23

Ginger Finds us a U-Boat

After a day or two at Aldergrove, doing air tests and landing at Nutts Corner to do compass swings, we were delighted on 2 March to be off back to Reykjavík, in a Mark I: 'L' for Leo. We had seven passengers, including a wing commander on his way to take up a job at Iceland Headquarters, and a load of spares and equipment. At the last minute, it was decided that we would do a short 'sweep' on the way to help round up a convoy (SC120) south-west of Iceland, which had become scattered due to bad weather and U-boat attacks. One of our chaps was out there from Iceland but needed some help as the convoy was so split up. We found some ships and a couple of escorts around 60 3ON, 28 15W. Ginger was picking them up like flies on fly paper and we buzzed around, signalling their bearing and distance to regain the main convoy. They were ploughing their way through pretty heavy sea but it was not at all bad in the air. It was a damn nuisance having all these bods with us though as they kept getting in our way; some of them were sick and a squadron leader (non-flying type) kept putting 'his oar in'. It was only a short trip as we did not have full tanks and after flying nine hours, we were pleased to see Reykjavík again after four weeks away.

Ginger and Joe moved into our hut. We packed up Harry's gear to be sent back on the next flight to the UK and soon had the hut warmed up and looking like home again. Nearly the whole squadron were up here now. The Mess became pretty full and DROs (daily routine orders) appeared on the Mess noticeboard alongside a Mayfly list (a list of skippers names, the top one being the one for the next trip; after each trip, you appeared at the bottom and work your way up). We had not bothered with such things when there were only a few of us. We now even got roped into the 'orderly sergeant'—the good old days were over.

However, we were getting a bit bothered about Joe. Ginger said he was good at his job and was okay in the air but sometimes, he would get very belligerent on the ground, especially after a few drinks. We gathered that he had had a pretty rough life, being brought up in a 'home'. He had married young, had a kid, and was convinced his wife was 'having it off' with another fella. The second night we were up there, we had to drag him out of the Mess because he was getting pickled, shouting, and being argumentative. We dragged him struggling back to the hut, protesting that he had no friends and the whole world was against him. We tried to convince him he had friends and we were only getting him back for his own good but he raved and ranted on till Ginger landed him one right on the chin and we dumped him on his bed. During the night, I heard someone staggering around and quietly said, 'Is that you, Joe?'

Ginger replied, 'It's okay, I'm awake too'. We then heard some rattling of the shovel and poker by the stove followed by a shout from Joe as he put his hand on the hot stove. Fred jumped out of bed and put the lights on. Joe was just approaching Ginger's bed with the poker in his hand. We all leapt on him; Ginger was sitting up with his boots in his hands ready to deal with him. For some reason. Joe seemed to 'have it in' for Ginger, maybe he was jealous of Ginger's DFM (distinguished flying medal). We gave him a real good rollicking, telling him that he could be court-martialled for this but for the fact that we were his friends, despite the way he was going on. Soon, he was crying like a big soft kid. We slapped some margarine on his burnt hand and we all got off to an uneasy sleep. The next morning, he knew nothing about it.

It was getting much lighter now, light by 8 a.m. and not dark till 5 p.m. so we fitted in a dropping practice and then got away to do a sweep out at 37 45W near convoy SC121; another aircraft was doing the close escort. We had now got enough aircraft and crews to start providing better cover. This convoy had already been attacked and lost several ships; we spent some time behind her in case any U-boats were catching up with her on the surface. First, we found a merchant vessel abandoned and obviously sinking some thirty miles behind the convoy.

We were just under the cloud base, in and out of bits of broken scud, with Ginger on the new ASV, when with all the confidence in the world, Ginger piped up, 'U-boat, 8 miles port side. Switching to forward aerials'. We turned till Ginger gave us, 'Dead ahead, 7 miles'.

We increased revs and boost—a rich mixture—opened the bomb-doors, and D. C.s were set for stick of six at 36-foot spacing. It was 6 miles away and we were still at 1,000 feet, skimming cloud. Fred gave our position to

Above left: Jack training at Basic Training in Torquay, May 1941.

Above right: Jack at Kitchener, Canada, after cross-country, August 1941.

Below: The American Niagara Falls.

SFTE Brantford. Middle row: Peter (fifth), Jack (sixth). Front row: Harry (last but one).

Above left: The Wings parade, 21 November 1941. Group Captain C. G. Johnson 'pins them on'.

Above right: Icebreaker in the distance.

H.M. CUSTOMS, NEWFOUNDLAND

No. 1006

PORT OF ..... Gander, Nfld.

This is to Certify that the

Capt. Colman ..... Master,

registered ~~tonnage~~ 21,000 lbs, with 2 men, registered in F.H. 451 – Hudson with the following cargo:

[H. M. CUSTOMS MAY 30 1942 NEWFOUNDLAND AIRPORT]
[H. M. CUSTOMS JUN 3 1942]

has been cleared from this port to the port of PRESTWICK, SCOTLAND or alternate landing grounds in U.K.

Given under my hand at the Custom House, GANDER AIRPORT, Newfoundland, this 30th day of May, 1942.

..... Collector.

A Hudson.

York railway station, including the W. V. S. Service Canteen where Jack's mother helped out.

Jack's wedding day with Mother (Freda) and Peggy, 30 September 1942.

Jack and Peggy with Heather and Peter Stembridge.

The wedding group.

Reykjavík airfield on a 'good day'.

A white Liberator.

Harbour and the main runway (top left), Reykjavík.

A U-boat in distress.

Possibly rescuing the crew.

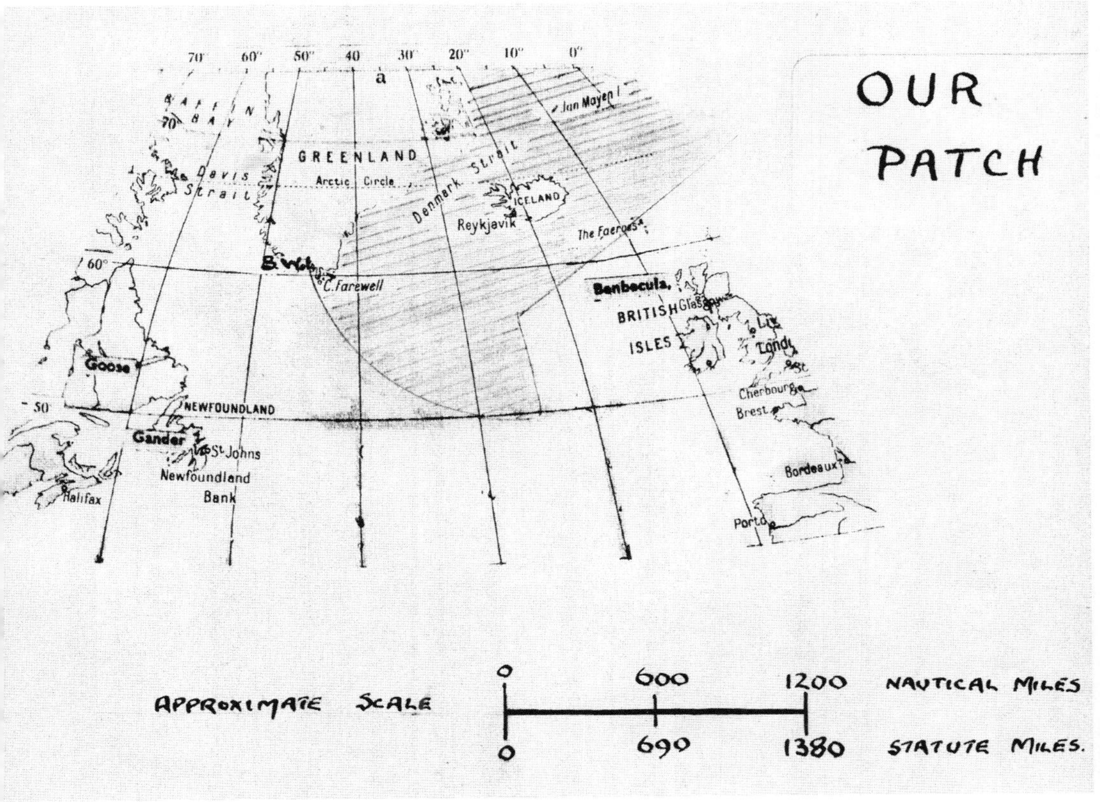

'Our Patch'.

An orderly convoy in calm waters.

Above: The east coast of Iceland.

Below: Drift ice in the Arctic.

Mark I Liberator 'L' for Leo just before they split up: back row: Ginger, Ron, Freddie, and Joe; front row: Fred, 'Little Titch', Norman, and Jack.

Above left: Formal portrait as a flight sergeant.

Above right: Outside our Nissen hut with Harry and Ron.

VLR Mark IIIA Lib 'T', August 1943, with Snæfellsjökull in the background.

Above: Greenland while searching for the enemy.

Below: Greenland.

An escort vessel.

Above: Vestmannaeyjar islands.

Below: A geyser.

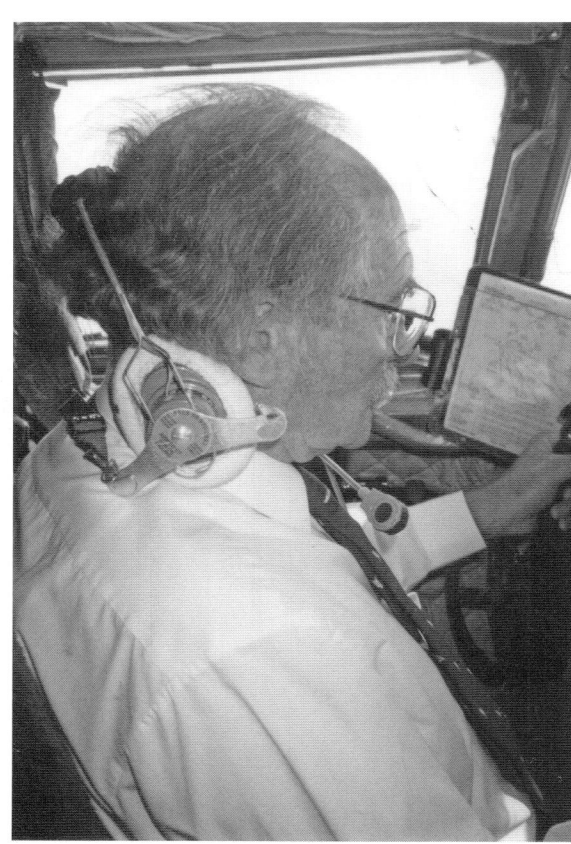

Left: Time in a 'front seat', fifty years on.

Below: Jack (far right) seems a bit outgunned at the Battle of the Atlantic celebrations fifty years on.

A CAM ship with fighter aircraft.

Convoy in calm weather.

Peggy.

Above left: Icebreaker to Prince Edward Island at Cape Bonden, February 1942.

Above right: Jack at Basic Training in Torquay, May 1941.

Ron, while Fred manned the forward gun and Joe was in the rear turret. With 5 miles to go, Ron was bashing out a sighting report; at 4 miles, we moved a bit to starboard and nudged Turbos open a bit more for 57 inches of boost, 2,700 revs then re-trim; 3 miles; 2 miles; right, down we went then there she was—a U-boat on the surface. Norman called 'Attack' so Ron knew to send '512' and hold the key down. We subscribed an arc to bring us diagonally across its track. It was going to dive or shoot back so we screamed down, trimming a bit tail heavy to help us pull out. As it was diving, we hurtled 50 feet above the waves, heading to cross its track some way ahead of the conning tower. We kept low for a few seconds. Joe shouted in glee from the turret 'Jesus Christ, the bloody sea is blowing up, and again, again, again, again, again. What a bloody sight, went hundred feet or more into the air—it's still coming down'.

Norman asked him if he saw the conning tower; he said he could not but there was a sort of swirl between the second and third eruptions. We reduced speed and circled around the disturbed area but there was no sign of wreckage, bubbles, or bodies. We dropped a marker and kept circling but still watched out in case any more of the pack appeared. We told ourselves that we dropped them just right and if Joe's swirl was in fact where she submerged, then there were two D. C.s on one side and four on the other, so if they went off at the correct depth, which we could not control, they must have badly damaged her. We reckoned she was a Type VIIC and could have given us a fight with her 37-mm and two 20-mm guns, but she got away.

After a little while, there was without doubt some oil on the surface, but this was no proof that we had got her; it could have been spilled from her tanks as she made a violent manoeuvre as they were open to the sea at the bottom, or it could be some oil they released on purpose to kid us. Perhaps we would never know, so our first attack would remain merely a 'possible'. We were recalled early so were back within nine hours and twenty minutes but we were home in time to celebrate in the Mess. Ginger had brought us luck but we kept a strict watch on Joe.

Fred and I spent quite a lot of time with the 'instrument bashers' to see whether, between us, we could devise some means of overcoming the severe compass 'dip' experienced when up in the Arctic. We all came up with various theories, most of which were soon 'kicked into touch' and eventually decided to modify two compasses, on one reducing the length of the north end of the needle in the hope that the extra weight on the south would keep the needle more or less level, and on the other, attaching a little wax weight on the south end to achieve the same effect. We realised that, even if they worked, they would not be accurate unless properly airswung when installed in the aircraft but we would not know which aircraft we were to have until too late. It was therefore decided to mount these two modified compasses on a wooden board with brass screws and take them with us when we went north again to see how they performed.

Before we knew it, we were off again on another trip. The trip itself was an eventful fourteen hours on a sweep in mixed weather but the events beforehand were rather traumatic. We were due to be called about 2 a.m., so after the preliminary briefing, most of us got to bed for, we hoped, four hours of sleep. Shortly after, Ron roused us, asking where Joe was. Ron, Ginger, Freddie, and I got up and went to the Mess and there was Joe, getting very well pissed. We dragged him out and once again, Ginger had to 'land him one' to keep him quiet. We dumped him on his bed and discussed what we were going to do about him. Deep down, we all liked Joe, in spite of these relapses; we really felt sorry for him and felt that, if only we could get him to feel that he was as good as the next bloke and part of a team, he would be okay. So, after some debate, it was agreed that he would not be fit to fly but, if Norman would agree, we would go without him, leaving him locked up in the hut while we were away and this would be his last chance. He would be out on his ear if he did it again, but we felt it might have the desired effect. Ginger and I went to Norman's hut about half an hour before we were due to be called and Norman agreed to go along with us and give him his last chance. It meant we would be one WOP/AG short, but as we were going in a Lib IIIA, Freddie could take the second pilot's seat for sessions while I helped out on the radio; I never thought that that WOP course would come in useful in circumstances like this.

Back at the hut, we roused Joe and drummed into him what we were doing and that we he must not show his face outside the hut, or put on any lights, or make any noise, or any smoke from the stove. There was some grub in the hut and he would have to do his business in a bucket. God help us all if we got diverted—we would all be in the shit then. To be on the safe side, we locked the door and made sure he did not have a key. Fourteen hours seemed a long time to us, but it must have seemed like an eternity to Joe, all the time wondering whether we would get back, without anyone twigging, and what would happen if we did not make it. On our return, we all split up to leave the aircraft and said we would walk to 'stretch our legs'. We found Joe, sitting in the dark, freezing cold; he could hardly talk, managing to get out a few words about it being the first time anyone had cared about him, tears ran down his cheeks as he put his arms around Ginger who said, 'Come on you daft bugger, make yourself look as if you have been flying and come to the Mess for grub, we are bloody starving'. After the meal, he had to spend another twelve hours in the hut while we slept but when we woke, Joe was rushing around with mugs of tea. We told him to forget the last thirty-six hours, except to thank Norman and apologise but if he let us down in the future, he would be for the chop.

No sooner had we arrived at the Mess for lunch, thinking that we would be free for a couple of days, when we were sent to do a little job before dark. A river was causing flooding around Selfoss, the principal town in south Iceland, due to slabs of ice having drifted down and becoming jammed in a narrow bend in the river. The flood waters were affecting the airfield at Kaldadarnes from where the Hudson Squadron operated. Our job was to take a series of vertical line overlap photographs of the area from 8,000 feet and also to bomb the ice to see if we could shift it. The weather was clear and we were quite excited at the prospect of seeing Iceland from 8,000 feet and doing a bit of bombing for a change. A bomb-sight was fitted, the vertical cameras charged with plenty of film, and the bomb bay filled with 500 lb SAP (semi armour piercing) bombs. We did not think that SAP bombs would be the best for the job but we only had AP and SAP bombs on the station for use against ships, so they would have to do, but we felt they would go straight through the ice and probably bury themselves in the river bed.

It was an interesting flight over land to this area of flat land, which showed some signs of cultivation, bounded by the sea to the south and ringed by high ground. To the north, the ground rose to a big glacier (Langjökull); almost ahead and furthers along the coast was another glacier (Mýrdalsjökull); and away beyond to the east, the vast Vatnajökull. Nearest of all, to the east, Mount Hekla, just short of 5,000 feet, was an active volcano with its snow-capped top. It had been quiet for some years, except for odd rumblings, but if it stuck to schedule, it was expected to erupt again within a couple of years of our visit; according to Icelandic folklore, it was the entrance to Hell. It was an unusual day for Iceland, at least at that time of the year.

We got the lay of the land sorted out and made several precise runs, taking pictures; the long shadows cast by the low sun should have given us a good idea of relief. We then started our bombing runs, only one bomb at a time because the area we wished to smash up was only small and the Icelanders would not be very pleased if we drop bombs all over the countryside. The bombs did not seem to be doing a lot of good; as we feared, some of them just seem to go straight through the ice with no sign of an explosion. Freddie altered the fuses to the very minimum and we dropped them from much lower; this seemed better as two did chuck up a lot of something into the air and we could see water swirling through this area before we set off for home. Reykjavík looked bonny with its lights twinkling as we approached from over land, a glow from the setting sun over the sea ahead.

The day after our bombing job, we were off again, not over the Atlantic but another trip to the Arctic to do a 'sweep' ahead of and to the east of a Russian convoy. We were to take a Lib IIIA, much to our disgust (as this meant no hot food) because the CO had decided that aircraft must have self-sealing fuel tanks on these trips. Fred collected our 'experimental' compasses, Freddie supervised the de-frosting, and at 6 a.m. on a cold, crisp, clear morning, we were on our way. Joe was behaving like a 'good-un' so we treated him quite normally and we were delighted that he was doing the same; he seemed much more settled already. The stars were twinkling brightly in their thousands as we flew round the coast of Iceland to the extreme easterly point, the radio was crystal clear and we even had the AFN (American Forces network) on one channel. The WOPs seemed to be logging lots of signals; none of them were for us but we decoded some for curiosity and came to the conclusion that there was a lot happening in the Atlantic, particularly with convoy HX228. We settled on course for a point just south-east of Jan Mayen Island, watching to see how the compasses were going to behave. Jan Mayan was a bit of a mystery; we had instructions about the central zone being fortified from the north, making recognition signals to a lookout post by lamp, then banking to sea to make recognition easier and not over-flying until 'R' is received, but we could not land there so there did not seem to be any point in over-flying it. Who occupied it, we did not know; they would not tell us.

Sure enough, the compasses started to stick. We found we could have all three pointing differently and by tapping them, you could get them to point more or less anywhere, but if it remained clear, we could check the course on the sun with the sextant and keep a note of which was the most reliable. As dawn broke, we were at about 69 00N—what a sight. The pinkish light extinguished the stars, the whole 360-degree horizon was crystal clear, the sea was covered in long lazy undulation but hardly a whitecap, everything was pinpoint clear, and the visibility unbelievable. As we commenced our 'sweep', we decided that with this most unusual visibility, we would fly higher than usual (2,000 feet) and open up the distance between legs as the new ASV was working well; this way we would be able to cover a larger area. The sea was as blue as a picture of a

South Sea Island with deep blue sky to match, yet it was bloody cold and somehow a bit 'creepy'. Although the four engines were happily droning away, you could somehow feel the silence outside and the solid coldness against you. We felt to be so alone in this vast nothingness. We were not used to such cloudless conditions and somehow it seemed wrong not to be surrounded by, or flying in, cloud. We remembered what had happened to one of our pigeons on our previous Arctic trip so stuffed screwed up paper in the tins around them and wrapped the engine covers around the tins to try to keep them warm.

Norman seemed to have his binoculars fixed on something and then beckoned to me to have a look. Through my binoculars, I can see something too—something white, almost on the horizon. Ginger said there was nothing showing on the ASV but we altered course for a look. As we flew towards it, we were mystified because it disappeared. Norman and I were both certain we saw something so decided to continue on this course, conjecturing as to what it might have been as a ship could not disappear like that; in any case, if it had been a ship or a U-boat, Ginger would have picked it up. After several minutes, we saw it again, but still about the same distance away as before. This time, it continued to come closer and Ginger reported a slight sea echo but nothing definite. Soon, we realised what it was: it was the edge of the drift ice. Beyond, the sea was becoming more and more covered with floating pieces of ice, all glinting in the sun and dazzling us. We noted its extent and resumed our sweep. The first time we saw it, it must have been over the horizon but the very cold air had bent the light rays to form a sort of mirage.

The weather held all day. The WOPs had been receiving all the time but had not picked up anything addressed to us. As it became dark, Fred got to work on the Astro in case we lost the stars and sure enough, Joe reported funny noises on the radio, which Ron confirmed were the Aurora; before long, the Aurora was in full glory—not like a cone this time, more like a curtain of vertical stripes flashing horizontally backwards and forwards across the screen, changing in intensity from dull to very bright. Looking at it tended to make you dizzy. However, this time, it was some use; although it buggered the radio and radio compass, as usual, it lit up the coast of Iceland, which looked like an evil black mass flecked with white. As we rounded the south coast, the big Vatnajökull reflected the changing colours as if she were herself lit up from the inside. Iceland was such a weirdly fascinating place. No diversions this time, the Aurora was still lighting the place up as we landed. Our compass experiment had only been a limited success, but gave scope for further thought.

We were all delighted by the transformation in Joe. If one or two others were going into town, we would make a point of asking Joe to join us; usually, he did. In the Mess, he would always be with one of us and left when we did without having to be dragged out; he also willingly took his turn at brewing up. He seemed to be quite happy now and was good amusing company. He and Ginger were hitting it off.

Things were hotting up in the Atlantic. Convoy SC121 had lost thirteen ships; convoy HX228 (the one we picked up signals from while on our last Arctic trip) had lost four ships and an escort destroyer; two other convoys were on their way across—SC122 of sixty ships and HX229 of forty ships—but they were not yet within our range. Intelligence reckoned that there were about thirty or forty U-boats looking for these convoys, which were not all that far apart. On 17 March, one of our crews was able to reach slow convoy SC122, but found only forty-eight ships, eight having either turned back or taken shelter off the Canadian coast due to bad weather and four had been sunk the previous night. We got away in 'L' for Leo on 18 March to meet fast convoy HX229 at 54 08N, 27 05W; she was further south than most of the convoys so that was why we had to wait until she got so far east. The weather was pretty lousy and when we found her in the afternoon, it was obvious she had been taking a hammering. The ships were spread out over a large area in anything but good order and the escort of a mere four Destroyers and a Corvette were charging around, rolling, pitching, and chucking up great clouds of spray. They were spread around, out of sight of each other, but using the R/T so it made it easier for us not having to use the lamp. Our first instructions were to help round up the stragglers, so we charged around like a sheep-dog, indicating the position of the largest group of ships, but we could only find thirty ships so it looked as if ten ships (a quarter of the convoy) had already been sunk.

The next job was to cover areas behind and each side of the convoy to at least force down any U-boats still in contact and finally to cover the area ahead. By now, it was almost dark but we were able to stay another hour or so; at least, our presence may have kept some U-boats down. Just as we were thinking about setting off for home, we received a signal: 'divert to Benbecula'. We have a laugh about this, in view of our previous experience there—at least they did not wait until we were nearly back at Iceland this time—so off we set on the five-hour leg to the Hebrides.

Ginger and Joe got cracking with the grub; this time, we managed to get some so-called steak, which the lads made a good job of, garnished with new potatoes from a tin. To be on the safe side, we passed our ETA to Benbecula in good time and asked for the BABBS to be available.

However, the clouds through which we had been flying for three hours or so disappeared about an hour out, and, having made doubly sure that Fred was safely on the flight deck, we let the BABBS operator bring us in, although there was no real need for him. This time, they did not tell us to get rid of our D. C.s.

The following day, we were told to take Leo to Aldergrove as Iceland was still unfit and Leo was almost due for a major service, so we made the pleasant little two-hour trip down the coast of Scotland to Aldergrove. At Aldergrove, we were surprised to find that some of the Squadron was still there. We thought they had all come up to Iceland, but it seemed that the Squadron strength was to be twenty aircraft and there were another five aircraft and some crews getting ready to come and join us. 'Big Mel', the flight commander I had spoken to before about getting my own crew, was also here, so I had another 'go' at him. He seemed much more receptive than the other flight commander, old Jimmy with the big tash.

The next morning, I felt that I may have made some impression on Big Mel as he sent for me to go with him on an air test on a Mark IIIA, which had just come out of a major service. As I made to get into the second pilot's seat, he beckoned me to get in the left-hand seat, taking the second pilot's seat himself. I very deliberately went through the cockpit checks, told him what to do as second pilot, and we were soon taxiing out. After more very deliberate, exaggerated checks, we were away and I was telling him to raise the undercarriage and bleed up the flaps.

We flew around for an hour or so, checking that the engines and all systems were working okay while the flight engineer made notes. We cut and feathered each engine in turn and did a mock drop on the target in Lough Neagh before coming in for the landing, which went off okay, although the runways at Aldergrove seemed very narrow. In the afternoon, we did another air test, this time in a Lib I and Freddie came with us as flight engineer, as well as a couple of ground crew. The routine was as before but we finished by doing some range flying on the new radio range at Nutts Corner and a couple of landings on the SBA at Nutts Corner before returning to Aldergrove.

The only calamity was when taxiing back in at Aldergrove. Big Mel pointed out a very narrow taxiway as a shortcut back to dispersal so I followed his directions as he knew Aldergrove much better than I did but soon, I found I needed more and more power to keep moving and in spite of the power, we came to a halt. Looking down at the wheel on my side, I could see it had sunk into the tarmac and had pushed up a bank of tarmac in front of it—it was the same on the other side—so we had to cut the motors and leave the aircraft to be pulled away backwards. This new taxiway was not supposed to be used by Libs.

The next day, it was another air test in the morning, some practice dropping with Big Mel in the afternoon, followed by some night take-offs and landings at Aldergrove and Nutts Corner using their SBA. I felt pretty sure that these two days of hectic flying were not just to help him do air tests but to check me out as a possible skipper. However, the following day, we were off on another trip, to meet what was left of convoy HX229 and then carry on back to Iceland.

For this trip, we had an addition to the crew: a shy young pilot officer, straight from the GR School to act as third pilot. We christened him 'Titch'. He had no experience on Libs. Compared to the rest of us wearing our 'diversion kit' of creased battle-dress, roll neck pullovers, stockings as scarves, and flying boots, he looked like a tailor's dummy in his new well-pressed best blue uniform, new flat hat, leather gloves, and Van Heusen semi-stiff collar. Norman persuaded him to change his gear before we set off.

At briefing, we learned that the two convoys, SC122 and HX 229 (or what was left of them), had now closed up. Between 16 and 19 March, they had lost twenty-one ships. One U-boat was thought to have been sunk by one of our Libs and many more suffered damage from the Navy escorts. Two had probably been sunk but attacks were still taking place in the dark, after the air cover had left. However, the combined escorts and strong daytime air cover seem now to be keeping the U-boats at bay. We were to be one of three aircraft either with, or close to the convoy.

We felt sure that on this trip we would bag a U-boat to add to our 'possible', especially when we picked up a signal '512' from one of the other Libs, meaning he was going in to make an attack, but it was not to be. Both convoys were now nicely closed up together, we spent five hours sweeping on the south flank without any luck but maybe we did some good, without knowing it. Norman let Little Titch sit in the second pilot's seat for the flight out and back so I was able to give Fred a break on the way home. On the way out, I went into the rear gun position for a while (no turrets on the Lib I) and this scared me to death, looking at the big fin and rudder on each side, which seem to be shaking about, especially when we get a bit of turbulence, as if they were likely to snap off at any moment. I decided it was best not to look but thought about those four bolts securing the tail plane.

Joe seemed to have taken over from Ginger as chef and produced delightful egg, bacon, sausage, and fried bread ,followed by tinned pears and Carnation milk and coffee. They seemed to get better rations in Northern Ireland than we did in Iceland. I resumed in the second pilot's seat as we approached Iceland. A moon was rising behind some cloud. The ground stood out very clearly—white all over; they looked to have had had a lot of snow while we had been away. Soon, the lights of Reykjavík were twinkling, reflecting on the water of the sea and the lake and brightening up the snow. The moon was no longer obscured and made a pretty picture as we came in to land, just like a fairyland with the big cathedral outlined against the snow and coloured lights reflecting off the lake. It was icy cold, dry, and crunchy as we slipped out of the bomb bay. Ron and Joe went to the hut to get the fire on while the rest of us went to the debriefing. Norman took charge of Little Titch, to introduce him to his new home; we dumped our kit and went to the Mess for grub and a few drinks before turning in. I had not written to Peggy for a week so I decided to do that first thing the following day, although it was always difficult thinking what to say because you could not say anything about what we were doing.

An American Squadron with amphibian Catalinas (or Cansos as the Canadians call them) had now arrived at Reykjavík and were living in a newly built camp at the other end of the airfield. When Freddie, Joe, and I were in town we met one of their crew in a cafe and they invited us back to their PX (the American post exchange was like a very superior NAAFI canteen-cum-social centre). Well, these guys had everything (except booze and girls): frozen chickens, meat, tins of fruit, frozen veg, infinite varieties of ice-cream, cigars, coke, and fresh eggs; you name it, they had it. They insisted we had a meal with them and we certainly did not need any pressing. What a meal—chicken, sweetcorn, potatoes, and peas followed by apple pie and lashings of cream, followed by coffee and finally cigars. They said they were allowed to take guests to a meal once a week and as we were allowed to take guests once a week into our Mess, we quickly came to an arrangement to entertain each other weekly whenever our respective flying schedule permitted. It soon became clear why the Yanks were so eager to entertain us; their PX was 'dry' and they enjoyed their 'Rye and Dry' in our Mess. They never overdid it though; in fact, they were rather quiet for Americans—maybe the Navy flyers were more restrained than the other American aircrew we had met. We gave them a bottle of Canadian Club to take away but they insisted on leaving us 1,000 Krona, telling us that that was the amount all their guys insisted on paying for a bottle of Rye and if we would not take the cash, they would not accept the bottle. This seemed ridiculous, 1,000 Krona was about £37 and the price in the Mess was about thirty shillings, but they were rolling in money that they could not spend and soon we were too. After a while, we had a tin stuffed with nice big 1,000 Krona notes—they were appropriately red blood in colour—and anyone who needed cash just helped themselves. It was useless paper really as we could not take it away with us or turn it into any other currency. From time to time, we gave some to the Mess committee to buy things for the Mess.

After all these months on the Squadron, I only now learned that the Squadron was commanded by a wing commander. I had never seen him, presumably because we had been on detachment in Iceland for most of the time, and until now, I had never heard anyone mention him. All this time, I had assumed that one of the flight commanders—a squadron leader—was the squadron commander. No one seemed to know where he was; maybe he was tucked away in the Officer's Mess, but I certainly never came across him.

24

The Critical Stage

With April 1943 came the news that I was to have my own crew. So, now, I was a 'skipper' without a crew. My first thought was that I must let my father know—he would be pleased—then I realised that he had been dead for almost a year. Norman wished me 'Jolly good luck' and said we must arrange for a photograph of us all to be taken by a Lib before we got split up and that we must also have a meal in town to together.

Big Mel had come up to Reykjavík and we got together to organise a crew. Two crews were on the point of being broken up because some of them had been twelve months on the Squadron and were due for a rest. Where possible, the lads could choose the skipper they went with, but it was not so easy when juggling about with those left from broken up crews and, if at all possible, I wanted a crew of all NCOs. However, things worked out great. Norman was very co-operative and let Freddie come with me while he took an officer flight engineer. Now, this was absolutely great because Freddie, as far as I was concerned, was the most knowledgeable bloke in the whole Air Force as far as Libs were concerned and, without being disrespectful, I felt it did not matter very much what the rest of the crew were like as long as I had Freddie. I tried to get Tug back as navigator; he seemed keen to renew the association but his skipper, a flight lieutenant, would not let him go. Mel suggested that we now leave things for a couple of days to see 'how the cookie crumbles' as word got around that I was making up a crew. In the meantime, I started thinking about Joe; he was good at his job, he was behaving himself perfectly now, and he was an amusing lad to have around. I was sure I could rely on him and if he could join me as No. 1 WOP/AG (assuming he wanted to), I was sure it would do him the world of good psychologically. I did not want

Norman to think I was trying to poach his crew so I dropped a hint to Joe over a beer that I wished he would be coming with me; that big broad smile spread across his wide, round face as he asked me if I really meant it. 'Of course I do, you silly bugger. Go and have a word first with Norman and then with Big Mel in the morning, but don't tell them I put you up to it', I told him, 'let's have another beer'.

Things fell nicely into place; in a couple of days, I had a crew and they looked a promising combination, at least they were a lively, cheerful bunch. Norman had agreed to let Joe join me, so that was three of us sticking together—Freddie, Joe, and me. We were joined by the following:

Chalky as second pilot—a tall thinnish lad with straight fair hair, which kept flopping down over his forehead, neat tash, had been a second pilot for about four months but his previous skipper had not let him do much handling on his own. He joined the Squadron without any OTU training so the last aircraft he actually flew himself were Ansons. At least, he already had some time on Libs as second pilot and seemed a nice lad. I decided that, even if it had to be unofficial, I would give him a bit of practise at landing a Lib because, to me, it seemed silly having a second pilot if he was unable to get you safely down in an emergency.

Dave the navigator had been on the same crew as Chalky. He came from some unpronounceable place in Wales, had dark curly hair, a ruddy face that seemed to be forever smiling, a lilting voice and always ready to start singing in the Mess—a real extrovert, such a contrast to Fred and the other navigators, so let's hope he was as good navigating as he was entertaining. Everything with Dave was 'luv-lee' in a musical voice: 'they're letting me fly with you, that will be "luv-lee".'

Eddie was a WOP/AG and been on another crew for a couple of months, medium size, dark straight hair but the bald patch on top, from some place near London.

Robbie or 'Rob' was a WOP/AG who had not done any ops but had been with the Squadron in Northern Ireland for a few weeks; a biggish dark lad from a Sheffield with an infectious smile.

We tossed to see whether Freddie, Joe and I, or Ginger, Fred and Ron should move hut; luckily, we won so Freddie did not have to move the, by now, rather elaborate electrical installation he had fixed up. We got settled down together in the hut and whenever the weather looked reasonable, we managed to get the use of an aircraft for some local flying, take-offs and landings, practice drops, air firing, range flying on the Keflavík range, and practise shutting down and re-starting engines. I was surprised to find that Chalky had never done some of these things before with his previous skipper. He seemed to be enjoying himself and enthusiastically set about compiling a little notebook for himself on the lines of mine; this brought to mind another thing the great O. P. had told me: that around 1,000 hours could be a dicey time for pilots as they began to think they knew all about the job—those that survived this period realises that you would never know everything, there was always more to find out, and you were always learning. He advised me to treat every trip as if it were your first.

We could not fly every day, mainly due to the very strong winds, sometimes accompanied by sleet and snow; in fact, one day, we nearly had to be diverted because the wind suddenly strengthened and was gusting over our landing limits so we had to hang around and pick the right time to come in. It would have been ridiculous to have been diverted when only on local flying. It felt great to be flying 'in charge' again instead of stooge for someone else. The days were getting longer now, just over twelve hours of daylight and getting more and more each day until soon, it would be light all the time. It was still bloody wet and windy though, but the worst of the weather must surely be behind us. I told Big Mel that our 'shake-down' flying had gone well and that we were ready to be put on the Mayfly list.

It was just a couple of days before we are called to ops and learned that we were to be the second aircraft away in the morning to meet convoy HX232 and stay with her till about two hours after dark. For the first two hours or so, we would be doubling up with the first aircraft. So far, the convoy seemed to be unmolested but nobody expected this inactivity to continue much longer. Dave and I provisionally arrived at a take-off time of 11.30 a.m. (GMT) and arranged to attend for final briefing at 7 a.m. We enquired which aircraft we were having, then Freddie, Chalky, and I strolled over to the flight for a look at the aircraft and a chat with the ground crew. We had got a Lib IIIA (Modified) (worst luck) so settled on 2,386 gallons of fuel, eight D. C.s, a spare drum of 5 gallons of hydraulic oil, and a spare 10 gallons of prop de-icing fluid, giving a take-off weight of just under 58,000 lb. Eddie had volunteered to look after the rations, so after a quiet night in the Mess, we all turned, in having arranged to be called at 6 a.m.

We awoke to a wild, wet morning, not yet quite light. The precipitation was a mixture of wet snow, sleet, and rain, with the temperature hovering around freezing point. It might be better by 11.30 a.m., but thank goodness, I had an engineer who was very careful to check for ice. Dave and I called at the Met and then at ops to see if the situation had changed, worked out a more accurate flight plan, and decided to put take-off back until 11.45 a.m. I liked the way Dave worked things out; he did not look anything like as serious as Fred used to do but he knew what he was doing okay, hummed away to himself and then remarked, 'That's luv-lee' when he checked his figures. We arrange to go back at ops an hour before take-off for any late information and to pick up the code cards and 'colours of the day', and then we joined the others for breakfast.

Dave and Joe came with me for a final briefing on codes, frequencies, convoy composition, and the like. As we drove up the tarmac to the aircraft, it had stopped snowing or raining but low clouds were floating swiftly across the sky. I thought, 'There will be some ice in those clouds'. As we approached, I saw Freddie busy with his broom on the wings; one day, he would surely get blown off and hurt himself. As we jumped out of the truck, I saw Norman walking around the aircraft. He came over, full of smiles, saying, 'Just come to wish you a good trip and good hunting. Good show'. We shook hands and he jumped in our truck.

I had a walk around the aircraft, checking that everything looked as it should do, then nipped up onto the catwalk. Walking through the bomb bay, I noticed chalked messages on the D. C.s, such as 'Good luck, Jack', 'This one's from us', and 'Drop this for me'. I climbed up onto the flight deck, tickled a pigeon who had its head looking out its tin, checked that Eddie had the grub on board, and settled in the left-hand seat. With twenty minutes to go, I decided to start engines. After the run up, I signed the form 700 and the ground engineer got out. We proceeded with the pre-taxiing checks, clearance to taxi, then, at the end of the runway:

Hydraulics	Booster pump on
Trim	Rudder 3 degrees right,
Elevator	Neutral,
Ailerons	Neutral
Intercoolers	Open
Mixture	Auto rich
Props	Max rpm (green lights)
Superchargers	Set to give 48 in Hg
Fuel	Check cocks with Freddie
Booster pump	On
Flaps	35 per cent down
Controls	Unlocked
Auto-pilot	Off
De-icers	Off

Generators	All four on
Gills	Closed
Hatches/bomb doors	Closed
Crew	All in position
Line up on Runway	Un-cage gyro

'Open throttle against breaks, check responding evenly. Release breaks, open throttle to 48 inches, revs should be 2,700. Call me out the airspeeds—105 knots, she should lift now; 108, okay. Wheels up (don't forget to brake them first), check wheels locked, 130 knots, start bleeding flaps up. Right, I've trimmed her, booster back to 43.5 on superchargers, revs 2,550. Level out at 1,500—try boosting 34 inches and 2,230 revs in auto-lean, wanting to settle on 140 knots.' I called out during take-off.

We turned to fly visually to Sangerdi while Freddie was busy checking cylinder head temperatures (230 degrees C); oil temperature (50 degrees); oil pressure (85 lb); fuel and hydraulic boosters were off. 'Tell Chalky to set 4 inches on turbos as there will be icing in some of these clouds. Trim. Airspeed has crept up, try reducing boost to 32 inches and slowly reduce revs to give airspeed of 140.' We were nicely settled on 140 knots as we passed over Sangerdi and set course for HX232 at 55 03N, 26 19W. After going through the rigmarole of engaging the auto-pilot, I scribbled out a roster for Chalky and I for the next four hours but I did not intend to be far from my seat for any length of time. We had about 480 miles to go to the south-south-east with an adverse wind component. We must watch this weather, particularly outside temperature, a dingy grey cloud base about 2,000 feet with here and there festoons of cloud coming down to the sea and odd bits of low cloud floating around. The sea looked pretty inhospitable, long deep troughs with spray whipping off the tops of the rollers—I thought that I would rather be up here than in a boat. I hoped Dave could get some drift okay as it would be difficult to spot a smoke or flame float in that sea.

I was pleased with the way Chalky flew the dog-legs for Dave to take drifts (nice and gently). He kept a good course too and reset the turbos and retrimmed every hour without having to be told. He also adjusted the revs as soon as he heard one engine out of synchronisation. He was a quiet lad, did not say much, but he was okay. I also liked the way he told Freddie if he adjusted the boost or revs so that Freddie could keep an accurate check on the fuel consumption.

Dave was also okay, always chattering away on the intercom, keeping us posted on what he was doing, which was quite nice really. When he was taking drifts, we got a running commentary, usually ending with 'That's luv-lee'. I paid a brief visit to see how he was getting on; his log was immaculate. I thought, 'what a contrast to dear old Tug, but let's hope he is as good'.

Joe seemed to be getting on great with Eddie and Rob. He had worked out their roster and they all seemed happy. Freddie, too, seemed happy with our new set up and I was delighted to be making the decisions again. In the back of my mind, however, was the thought that with this wind, the centre of the low was obviously to our west and if it followed the course of most lows, it would be heading towards Iceland. How deep was it likely to be and would it be over Iceland by the time we returned? I tried to remember what O. P. had told me.

We were about half an hour late in arriving at the convoy due to stronger headwinds than expected but by then, we had run out of cloud and the sea was just a moderate Atlantic swell. Radio silence was being maintained and the convoy was complete, so was this just a lull before the storm as the U-boats would surely be back soon to follow up those successes of last month. We saw the other Lib as we both flew near the SNO's ship. It seemed funny to see another aircraft right out there; it looked so small too. I was pleased with the way Dave worked out some of the rather complicated search patterns the SNO asked us to fly, especially a moving 'V' pattern ahead of the convoy—one of the trickiest for a navigator. We stayed for nearly a couple of hours after dark but could not signal to the convoy after dark, just watch them on the ASV. The sky was clear so Dave was able to get some good Astro fixes.

On the way home, we ran back into some cloud but even before the stars disappeared, it was obvious that we were going back like a 'a bat out of hell'. Dave reckoned we had a 65-knot wind behind us; there was a bit of background interference on the radio but nothing serious. However, we could not get two radio bearings suitably placed to give us a decent fix. I asked Joe to call Reykjavík for a landing forecast, which came back giving us 30 knots about 15 degrees off the runway, cloud 8/10ths at 2,000 feet. That seemed okay if it stayed that way as we should be okay 30 degrees off the runway at 30 knots.

Somehow, I had the feeling that we were making more speed than even Dave thought. I did not want to go rushing too far north past the west coast of Iceland, or worse still, be too far east and plough into some high ground, so I tuned into the Keflavík (Meeks Field) radio range on 320 K/cs and was delighted to faintly hear 'N's' and the 'VT' call-sign. I also got Joe to watch on the forward ASV aerials in case we were too far east. I was just thinking that I hoped to goodness we would not be diverted as it would take us a hell of a long time to make Benbecula with this wind, when I thought I heard a background steady note coming up on the range. Now which leg could it be? Joe had nothing on the ASV so that seemed to check that we are to the west. Happy that I had found the west leg, we turned around and flew in. Soon, Joe picked up land ahead; we were back in just under three hours.

Shortly after we told 'Arctic Fox' that 'Snow-goose S sugar' was coming home to roost, Big Mel came on the R/T to say we would be using the short runway. We were to approach from over the town to land to the south-west as the wind was 45 knots and gusting but only about 5 degrees off this runway. He added that he suggested I came in higher than normal with plenty of power on; he would be in the tower and advise overshoot if it was gusting while on the approach. I told him I proposed to complete a circuit before coming in.

Approaching Reykjavík, I could see the town still lit up although it was well after midnight. I figured that you could not be too specific in conditions like this as regards approach heights and speeds as it was a case of compromise: enough height to make sure you did not land short but not so much that you overshot; enough speed so you could knock a bit off with safety if you are going to overshoot but plenty of spare power left to bang on if you were going to be short. We were about 44,000 lb so I came in at 120 knots instead of 103; our ground speed would only be about 75 knots so we would pull up in time and I would roughly halve the length of the approach.

We commenced our pre-landing checks:

Hydraulic booster	On
De-icers	Off
Brake-pressure	900 to 1,050 lb
Gills	Closed
Intercoolers	Closed
Undercarriage	Navigator clear of nose. Airspeed below 146 knots. Select down.

Check down by closing throttle for horn to blow.
Freddie to make visual check

Fuel boosters	On
Mixture	Auto-rich
Props	Max rpm (2,400)
Turbos	3 inches

Flaps	Airspeed below 133 knots, 20 per cent down
Crew	All in position

We were ready to join the circuit. I told Chalky not to brace the rudders on landing until I told him to as I might need to use the rudders after touchdown to keep her straight. As we flew into wind, more or less over the runway, we seemed to be moving very slowly. We went well past the runway, then commenced a port turn downwind. The lights below seemed to slide sideways underneath us and then, on the port side, the lights on the airfield and town seemed to flash past at a hell of a speed. It only seemed like seconds before it was time to turn back into the wind for the approach yet, as we were turning, the lights were still drifting further away. On completion of the turn, the town and airfield seemed miles away ahead of us so I decided to maintain height. Chalky was calling out the airspeed: '125, 125, 125.' The lights were sluggishly getting nearer and we were rocking about a bit.

There was quite a bit of drift; I had the nose pointing about 10 degrees off the runway in order to stay in line with it. I thought, 'I mustn't knock this drift off until the wheels are just about to touch, otherwise we'll be off the runway. 125–750 feet, 125–750 feet, Harbour lights to starboard—just about at the coast. I'll start losing height, off with a bit of throttle, 125–700 feet ... 125–650 feet ... 125–600 feet ... 120–550 feet ... 50 per cent flap—not full ... 120–425 feet ... 120–300 feet ... bit of power 125–200 feet ... 128–100 feet ... she's rocking a lot ... 125–50 feet ... over end of runway ... ease throttles back... kick-off drift ... squeal of rudder ... we're down ... lots of rudder to keep her straight ... nearly stopped already ... brace the rudders ... thank goodness for nose-wheel undercarriages—no nasty blanking off effect as the tail comes down, wonder why British aircraft don't have them? Would not like to have been landing a Hudson in this.'

Turbos	Off
Generators	Off
Flaps	Up
Gills	Open

Now for the tricky bit. At the intersection, she would not turn out of wind to get to the dispersal; she was as stubborn as a mule. With her large fin and rudder area and big flat side, she just would not turn out of wind; like a big shuttlecock, she whipped back into wind so not wanting to damage the nose wheel, we stayed where we were until the ground crew came up with chocks. We shut down the engines and left the ground crew to try to tow her away. When we got out, we could hardly keep our feet. It seemed we were nearly diverted, but Benbecula was closed due to low cloud and rain.

Freddie and I agreed that we seemed to have got a pretty good crew. They all seemed to know their jobs and got on with them with a minimum of fuss. Joe and Dave kept us amused and we were particularly pleased with the way Joe had changed; he looked after the other two WOPs like an old hen looking after her chickens. We introduced the new lads to our Yankee pals, who brought us things round from their PX. The argument always ensued when we insisted we paid for them, as they did for their Canadian Club, so soon we had a nice supply of tinned ham, peaches, and other goodies in the hut.

The weather continued to be damn rough. Some days, no one could get off and just about every crew had twenty-four hours on standby, already briefed, and ready to get away quickly if the weather allowed. Those who did manage it were diverted but somehow some 'top brass' from the UK arrived on the scene and gave a 'pep talk' to all those air aircrew who were available.

An RAF chap told us about the difficulty Coastal Command were having in getting enough Liberators. Although the Americans were now churning them out fast, the Americans themselves wanted more and more of them for Europe and the Pacific. We only had just over sixty VLR Libs for three squadrons and had agreed to release some of those due to come to us to the Canadians so that they could operate Libs from Newfoundland, instead of the present short-range Digbys, and thereby close the air gap on the Northern route but it would be another four to six weeks before these were operational. He also referred to the RAF activity over the Bay of Biscay, saying how the sightings had increased since the introduction of the new radar and the success of the Leigh Light attacks, although with considerable loss of aircraft (I thought about Peter). Bomber Command had attacked the U-boat pens in the Biscay ports with the loss of over 100 aircraft but it would appear that even the big Tallboy bombs failed to do any significant damage. He also told us about some reorganisation of Group Headquarters and in communication procedures.

A very amiable Navy chap put us much more in the picture. The merchant shipping losses over the last twelve months had amounted to an enormous tonnage (he said what it was but the figures meant little to us, except that it represented a hell of a lot of ships); the North Atlantic loss alone sounded almost as much as the total. He referred significantly to convoys HX228, HX229, and SC122, saying that if losses carried on at this rate there would be no invasion of Europe and we would be out of the war. This was the critical time of the war; we had to beat the U-boats or we could not carry on. He was very generous in his praise, saying that even though we may fly many hours without ever seeing a U-boat and feel we were doing no good, our very presence was doing good because shipping losses were much lower in areas with air cover than they were elsewhere and the sooner we had continuous air cover, the better. He then informed us that from then on, we were aiming to take the offensive against the U-boats rather than remain on the defensive.

> Fortunately, we now have most of the Escorts back which were deployed to support the landings in Africa, more 36 knot Destroyers as well as the slower Corvettes and some new Frigates. We now had a small escort Carrier *Bitter* sailing with some convoys and in another few weeks we will have some MAC ships (merchant aircraft carriers) which are grain ships or tankers which have had their superstructure removed and the flight deck constructed so that they can carry three or four Swordfish. We have formed three 'Escort Groups' of fast ships stuffed with anti-U-boat weapons and manned by experienced crews and shortly hope to form another two. We will then have at least three of these 'Escort Groups' at sea at any one time ready to be directed to a threatened convoy or on to any Wolf Pack we may detect by one means or another. These 'Escort Groups' will not form part of the convoy's close Escort; they could be positioned between convoys, ready to dash to whichever is threatened. The big advantage will be that, as they are not providing close Escort for the convoy they will be able to remain with U-boat contacts and track them down to destruction, instead of having to break off an engagement to return to the protection of the convoy. We are now on the attack – not the defensive – and you are an important part of this offensive, between us we will hound these U-boats to destruction – if we don't everything else, the Army, Air Force and Navy are doing will be a waste of time as we will just run out of supplies. Our American friends are providing escorts for the convoys on the southern route and to Gib but we, and the Canadians, have total responsibility for the northern routes although the Americans may provide some escort if there are any of their troop ships in the convoy. Our Queen Mary, as you will know, dashes across on her own with British and Canadian troops. The Americans are also forming an 'Escort Group' to operate with carriers in mid-Atlantic down towards the Azores to try and catch the wandering re-fuelling supply U-boats.

Another Naval officer then gave us the rundown on some changes in recognition and communication procedures as between ships and aircraft and some changes in frequency. Also, he shared the news that intelligence indicated that the U-boats had been issued with instructions to fall into packs of between twenty and forty before attacking the convoy and that they should stay on the surface and provide each other with protective AA fire rather than dive, unless they had plenty of time to dive safely.

An RAF officer then caused a lot of caustic comment from us when he informed us that research had shown that it was better to drop depth charges from 100 feet rather than 50 feet. Previously, we had been told that over 50 feet, there was a possibility you may blow your tail off and there was plenty of sarcasm from most of the skippers when this 'wingless wonder' talked about dropping from 'precisely' 100 feet. Had he ever seen the Atlantic where even on a calm day, there may be twenty-foot rollers, an altimeter that was useless as you did not know the sea level pressure anyway. One wag suggested we should call up a U-boat for a QFE (altimeter setting) before going in; all you could do was estimate and we all had admitted we were probably a bit high anyway, we merely got down as low as we dare and hoped for the best. The Naval officer, who had obviously been to sea, nodded with a smile. We had heard tales about non-co-operation between the Navy and the RAF, but we all agreed that as far as we were concerned, the Navy chaps were all the greatest—they were down-to-earth, practical, and great to work with as they tried to keep you in the picture as far as they could and treated us as equals with a common job to do.

Enquiries as to when we were likely to be getting the new Mark III, 10-cm ASV revealed that in the inter-Command battle to see who should have these new sets, which were in short supply, Bomber Command had 'won'. They were given priority and using them as a bombing aid called H2S (an airborne ground scanning system, for identifying targets, day or night at an increased range, allowing all weather bombing). After putting up a fight, Coastal Command managed to get the Air Ministry to allocate forty of these sets to Coastal and they were being fitted into Leigh Light Wellington squadrons operating in the Bay of Biscay as it became obvious that the U-boats in transit through the Bay were picking up the transmission from the Mark II ASV as the number of sightings had dropped off significantly. We would get them in due course, but it may be a long time yet.

We also enquired whether anything was being done to find a compass that would be reliable in the Arctic. We learned that some work was being done on a 'Gyro-compass', which would have a main unit, perhaps somewhere near the tail of the aircraft, with 'repeaters' on the flight deck and in the navigator's compartment. It was hoped that the combination of a magnetic compass and a gyro would overcome the dip problem; the 'boffins' were working on it but we could not expect anything in the immediate future.

We also learned that the Arctic convoys were to be suspended during the approaching 'summer' as it was deemed that losses during the period of twenty-four hours of daylight, when they were subject to continual air attack, were un-acceptable. This would release more escorts for North Atlantic work. There was also a RAF squadron of Catalinas that had been operating from a river near the Kola Inlet to try to give some cover to the convoys after they left our limits, although the Catalina could not cope with the German bombers and torpedo aircraft, only warn of their approach. We gathered that the Russians treated these Catalina crews almost as though they were prisoners, hardly allowing them off their base, which was surrounded with barbed wire.

Another bit of information to emerge was that soon, some of the Mark IIIA Libs would be further modified to carry even more fuel. Auxiliary wing tanks were to be fitted consisting of three cells on each side, to carry a total of 374 gallons, which would be transferred to the main tanks via transfer pump. Also, the capacity of the bomb bay tanks would be increased by 170 gallons to 670 gallons, which would be transferred by pump and a four-way cock to the cross feed and the appropriate engine. With 1,960 gallons in the main wing tanks, this would give a total of 3,004 gallons. This would be 618 gallons more than the present Mark IIIA and 504 gallons more than the Mark Is. At economical cruising, this could extend endurance by about four and a half hours. It transpired that the Yanks had now increased the maximum permitted take-off weight in ideal conditions to 62,000 lb, which required a lift-off speed of 114 knots as against our lift-off of 105 knots at 58,000 lb. The RAF were to carry out trials for increased take-off weight and would soon be issuing new data on take-off speeds for various wind conditions, weights, and runway minimums. The extra 618 gallons would weigh 4,450 lb, so, even if we increase take-off weight to 62,000 lb as per the Americans, we would still have to cut the D. C.s by one. It is not therefore contemplated that all the aircraft will be so modified as in some cases it may be better to increase the number of D. C.s than increase the range or endurance. In any case, it would be June or July before any with increased tankage were available.

The Critical Stage

The gale force winds seemed to go on and on, several times whipping up so much that we had day and night sessions sitting in aircraft with engines running to keep them from being blown about. Then, during a relative lull, we got away in an aircraft that had not many hours to go before due for a major service, with instructions to land at Aldergrove and then bring another aircraft back, which had had its inspection, if and when the weather allowed. For us, it was only a short trip but in atrocious weather and after ten hours, we were jolly glad to be cutting the motors at Aldergrove.

The next morning, we learned that there would not be an aircraft ready to go back to Iceland for at least a week and later in the day, the Station Commander informed us we may as well have seven days' leave. So, it was off to Larne for the night boat to Scotland. At Larne, we found there was some doubt as to whether the boat would sail due to the sea state, which was very rough. However, we got away okay and the following afternoon, I paid a surprise visit on Peggy at the Probate Registry. It was nice to be away from all that wind, and the daffs were out on the grassy bank outside York Station. For six days, I was going to be with Peggy. She said I looked tired (I was not surprised) but a couple of days put that right.

While I had a lovely few days, I could not help from time to time, thinking about those blokes still on the sea and at times felt like telling people about them, but I kept my mouth shut as they were not really interested. I did not even tell anyone I was now a 'skipper' but if Dad had been here, he would have been interested. Mother showed no emotion at all. She seemed to be thoroughly enjoying helping on the station canteen and singing at the piano with the Canadian soldiers who visited her.

Peg's Auntie Muriel let us have the use of her caravan—an old wooden, four-wheeled, horse-drawn one, now fixed up nicely as a static, in a field which she owned at the top of Stepney Road at Scarborough, not far from the scene of my very first flight. We had a wonderful three days there. Spring in England was perfect, all the flowers and trees bursting forth, a magnificent view over Scarborough by day, I wore my civvy clothes, we took photos of each other on 'Towzer' (Auntie Muriel's Shetland Pony) and we were not in the least bothered about the 'blackout' as night fell. Looking towards the sea by day, I still gave the odd thought to the chaps on the ships, going through hell so we could keep this lovely country of ours. All too soon, we had to return to York and I kissed Peg goodbye as I set off for the station. I did not want her to 'see me off'.

25

The Big Battle of the Atlantic

It may have been spring in the UK but it did not sound as if spring had yet arrived in Iceland as, after doing an air test on an aircraft that had just been serviced, we were told that Reykjavík was closed due to high winds. This went on for three more days, then there was a rush to get away quickly on a direct transit flight to Iceland as the weather had moderated but we carried enough fuel to get back if we could not get in. On the flight, the only point of interest was that early on, we sighted the *Queen Mary* with a very big escort heading westward. We kept well clear but, through the glasses, she was a most impressive sight, throwing up a big white bow-wave, which we spotted before seeing the ship herself. She seemed to be painted overall in a dull grey; she seemed fairly steady but the escort cruisers and destroyers were pitching about in the fairly choppy sea.

Winds at Reykjavík were still upwards of 40 knots but thankfully almost in line with the main runway. Control warned us that the wind was occasionally gusting to 60 knots and to be prepared to overshoot but coming in on the main long runway from the north-west, the wind would only be about 2 degrees off the runway. This was good. The approach was over flat ground, then over an inlet of water and the runway had been extended, almost to the water's edge but I decided to do a circuit first to size up the situation. Cloud was only about 5/10ths but they were very 'ragged' squally looking clouds and in places, the sheltered water in the inlets seemed to be very ruffled. The wind-sock seemed to be sticking straight out but, sure enough, as near as damn, it was pointing straight up the runway. This, I decided, was another case of coming in with bags of airspeed, plenty of height, and not much flap.

Soon, we were on the approach. It was a bit rocky but we were keeping a nice angle of descent and although the runway was only slowly getting nearer, we had bags of airspeed to keep good control. Just over the runway threshold at about 50 feet when 'whoosh'—a huge gust of wind seemed to lift us and toss us to starboard as easily as if we were a dead leaf. We had no runway insight. Simultaneously, I shoved the throttles fully open and told Chalky 'Gear up'. Mercifully, the Pratt and Whitneys all responded quickly and evenly. Freddie, as usual, was kneeling between Chalky and me; I felt his hand come on top of mine to take over the throttles to make sure they did not slip back. I told Chalky to leave the flaps at half down as I did not want to risk the wheels dropping down if we used the hydraulics on the flaps before the wheels were properly locked up. We safely climbed up again to sort ourselves out for another approach. For a moment, I thought I had run out of 'pebbles in my bucket' but thank goodness, we had practised 'overshoots' together as a crew. The odds must surely be pretty hefty against us hitting another gust at such a crucial spot next time.

At debriefing, the Naval officer seemed most concerned about us having 'bumped into' the *Queen Mary*, so we must not mention this to anyone, at least not for a week. We assumed there must be something special about that trip, particularly as it was escorted.

The only thing in Iceland to let you know that summer should be on its way was the longer hours of daylight. The weather was still like mid-winter, but daylight was from about 3.30 a.m. till 8 p.m., till in another month, when it would be light nearly the whole twenty-four hours. Freddie, Chalky, and I had a night out at the pictures in Reykjavík where we saw a new film *Desert Victory*, which was made during the fighting in North Africa and made us all feel that it was not at all bad being Stationed in Iceland after all. The supporting film was *Hawaiian Moonlight*—a bit of a contrast.

We had a meal afterwards but both Freddie and I got the impression that the locals were beginning to get a little friendlier towards us or maybe they just preferred the reserved English to the Americans who were always trying to chat-up the local girls. However, I went back to the hut to write to Peggy; those had been a lovely few days at Scarborough. I also found an income tax form for completion in the post when we got back.

We were soon at the top of the Mayfly list as several crews were away after diversions due to the weather—one crew were in Newfoundland, another in Labrador (Gander and Goose), and another in Ireland. We were disappointed to find that we were not going into the Atlantic, where there seemed to be some 'trade' about but up to the north-east. There seemed to be some idea that some '*Milch* cows', the big re-fuelling U-boats, may be making their way from the German building yards down into the Atlantic by passing north of Iceland and then into the Atlantic by the Denmark Strait so, we were given an area to 'Sweep' and then, on the way back a crafty idea of sending a lot of signals pre-fixed with a different call-sign to make it seem that they were coming from different sources but carrying a certain letter to let our people know that they were bogus so, after take-off just before dawn we skirted the south coast of Iceland, little of which we could see due to cloud, and set course to the north.

It was the first time that Chalky, Dave, and Rob had ventured into the Northern Latitudes, the area of crazy compasses and the Aurora, but maybe the Aurora did not 'work' during daylight. At least, you would not be able to see it but did that mean that it would not be there to bugger up the radio? There was so much about flying up here to still find out. Shortly after leaving the coast of Iceland, all the cloud disappeared to reveal a deep blue sea, speckled with snow white 'white caps', all beneath a cloudless deep blue sky. In a little while, even the 'white caps' disappeared, except for the odd lazy one, which had us fixing the glasses on it, in case it was being caused by a periscope. From my limited experience of here, it seemed that it was both fantastically clear and cloudless or 100 per cent cloud and a roaring gale—nothing in between. We were soon into our routine. Chalky and I took thirty minutes turns and all eyes scanning our sector of the sea except for the WOP on the set and the ASV. Chalky and Dave kept making amusing comments about the compass, Joe chirped up on the intercom to tell Dave we must be flying the wrong way because one of the pigeons had its tail sticking out of the tin, instead of its head; that reminded us to keep them warm because, in spite of the bright sun—so bright we needed our sunglasses—it was about minus 20 degrees outside (and inside). Dave was trying to take some readings on the sun with his sextant, to check on our heading; he seemed to get some fairly consistent readings. Joe reported from the rear turret that he was 'as cold as a witch's tit'.

The sea conditions would have been ideal for making an attack, but in that cloudless sky, we would almost certainly have been spotted before we could have pulled it off. However, there were no sightings, only a few false alarms, and it was time to head for home. The radio has been behaving itself so it was time to start sending the bogus messages we had been given. Some of them we could decode and seemed to be intended to appear as if they had come from different ships, others seemed to be complete rubbish. We speculated as to what these were all about: were they to make the Germans think there was a convoy on its way to Russia (which we knew there was not)? Were they to test whether or not the Germans knew our SYKO code? We would never know; even the ops folk at Reykjavík probably did not know. We received a reply to some signals, which we knew by the pre-fix was also bogus.

Flying back south-west towards Iceland it gradually became less cold and in due course, while thinking what a change it would be to complete a trip in daylight, a bank of cloud appeared on the horizon.

We were gradually closing with this bank of cloud, which appeared to be at an acute angle across our track. As we approached, the cloud looked darker and darker—a very dark grey, extending from sea level to goodness knows how high. There was already some high cloud above us and way out on the starboard bow, we were slowly closing with this solid-looking grey wall. I asked Dave what the wind was and doodled on my little chart, sketching in isobars and a line for this front, all the time watching the outside temperature gauge. This must have been a 'warm' front; the outside temperature had risen to just about the worst it could be: about minus three. The warm air behind the warm front would be pushing up over the lower cold air, so it could be above freezing higher up (an inversion). Precipitation could therefore fall as rain but as soon as it fell on us at only minus three degrees, it would freeze on us and we would go down encased in a block of clear ice. We had to avoid this situation.

For a start, I told Dave we would alter course about 25 degrees to port to fly roughly parallel to the front. I told Joe to call Reykjavík for a landing forecast thinking that, if we were likely to be diverted to Benbecula or Northern Ireland, there was no point passing through this front only to have to fly back through it again. We received a favourable landing forecast so, still watching the outside temperature like a hawk, I made plans for getting through it safely, still minus three. We could not go down to find warmer air so we would have to go up until it is cold enough to be safe. Leaving Chalky to watch things for a while, I went to the nose to have a chat with Dave and explained that we would climb until the temperature was down to minus twelve, then, when on the same latitude as the south coast of Iceland, we would turn starboard onto due west to get through the front as quickly as possible, hoping that we would get a bit of help from the ASV in picking up the coast of Iceland. Fortunately, it worked like a charm; as we flew through the front, it became very dark and even the thick snowflakes looked dark grey, but they flashed by without sticking. After what seemed quite a long time, it became brighter, the cloud began to look like separate lumps rushing by, and we emerged once again into sunshine. A lucky radio bearing on the bacon at Vesturhorn (as this Naval beacon is only 'on' for five minutes every half hour) confirmed we were to the south so we altered 20 degrees to starboard and shortly, the white tops of Vatnajökull appeared dead ahead; if we went 10 degrees to port, we would be okay. It was a nice gentle let down as we converged with the coast—no more cloud, just a nice sunny late afternoon with a fresh cool wind as we settled down at Reykjavík. Chalky remarked afterwards that he wondered whether I was doing the right thing when I climbed to get through the front; I told him I once met an old man called Zig who told me about minus 12 degrees.

The ops board showed convoy SC130 of thirty-eight ships had recently left Halifax. It was not yet anywhere near us but the Canadian Lib squadron was just about ready for operations and we gathered that we would be making an all-out effort in support of this convoy now that most of the diverted crews were back. The first of our crews, with 'Smoky', the only other flight sergeant skipper, got away on 15 May in the early morning, followed by another later in the day. From now on, it was two or three aircraft a day, doubling up for some of the time. We started off at the bottom of the Mayfly list, having done the Northern trip, but our turn came on 19 May. There had been an almost continuous battle around the convoy for four days; there seemed to be at least three packs in contact and two of our chaps were confident that they had made kills but the best news of all was that there were still thirty-eight ships.

At last, I was to have a Mark I and out of our five Mark Is, it was to be dear old 'P' for Peggy. With eight D. C.s, eighteen magazines of cannon ammo and 2,500 gallons of fuel, we headed off to 54 42N, 33 11W to meet SC130, feeling sure that there surely must be something on this time. Joe delighted in making hot tea and coffee and frying eggs on the way out. We got the D. C.s set and the ammo loaded in good time and all went to the loo so we would not have to bother when we got to the convoy. As we approached, we heard plenty of talk on the R/T, all very calm and correct. We announced our arrival and got a very polite and gentlemanly acknowledgement. Robin, one of our flying officers, was around as well; he had been there since before dawn.

We were sent a little way from the convoy to join one of the escort groups; they seemed to be working in pairs, sometimes both steaming at full speed, sometimes almost stopped, and sometimes one almost stopped with the other steaming at full speed across the others track. We were told to search an area a few miles south of the escort group. The weather was just right and the sea fairly calm but there were broken clouds at about 1,000 feet, throwing patches of shadow on the sea. I was thinking to myself whether to attack if it was only a 'half chance' or whether to save my D. C.s for a certainty and direct the escort to the area of a 'half chance'. I had the D. C.s set for a stick of four at 45 feet spacing so that would give us two attacks, but if the chance came near to the end of our time, I would attack anything and give them the whole lot.

Suddenly, Chalky, pointing on the starboard bow, shouted, 'There's two of the bastards'. Everything went forward (throttles, pitch, and mixture); the bomb doors opened; and the nose went down, turning into the nearest one. Luckily, this put them more or less in line so that, while attacking one, we were not exposing our side to the other. I turned to try to bring us diagonally across the nearest boat's track and gave a few quick bursts on the cannons. She was diving but the other bugger was not, just coming up to the first. The decks were awash now.

'Press the tit,' I said. 'Little orange lights are coming up from the other one, seem to be suspended in the air and suddenly gather speed and flash past. Must try to turn straight towards her, keep the wing out the water. I can't pull her around sharply enough—where the devil is she? I've lost her.' Popping up a bit and completing the turn, we spotted her diving, deck already awash. I tried to haul the Lib around but she got away, just a swirl in the water. We circled, dropping smoke floats, dye, and flame floats and stay circling until a Destroyer and Corvette arrived and took over. Did we get the first one? We felt confident we did.

The escort vessels arrived in about thirty minutes and started doing high-speed runs in different directions, then appeared to be firing Hedgehogs judging by the splashes in the water. They did this several times and then there was an underwater explosion, not as high as a depth charge, just a little white mound, which spread and spread. It looked as if they had got a U-boat as we understood that the Hedgehogs only exploded when it came in contact with an underwater object. Maybe, between us, we had got them both; we hoped so. We were told to continue searching just a little way away. I suddenly thought about those non-sealing tanks—had a round from that second U-boat punctured one? I asked Freddie to check the gauges, but he already had.

I spotted the next ones, three of the devils moving at some speed about three miles away. It was the white wakes that gave them away. Off we dashed again while Dave quickly gave the position to Eddie so that he could tell the escort on R/T and send the routine W/T message. This could be tricky. Were they going to stick together and fire? We were descending towards them at 260 knots. 'They've seen us. They're diving. Bugger it, they'll have gone. Shit, they are all going down together. They've gone.

Another few seconds and we would have made it.' I decided it would be a waste to drop the D. C.s so let go a smoke float and then came around again to drop some dye and more smoke floats. We called the escorts and hung around. This time, it was one of the new Canadian-built frigates and a Corvette. We heard on the R/T that Robin was on his way home but 'Red' had come to join us. He sounded to be on the northern side of the convoy and Robin had also had some sightings in that area. There must be bloody dozens of U-boats around this convoy, but, as far as we knew, no ships had been sunk—at least, not yet.

As soon as the escorts arrived, they asked us to investigate another contact about five miles away. We set about a rather tight square search from where we could just see the convoy almost on the horizon. Freddie had recalculated the fuel situation because at times, we had been using fuel at the rate of 540 gallons per hour instead of about 146 gallons per hour and Dave calculated that we only had a little over an hour to go before we would have to leave for home in order to have the regulation reserves for possible diversion; if only the weather in Iceland was more predictable. With only about three-quarters of an hour to go, Chalky spotted another two flat out on the surface. God, that made seven we had seen. The routine was automatic now but I tried to keep height for a while, hoping to be less easy to spot against the bottom of some clouds.

It looked as if we had foxed them. They were still moving fast on top. Bomb doors open, I decided that one of those two would get our four remaining D. C.s, even if it dived. Just as we started our dive, they must have seen us. The bows went under and I was talking to 'P' for Peggy: 'Come on girl, hurry up, they're going to beat us, come on, come on, you can make it.'

However, the conning tower of the one I had picked was just going under. I pressed the cannon tit in annoyance, knowing we were too far away. I then let the D. C.s go where I thought she may now be but it would be a chance in a hundred that they cracked her. Anyway, they may have shaken her up a bit, so I pulled up a bit and did a tight turn and dropped more smoke floats and flame floats. 'We'll chuck out all we've got left and hang around for the escort.' Time was getting on; Dave said we should be off in fifteen minutes, yet there was no sign of any escort ships yet.

I discussed the fuel with Freddie. We decided that we could stretch it to an hour and if necessary, cut two engines and fly on at a reduced speed to make a diversion airfield if it came to the crunch. The smoke and flame floats had gone out but the dye was still discernible so we dropped what dye we had left and were relieved to see an escort frigate approaching at about 20 knots. We bade him a quick 'Farewell and good hunting' and set course for home. The time had passed like a flash. This idea of having escort groups separate from the close escort to the convoy seemed to be paying dividends; they were getting them before they got into the convoy itself but they must be using a hell of a lot of fuel if they were dashing about all the time, like they seemed to be doing. It was to be hoped they could re-fuel from a tanker in the convoy. So, it was time to relax. We had seen seven U-boats and attacked two, although the second one was unlikely to have been damaged; one U-boat had even had the cheek to fire at us. Joe soon had the coffee made and set about doing sausage and beans. It was nice to be in a Mark I again and good old 'P' for Peggy had not let us down. I knew she would not, even though she got shot at.

We were lucky that the weather at Reykjavík had been behaving itself for these last few days, enabling us to get so many aircraft away and back again. Reykjavík looked especially nice as we came in about 7 p.m. It was still light too; that was a change. After a very long debriefing and a meal, we still did not feel tired, so we celebrated our trip in the Mess until almost midnight. News of our success had preceded us and with three of us fairly confident that we had made 'kills', the atmosphere was very jubilant. I noticed Joe and Chalky gesticulating to a little group, obviously showing how we went in for the kill. Other crews had made more than one sighting but nobody else had seen as many as seven. The news from ops was that there were still thirty-eight ships in the convoy, with no losses so far. One crew was still out there and three would be off the following day (20 May); after that, she should be through our area and then be within range of the Lib Squadron, which was now operational in Northern Ireland and would have cover the rest of the way from Libs, Forts, and Sunderlands. It was not long before Dave was leading the singing. We all seem to feel that now we were, at least, after many monotonous flying hours, doing something worthwhile. I looked at Joe, who seemed so pleased with himself and behaving himself. He had had a fair bit to drink like the rest of us, but he was just enjoying himself and not being at all difficult. I thought how worthwhile it had been sticking our necks out for him shortly after he joined us; he was a different lad altogether. We all left the Mess together, with a bit of singing as we made our way to the hut and slumped on our beds. Before dropping into a deep sleep, I thought, 'What a different feeling you get over a kill, at least I hope it was a kill, when you are the skipper, then when you are only the second pilot.'

We did not wake up until tea-time the next day. In the Mess, we learned that there had been two more sightings but still no ships lost so it was another rather noisy night in the Mess. We also heard from ops that two convoys—HX237 and SC129—had arrived after taking a more southerly route. They were accompanied by one of the new escort carriers, which was able to give cover to both convoys and although between them they had lost five ships, it was believed that at least five U-boats had been sunk. We wondered whether these escort carriers may put us out of a job but the Naval chaps assured us they would not as there were only a few such carriers and often the weather would be too bad for them to fly off and land aircraft.

It appeared that four packs of U-boats attacked SC130 between 15 and 20 May. They failed to sink a single ship, but five U-boats were lost. As events turned out, SC130 was the last north Atlantic convoy to be seriously threatened by the U-boats as Dönitz could bear losses of this magnitude no longer. Faced with the proven ability of enemy aircraft to locate the U-boats by radar, and the skill of the surface vessels in following up sightings, Dönitz temporarily, at least, was forced to withdraw from the conflict, withdrawing his boats from the convoy routes on 24 May. Intelligence, however, pointed out that more U-boats were being fitted with two four-barrelled 2-cm cannon plus an automatic 3.7-cm cannon, so although they had temporarily withdrawn to lick their wounds, they would be back.

26

Diverted to Gander

We climbed the Mayfly list like a rocket and we were soon off again to cover a westbound convoy (ONS8), which was taking a very northerly route, to pass within fifty miles of the tip of Greenland. We were favoured with another Mark I so that Joe could demonstrate his cookery talents, and took-off nearly three hours before dawn, making for 59 10N, 37 21W. It was a nice ride for an hour or so in spite of the Aurora having a spectacular last fling. Then, there was no sign of the Aurora, although the pulsating static was still there, but no stars either, so we were under the cloud. We made a quick check on the outside temperature, which seemed okay, well above freezing, then soon, we were being lashed by rain. After a while, we seemed to be out of the rain and a burst on the landing lights confirmed that we were in pretty thick cloud and better wind the altimeters down 20 mbar to be on the safe side.

Then, the old St Elmo's fire started off; this pretty coloured ring of light round the prop tips fascinated Rob after his initial concern, as he had not seen it before. Little tufts of coloured light like candy floss appeared on the nose ASV aerial, and then floated off. I began to get bloody scared myself as the ring around the prop tips got brighter and brighter until the whole of each prop looked like a great big luminous disc of changing colours and bits seemed to be flying off—maybe it was only imagination but lumps of this light seemed to come right into the cockpit with a crack—but now, the tufts of glowing candy floss on the ASV aerial were getting bigger and bigger and flying off at the windscreen. God only knows whether or not it was an illusion but I could have sworn they came through the windscreen and floated around in the flight deck like some evil, weightless genie. Instinctively, we were all swatting at these floating spirits that seemed to leer back at us as they continually turned from blue to green and back again. We were trying to beat these things away with anything we could lay our hands on (a map or a ruler) but they seemed to keep on coming and after floating around the flight deck for a while, they seemed to disappear down into the bomb bay. Dave was fighting his own battle down in the nose and asked what the bloody hell was going on. I tried to sound unperturbed, telling him that it would not do any harm and that we would soon be out of it but I did not feel all that sure. I felt sure I could hear cracks coming from them sometimes and thought about all that fuel we had on board. Eventually, they seemed to die down. The props just had a ring around the tip, the tufts on the ASV aerial became smaller and seemed to stay put and we seemed to have got rid of the bits floating around inside. Dave said the nose was clear so I asked Eddie to make some coffee as we certainly needed it. That was a display and a half of St Elmo's fire.

As things got back to normal, Dave announced that we were almost at 59 10N, 37 21W and it was only a few minutes off sunrise. Joe reported a lot of sharp crackles on the W/T, indicating that there was thunder about, which, oddly enough, was about the first time I had encountered thunderstorms on this job. We were in cloud and our accurate height was anybody's guess. I asked Joe to go to the ASV and see if he could find anything. At our ETA over the meeting point, we commenced a square search. For over an hour, we had no contact then Joe thought he may have something. I had a look at the screen and could faintly see what he was talking about; he was getting as good as Ginger had been on the ASV. We closed with this blip and yes, soon, there were several blips but we were still in cloud and for all I knew, this cloud may come down to the sea. I told Dave we could fly westwards along the convoy's track, hoping that soon we may get out of this cloud, then we could let down and fly back towards it in visual contact with the sea. The main thing going through my mind, however, was that if all this muck we have been through was moving to the north-east as was the usual pattern, it would be bloody nearly over Iceland by the time we were due back. As it was a hell of a way to Northern Ireland or Benbecula, I had a look at my little knee chart and decided that Gander or Goose were the places to keep my eyes on—God bless O. P. Zig and O. P. gave me a lot of good advice—how lucky I was to meet them. I told Joe to keep a keen ear on anything he could pick up about weather; he said there were still a lot of loud cracks and still thunder around.

After an hour, we were still in cloud going away from the convoy, ahead of it. We had been showered a couple of times with hailstones, which sounded as if we were being pelted by 1,000 shot guns. I concluded that we must be flying through an occluded front because there would not be thunderstorms in a normal warm front and then, almost as if by magic, we merged into sunshine and totally clear air. We were almost due south of the tip of Greenland and in really nice weather, but we must turn around, descend, reset the altimeters by guessing our height, and get back under the cloud to find the convoy. Back under the 'clag', in an hour and a half, we should have picked up the convoy.

We were driven down to about 250 feet, sometimes in heavy rain and almost nil visibility, and began to realise that we were not going to be able to do very much, even if we did pick up the convoy. I thanked goodness I did not try to come down through that cloud, as in places, it was right down to the deck. When we thought we were back at the convoy, we did another square search with Joe once again on the ASV. After a while, Joe spotted something; there was no R/T to be heard, so that was a good sign—it would seem that they were not being bothered by U-boats. We closed with the blips on the ASV, Chalky with his finger on the trigger of the Very pistol, ready to fire off the 'colours of the day' as soon as we made visual contact.

Soon, we spotted a ship, then another, and Chalky was busy firing off the Very cartridges, but these were all merchant ships. We buggered around until we spotted an escort vessel and tried to keep him in sight while we made contact with the Aldis lamp. Joe then told me he had a signal for me. He handed me a message, which I decoded. It read something like, 'Do not return to Reykjavík, acknowledge and stand by'. We cleared off a few miles from the convoy, acknowledged the signal, and included the code for 'convoy met'.

As we set course back to the convoy, I tell the lads that it looked as if we would be going to Gander, Goose, or BW1 on the tip of Greenland. We knew we were not going to be any earthly use to the convoy as we would only be able to see one ship at a time and we could not get in position to attack a U-boat in this weather, even if one obligingly surfaced right in front of us. Goose looked to be slightly nearer than Gander, which Dave confirmed, and gave me an approximate distance and time. Freddie gave me the fuel situation and endurance; we had plenty of fuel. In another few minutes, we got another signal, 'Leave C/V, proceed Gander, acknowledge then call Gander on H/F'.

We climbed up into the murk and set course for Gander. When a few miles further from the convoy, we acknowledged the signal and called Gander. The convoy would have been listening out and received these messages so they would know we had left.

I got quite excited at the thought of seeing Gander again. I hoped to meet some of the Ferry lads, perhaps even be able to work a quick trip to Montreal for an inspection like 'NEM' did when he was diverted there and needed an engine change. The Lib boys at Gander would be interested to see a Mark I. I hoped they were not in fog; if so, there was always Stephenville. We had bags of fuel to make that, and could even get down to Dartmouth if necessary. We got the weather for Gander; it sounded okay although a wind of only 5 knots could be a bit ominous. I looked at the chart to refresh myself on Gander as I had not previously approached it from this direction and then studied my little notebook.

We settled down for the best part of five hours at 140 knots. After a couple of hours, we suddenly emerged from cloud into an almost cloudless sky above a clear blue sea just flecked with gentle white caps. It was 'luv-lee' for Dave. We flew a couple of 'dog-legs' so that he could take some drifts and calculate a wind. We sent an amended ETA, then settled down to enjoy some food (Robbie was the cook that day) but we maintained a watch all round. We did not want to miss anything and we kept the D. C.s fused, just in case. We speculated that we should get some good food in Newfoundland; I thought of those Canadian steaks followed by apple pie and lashings of cream. We kept picking up signals from Newfoundland; in fact, signals from all over the place. Weather for Goose did not sound too clever: snowing with visibility of 200 yards. Another signal reported Reykjavík at visibility of 200 feet, raining, and 40 knot winds, so they must be already getting the rubbish we had flown through.

We chatted about the display of St Elmo's fire. It really was weird in the dark, seeing those bits of glowing candy floss floating around inside the aircraft. What a queer place the Atlantic was—one minute, filthy rough weather, bouncing up and down and may be picking up ice; then queer balls of fire floating around like weightless genies; then beautiful clear blue skies like this and smooth as silk. The sea, sometimes a dirty grey, whipped up into huge waves, the wind whipping the tops off in the foaming spume, tossing big ships around like toys and sometimes like this, deep blue flecked with lazy little whitecaps.

With about an hour to go, a layer of high cloud had formed above us and there were a few clumps of low cloud around. It was a bit misty ahead but nothing to bother about. I told Joe he could put the ASV on now. After a while, land showed up. At maximum range on the starboard bow, we had converged with the range leg and stayed in it, flying at 280 feet so there could not be much wind. We were flying into Bonavista Bay and I could see all the little islands. We popped up to 2,500 feet to comply with local regulations. We could see the long inlet leading to near Gander. Joe picked up the identification 'GR' on the ASV beacon at Gander. Funny thing, I had not noticed these islands in the bay before, then I was always going the other way and was too busy trying to keep an overloaded Hudson in the air without gobbling too much fuel to be concerned about looking out at the scenery.

In a few minutes, we were over the airfield and cleared to land on the very wide 09/27 runway. The airfield looked much quieter than when I last saw it: a couple of lonely looking Hudsons, a Mitchell, some Digbys, a black Lib, and three or four white Libs over in the far corner. The lads were a bit surprised when they saw local time on the clock in the control tower. Iceland local time was the same as GMT but here it was, three and a half hours earlier. They must have been the only country in the world to have a half-hour difference, perhaps to make the point that they were a separate crown colony and not part of Canada.

In some ways, Gander was a bit of a let-down. There were no Ferry people there who I knew. I thought the chaps on the Lib Squadron would be pleased to talk to someone from Iceland but we could not find any of them. We learned that they were not yet all operational and not up to full strength. There were none of them in the Sergeants Mess, to which we were taken; it seemed they had their own set-up at the other side of the airfield. After a jolly good meal—fresh meat and lots of trimmings—Freddie and I decided we would walk over to the aircraft to make sure she was being taken care of. We found she had already been fully refuelled to avoid condensation and we decided that we may as well leave it all on when we got away, in case we got back to Reykjavík to find we were diverted to Scotland or Northern Ireland. We pop into Control, where they told us that Iceland is 'zig' with strong winds, rain, and low cloud. It was a very nice evening here.

Back in the Mess, we found the lads were having a real old sing-song and booze-up. Dave was already leading the singing, then one of the local lads produced a guitar and sang some country songs. However, the highlight was when Rob called for 'Hush' and announced that Eddie would render the original version of 'Eskimo Nell'. Eddie, glass in hand, mounted a table and commenced: 'Dead-eyed Dick and Eskimo Pete set out for the Rio Grande...' Eddie progressed through the whole twenty-odd verses. The interruptions became louder and more frequent so that he had to keep stopping; he would forget where he had got up to, take a swig, and then go back a line or two to pick it up again. One of the lads asked if there were any Eskimos in Iceland; if there had been, I think he would have gone back with us. We went out like a light soon as our heads hit the pillow, as although it was only just approaching midnight local time, we had been awake for getting on thirty hours.

No one woke us the next morning so it was after 10 a.m. local time before anybody stirred. After a very good breakfast-cum-lunch, Dave, Freddie, and I visited Control; they had no instructions for us. We then went along to the Met office. They expected Reykjavík to be okay overnight and the next morning, with a slight following wind component at 6,000 feet, we provisionally decided to take-off about 2 p.m., which would be 5.50 p.m. GMT as it looked as if it would take us between ten and ten and a half hours. This would mean that Dave would be able to get Astro fixes around the area where they would be most use as there would only be a few hours of darkness with us flying north-east. We would arrive at about 4 a.m.

I thought, 'Jesus, that's as long as going to Prestwick in the Hudsons; but we wouldn't have been able to go without a stronger wind than this. Airspeed 140 and we are only planning on a ground speed of 157 knots. We can't go really high to get better winds because we have no oxygen but not to worry, we have plenty of fuel'.

Freddie checked that the aircraft has been serviced with oil and what have you, so we arranged to pick up a briefing folder from Met at 1.30 p.m. local and take-off half an hour later at 5.30 p.m. GMT. We told Control what we were going to do and filed a provisional flight plan. Then it was back to the Mess to tell the others what we were doing and to arrange some rations. We wanted to buy some of those lovely fresh steaks to take back to the boys in Iceland, but we had no proper money—only our 'diversion currency' of fags and nylons, which you could swap for anything in Scotland or Ireland, but the folks here had plenty of such things. Anyway, one of the cooks in the Mess took pity on us and gave us a cardboard box full of meat in addition to the rations for the trip, and one of the chaps gave Eddie a huge fresh salmon in appreciation of the previous night's entertainment.

We were a happy little crew as we left Gander, with no need to worry about whether or not she would lift off or how the fuel was going. The sun was shining; at 6,000 feet, it was as smooth as silk and the wind was so light that it could hardly raise a whitecap on the blue sea. There was not much Dave could do. One of the WOPs got him a few QDMs on H/F but they were not really much use. There seemed to be a lot of traffic on the W/T; some of it was weather information but all for places behind us, most of it was just routine stuff. Freddie or one of the WOPs had a turn in one of the front seats and we kept a constant look-out from upfront, just in case there was anything to be seen. With Chalky and Freddie upfront, I had a rest on the bunk and went flat out for over an hour but nothing had changed when I woke up. Talk ensued as to when we were going to get stuck into the steaks. Eddie was going to be cook and as he could only do one steak at a time, it was decided he would have a start shortly so he called each of us up in turn with 'This is the chef speaking. How would you like your steak doing, sir? Medium or well done?' We had fresh potatoes too (not tinned ones), and fresh milk to go in the coffee. It would have been a bit of a let-down if we had been in a Mark III. We decided we would leave the tinned fruit and biscuits until much later.

Dave had been flying short rhumb lines on the forecast winds but thought they were freshening a bit from the state of the sea, although we were too high to take proper drifts, he had made a slight alteration based on 'intuition'. The total trip was about 1,650 nautical miles. In another forty-five minutes or so, around 10 p.m., it would be getting dark, then he would be able to get some Astro fixes and we should be about 220 miles off the tip of Greenland, way out on our port side. There should be little moon but as it was in the first quarter, it would soon set somewhere behind us. Just then, we saw a line of cumulus-looking cloud way ahead. It seemed to extend across our path and way into the distance towards the north, but fizzled out towards the south. As we got nearer in the fading light, I could see that it was definitely cumulus but it did not look angry and Joe assured me that there was no static on the W/T. It was not the usual cloud associated with a front, just our luck to be running into this as it got dark when we wanted some Astro shots.

Looking at the little map on my clipboard, I reckoned that this cloud was probably formed by a stream of bloody cold air coming down the east coast of Greenland, meeting the warmer, moist air over the Atlantic, cooling the latter so that cloud was formed but you would think that would create sea fog, not rising cumulus cloud; however, funny things did happen around here so I knew to watch the outside temperature closely and prepare for a bit of turbulence. There should not be any trouble with freezing rain. Just as it got dark, we entered those clouds; there seemed to be no advantage in altering height. It was a bit bumpy but the temperature was okay—no icing—although it had got very appreciably colder. In twenty minutes, we were through the cloud and out into clear air, where our friends were all brightly twinkling down on us to show us the way.

Being in a Mark I, the astrodome was up on the flight deck, not in the nose like it was on the Mark III, so Dave got himself on the flight deck, armed with his sextant, some paper, and a pencil. He gave me his chronometer to note the exact time when he called out as he took his shots, then disappeared back into the nose to do a bit of working out. After a while, he came on the intercom: 'That's luv-lee, skip. Absolutely beautiful, luv-lee little cocked-hat. No more than a tenth of an inch on all three slides of the triangle which puts us just a little bit to the north but keep the course and I will take some more shots in another twenty minutes. If they are as good as the last ones I'll have a "spot on" wind, then I'll give you a new course. Absolutely luv-lee, boy-o, beautiful.'

'That's splendid, Dave,' I replied. The second shots were almost as good as the first. Dave was happy with his new wind and we slightly altered course to starboard. ETA was now 4.05 a.m. Roughly four hours to go, we decided we would have some hot coffee and get stuck into the fruit and biscuits. I told Joe that we might as well put the ASV on; he need not stay glued to it. If we saw something all well and good, it may be of interest to the ops chaps at Reykjavík, but the main idea was that, if those U-boats were listening out for our ASV, if one should hear it, it may make them dive and slow them down because this was the time when they would be moving fast on the surface to get into position.

The thought goes through my head that while we had those friendly stars above us, down there in the darkness, our enemies, the U-boats, were probably dashing along the surface to get into position to attack the convoy at dawn or forming themselves up into wolfpacks to lay in wait. We hoped it would not be long before we got the new tackle. I realised I had been with two smashing crews; you could not find a better bunch of lads anywhere. Each one of them was thoroughly reliable, you knew they would do the right thing at the right time, and, by Jove, I had some good navigators, old Tug on the Hudsons, Fred, and now Dave. They had to keep at it for the whole trip, they had never let me down, and sometimes how they found a convoy was almost a miracle. Also, Freddie, as an engineer, was worth his weight in gold. However, I bet everyone on the Squadron thought he was with the best crew.

The first sign of twilight was well before dawn so Dave hurried to get another three shots for a fix before the stars deserted us. Then, slowly, the big red sun slowly rose above the horizon almost dead ahead. The sea was a pale blue but slightly more speckled with whitecaps than when we last saw it. Dave confirmed from his fix that the wind had freshened. We were a little to the north and ahead of ourselves but I told him that we would not amend our ETA as we would use up the spare time letting Chalky have a bit of practice on the Keflavík range and he could 'put his feet up'. The range was coming in nice and clear, so on a sheet of paper, I drew out the legs of the range, marked in the 'A's and 'N's so that I could keep pointing out to Chalky where we were. The low sun was almost straight in our eyes and glinting on the icy slopes of Snæfellsjökull way out to port, then the low black outline of the southern peninsula appeared ahead. Only a couple of very slight corrections kept us on the edge of the beam. We crossed the coast and Chalky seemed really chuffed as he saw we were going to pass right over the four masts of the range station. Everyone seemed to be fast asleep at Keflavík as we passed over the airfield where the red beacon was still flashing 'KF'.

We took out the auto-pilot and took it in turns to hand-fly the few miles to Reykjavík. We heard Control talking to one of our chaps who was ready to taxi out for take-off so we gave them a brief report on the weather and winds in case they were going in that direction. It was a lovely calm, sunny morning so I decided this was a good opportunity to let Chalky have another landing. We agreed as to who was going to do what and that I would do the brakes after landing, so he braced the rudders. He brought her down very nicely. What a lovely crisp, sunny morning—one of the rarer faces of Reykjavík.

We kept the meat and the salmon in the hut when we turned in as we did not want it all to go before we got up for dinner. When we took it along, the cooks were delighted. They cut the steaks up into smaller pieces to make them go around and the following day, we all had a bit of salmon, which was a hell of a change from the dried fish we usually got.

27
The New Wingco

With lengthening hours of daylight (it never seemed to get properly dark at all now), morale was really high. Not only were we finding and sinking U-boats, but we were beginning to get some of the further modified Libs designated 'VLR IIIAs', and also a new weapon. Messages of congratulations were appearing on the noticeboards; most significant of all was the recent arrival of a wing commander as squadron commander.

The wing commander (called the 'Wingco') was one of those rare characters, immediately liked and respected by everyone from the AC2's up to the two Flight Commanders. Everyone would do anything for the Wingco, yet he never needed to use the big stick. Mechanics would work all night to make sure the aircraft were in top condition. He could be friendly with everybody without losing any respect. We felt we were lucky to have such a great leader and felt sure he would do everything he could for us. Where he came from, we did not know, only that he was quite young and had been awarded the OBE. We later learned that his father was an air vice-marshal and inspector general of the RAF. Most of the time, he dressed just like us. He had a big dog, a brown and white Spaniel, which followed him everywhere, but as dogs were not permitted in Iceland by law, it had to stay on the station. About the same time as the Wingco came to take charge of us, a group captain arrived as station commander. Known as 'Groupie', he had ideas of holding a 'station parade' every Friday morning. The Wingco did not see any point in that sort of bullshit, so he let it to be known that as he did not have a crew of his own, he would go with whoever was going on an op over the parade period and for those aircrew who were not either away or resting, he would fix some practice dropping or an air test. To my knowledge, no one from the Squadron ever attended one of these parades, except maybe the adjutant, who apologised for everyone else being tied up on some important job. After several weeks, the parades seem to fizzle out.

We soon had three of the VLRs with the extra auxiliary wing tanks to give us a total of 3,004 gallons and were cleared for an increased take-off weight of 60,000 lb 'subject to suitable conditions'. We fitted in some practice dropping and firing on these new aircraft to get used to a few other modifications but, of course, we did not take-off fully loaded on these trips, otherwise we would have had to stay up for hours and hours to get down to the safe landing weight. A fully loaded take-off would have to wait for the real thing.

A new weapon was shrouded in secrecy. A device produced by the Americans—which they called 'Fido' but the RAF christened as 'Oscar', presumably because there already was a 'Fido' in the RAF—it was a system of burning an enormous amount of fuel from burners down the sides of certain runways in the UK for getting down in fog. Our Oscar was a sort of cross between a depth charge and a torpedo. It was a chubby thing with a propeller, fins, and rudder at the back, with the conical head containing 600 lb of Torpex explosive, more than twice as much as in a depth charge. The idea was that an acoustic device in the nose would 'home' in on to the noise from a U-boat's engines, and off it would go at between 12 and 14 knots, exploding only on contact. It could detect noise up to 1,500 yards away but if no sound was detected, it would go around and around in an upward circular pattern looking for sound. As soon as a sound was picked up, it would set off after it. After fifteen minutes, the fuel would run out and it would sink. On most trips, we would be carrying one of these things in place of three depth charges but it was not to be used against a U-boat on the surface or only in the process of diving—that was still a D. C. job—it was only to be used if the U-boat was completely under before we got there and even then, only if we were over the swirl pretty quickly. It was not to be dropped indiscriminately because they were expensive and, like most things, in short supply. It was suggested that the Americans were so confident in it that they were claiming a kill whenever they dropped one, but it was stressed that the RAF would need conclusive evidence before being credited with a kill as there may be some evidence of an underwater explosion but there also may not.

We must not drop within five miles of the ship in case it chased the ship, but there did not seem to be any risk of it pranging the aircraft, which was always a possibility with a D. C. We learned about the bits and pieces attached to it, which activated the motor and gyro when it left the aircraft, about making it safe and fusing it, all of which could be done in the air in a Lib. However, the Catalinas were taking off with one under one wing and D. C.s under the other so they had to be already fused; this amused us because the one under the Catalina's wing was there for all to see yet ours were brought out to the aircraft on a bomb-trolley, covered with a sheet 'in case anyone was watching through glasses from a nearby house and tipping off the enemy'.

Periodically, extracts from signals kept appearing on the Mess noticeboard. The Admiralty stated:

> I am commanded by My Lords Commissioners of the Admiralty to forward, for the information of the Air Council the following extracts from the report by the Senior Officer of the Escort of convoy MX.128 which arrived at the Clyde on the 20 December 1942:
> 'No attack was made on the convoy. The Liberator aircraft from Iceland undoubtedly contributed largely to its safe passage. By attacking and harassing the U-boats and by effective reconnaissance and information given to the escorts, they were of invaluable assistance.
> I am to say that My Lords conquer in the above extract which is typical of many, and wish to add their appreciation of the excellent work done by the Liberators from Iceland (C) and the United Kingdom during recent months under very trying weather conditions.

The Air Ministry noted:

> I am commanded by the Air Council to refer to Admiralty letter of the 27 April 1943, in which their Lordships expressed their appreciation of the good work done by the Liberators from Iceland (C) and the United Kingdom throughout the past winter. I am to say that Council were pleased to note this letter and concur in Their Lordships remarks.

The commander-in-chief of Coastal Command remarked:

> I have pleasure in forwarding, for your information and that of the Squadron concerned, copies of letters expressing the appreciation of the Lords Commissioners of the Admiralty and Air Council, of the work of the Liberators in the NORTH ATLANTIC during the past winter. I need hardly say that I heartily endorse these expressions of appreciation, which have been duly acknowledged.

On more recent operations, the following signal was received from the senior naval officer of the convoy after an eventful two days: 'Composition unchanged—Liberators as good as ever'.

From squadron commander came: 'Keep the service ability up to the very high standards attained, and the aircrews will do the rest'.

The next trip was for take-off early one Friday morning, so as half anticipated, the Wingco said he would come with us. In briefing, he paid very full attention but told me to carry on as I would normally. I did not know whether he knew much about Libs or whether he had experience at dropping D. C.s but those were not the sort of questions a flight sergeant should ask his squadron commander so I decided that all I would do was to 'play it by ear' and not let him put me off. After studying at the Met, we parted, going to our respective Messes for our meal.

As we converged on the aircraft, I saw the Wingco with a peaked American-style cap on top of his flying helmet, a hunting horn slung round his neck outside his Irvin jacket, and his dog. We had a Mark I, which I thought was rather good as Freddie could have his own seat and there would be a bit more room than in the Mark III. The Wingco and his dog accompanied me as I walked around, making the customary external inspection of the aircraft. He had a word and a joke with the ground crew, the dog cocked his leg up on the tyre, and we bobbed under the bomb-doors, up onto the catwalk for a quick look at the D. C.s (no Oscar for us as they seem to be in short supply), the Wingco lifts his dog onto the flight deck, and we followed.

The Wingco said he would be all right standing behind us so I started the old routine with Chalky and Freddie—routine checks, engine starting, warming up, more checks, running up, pre-taxi checks, call the Tower—then I looked around at the Wingco, who I noticed had plugged into the spare 'jack box' with the hunting horn still dangling on his chest. He nodded and I started to taxi. At the end of the runway, I cleared the engines, did another mag. drop test, lined up on the runway, finished pre-take-off checks, and we were away.

On the way to Sangerdi, I checked temperature, pressures, and what have you with Freddie, then told Dave it was okay for him to go to his office in the nose. The Wingco looked happy with his dog curled up at his feet but I could not expect him to stand up all the way. I told him that I usually made out a roster for an hour each on the way out and back, and asked if he wanted to be included. 'Of course,' he replied, so I drew out two columns, one for the left-hand seat and one for the right, so that I was alternating with him in the left; Chalky being in the right with the

Wingco and Freddie with me. The Wingco took my seat and explained to me that the hunting horn was to blow if we make a sighting as the note was very penetrating and carried anywhere in the aircraft—much better than the alarm bells. He warned everybody on the intercom what he was going to do and gave us a demonstration; he was right. The noise made the dog lift his head up but he soon settled down again, sprawled all over the flight deck floor.

One of the lads soon made some tea and I stood for a while, feet astride the dog, watching the Wingco sitting there as relaxed as if he were in his favourite armchair, his right hand hanging down and casually stroking the dog. Then, he would nonchalantly adjust a knob on the auto-pilot to keep us spot on course and another to maintain altitude. I was glad to see Chalky make a slight throttle adjustment with a little pitch alteration to synchronise the engines.

I popped below to the galley where Eddie was sorting out the rations. We put our helmets aside and shouted in each other's ear (as we did not want to broadcast over the intercom) – remarks that we seemed to have got some good rations this time. I told Joe on the W/T to make sure he did not miss anything and pass the signals to whoever is in the left-hand seat, then I popped into the nose to see Dave, suggesting that he flew plenty of dog-legs, especially if he suspected a change of wind, as we wanted to hit this convoy dead on.

Going back onto the flight deck, I saw the Wingco had just disengaged the auto-pilot, was re-trimming, and then put 'George' back in. I thought to myself, 'This chap is okay he knows what he's doing all right'.

I reminded myself that I must not overlook watching the weather, temperature, and what have you because it was up to me to make decisions, even though we had the CO with us. He showed interest in the small-scale Atlantic map I always carried and the weather lines I marked thereon and also in my little pocket notebook.

After four seat changes, we were nearing 56 23N, 30 08W, where we hoped to meet HX242. The weather had been kind as for only about an hour, we had been forced down to about 800 feet in rain, then maybe a couple of hours in the clear, but now it was dull with a layer of fairly high cloud and a moderate sea. I asked the Wingco if he wanted to continue on the roster basis when we met the convoy as while 'on the job', Chalky and I usually stayed in our respective seats. He said he wanted to do his stint so I made another roster so that one of the three of us would be off, either he or I in the left seat and when Chalky was off I would be in the right-hand seat.

I congratulated Dave when the convoy came into sight on the second leg of a line ahead search, which he commenced when he reckoned we were at the datum point. The sea state look almost ideal for spotting and attacking U-boats but the cloud was too high to give us any useful cover. Contact was made using the lamp. We learned that they were not aware of any U-boats and we were sent off to do a creeping search ahead, just to the south of this fast, eastbound convoy. The ships were in very orderly formation and most of them seemed to be riding very deep in the water; some had lots of deck cargo, vehicles, and large crates. At a good distance from the convoy, we transmitted our 'convoy met' signal. As we progressed with the search, the visibility fell so I had to tell Dave to alter the distance between legs, although this was only really necessary in one corner of the area. Search completed, we returned to the convoy for further instructions; this time, we were sent to search a rectangular area commencing some twenty miles to the south. The swap-over routine was working well, each pilot getting the third hour off, with the extra pair of eyes usually looking out for good measure.

We had now been with the convoy well over four hours. The Wingco had fed his dog, which caused no bother at all, except we had to watch out that we did not trip over him. With the Wingco and Chalky 'up aloft', I crawled into the nose to see Dave and maybe give him a little break as the poor navigator got no let-up when we were flying these search patterns. While I was down in the rather confined space of the short-nosed Mark I, leaning over Dave's navigation table, I heard the power suddenly increase and the props wine into fine pitch. I was pressed back against the sides as we went into a hell of a bank and at the same time, the shrill note of the hunting horn penetrated the air. For a few seconds, I could not move, pressed against the side of the aircraft, then we seem to level out and through the Perspex nose, I could see we were in a shallow dive.

I did not stay to look out of the nose. I thought I had better get back upstairs so started crawling back between the nose wheel and the side of the aircraft. There was not much room and my Irvin jacket got caught on something to slow me down a bit. By this time, I was aware that the bomb doors were open and just as I was coming out from under the flight deck, the cannons went off with a hell of a noise and clouds of cordite. Freddie had just dropped down there and was undoing a cannon magazine from the rack so I started to get one out of the rack on my side. Just as I got it out, we must have come out of the dive as it felt to weigh a ton instead of 56 lb and I all but dropped it on my toe. The firing had stopped so Freddie whipped off two magazines and replaced them with the full ones. I heard the power reduce but could tell we were in a steep-ish turn. I had not seen a damn thing outside.

I jumped up onto the flight deck and found the Wingco circling some white frothy water and a smoke float. The Wingco had everything under control. Joe had bashed out '511' and held the key down as we went in. Eddie, who was on one of the beam gun positions, had put a smoke float down the flared chute and the Wingco was speaking to the convoy escort on the R/T. As we continued circling, I learned that Chalky had spotted a U-boat a long way off, which seemed to be travelling away from the convoy. The Wingco immediately turned onto it but it dived long before we got there. He fired the cannons a long way off, more in annoyance than anything as they were unlikely to do any damage and had dropped a stick of D. C.s a good distance ahead of the swirl. The explosions would have shaken them a bit but he did not hold out any hope of having done any serious damage as by then, it would have been too deep and may also have made a violent alteration in course as he dived.

The senior Naval officer with the escort asked us to remain in the vicinity as they were sending two vessels. We kept dropping smoke floats and circled at about 800 feet but also kept a good look all-round in case she came up again. We worked out how much longer we could stay and still leave enough fuel for possible diversion. We decided that two and a quarter hours was the maximum. It was about an hour and a half before we saw two vessels approaching at speed; we directed them towards us on the R/T. It would seem they had not seen us yet so Chalky remarked that they did not seem to have such good lookouts as those on the U-boats. Then a steady light told us they had seen us. Shortly, they told us on the R/T that they had our smoke. We dropped another float in case one went out before they got there. We wished them good hunting, told them which way the U-boat appeared to go before it dived, and bade them a very good night.

We had a very pleasant and relaxed trip back. Eddie excelled with the meal—soup, tinned meat stew with tinned potatoes, tinned fruit with Carnation milk, and a constant supply of coffee. When not 'on duty', the Wingco moved around and chatted with everybody. We mused about how unlucky we were—if only we had some cloud cover or we had been carrying an Oscar. Was he just an odd one who may not have known about the convoy as he seemed to be going the other way?

It was dark now, with the Wingco and I together at the front. The Wingco turned his interphone to 'compass' and heard me listening to the Meeks Field range. He turned to 'call' and asked me if I used the range very much. I told him, 'Just as a standby aid. Dave doesn't need it but I got used to it on Ferry Command and like to keep my hand in'.

He smiled and said, 'Can't we have something more interesting?' I went over to the 'command' set, found the AFN and we listened to Tommy Dorsey and Frank Sinatra.

When approaching Sangerdi, he asked, 'Mind if I do the landing?'

'I'd be delighted if you would, sir,' I replied, 'I'll do second pilot'.

Just as I was about to call Reykjavík for landing clearance, he reached over, pushed my mike aside, saying, 'I'll do it'. With that, he put a hunting horn to his lips and blasted out a 'Tallyho' into his mike. Immediately, we received full landing instructions and the Wingco did a tight circuit and put us down smooth as silk—what a great guy.

As we neared the longest day, things seemed to have gone very quiet. Ops became less frequent. We kept seeing reports indicating that over the last two or three months, the number of ships sunk had fallen substantially and that the number of confirmed 'kills', both by shore-based aircraft and ships, had more than doubled. The number of sightings and kills in the Bay of Biscay was increasing, possibly due to the new Mark III ASV, and a lot more aircraft were now operating in the bay. I wondered how Peter was getting on.

With more time off, and almost perpetual daylight, we went into Reykjavík a lot more. Most days were overcast for at least part of the time and, on average, it would rain every other day, although not continually and occasionally, there was a completely cloudless day with temperatures reaching the low 60s. On a clear sunny day, everything looked so crystal clear with the white peak of Snæfellsjökull, catching the sun, 70 miles away across the blue water of the bay.

We would wander down the main street (Laugavegur) looking in the shop windows, remarking about the extraordinary number of bookshops, stop for a coffee and cream cake then carry on into the Old Town with its timber houses with colourful corrugated iron roofs, down to the harbour, where we would stroll along the jetties, watching the fishing boats unloading. The spectacular time to go down to the harbour was about 10 p.m. on a clear night with just a bit of high cloud to the north. Freddie and I strolled along there one night after we had spent some of our American friends' whiskey money on sampling an exotic starter of pickled fish followed by smoked lamb, cream cake, and coffee. The sun, like a huge yellow ball, was low in the sky, casting a wide yellow ribbon on the surface of the smooth water. Above and behind the sun, the clouds were a brilliant yellow, striped with bright and dark crimson.

We sat on a wall just watching as the sun slowly moved sideways and very gradually lower. Other people strolled slowly by, and sat down to watch, some couples, arm in arm. I wished Peggy were with me. The colours in the sky seemed to intensify, the patterns changed a bit. The sun, still moving sideways, was now getting very near the horizon. The sky above seemed to suddenly brighten up and streaks of colour flashed across the sky, bending and curling as if someone was waving a long horse tail to and fro. Just a tiny bit of the top of the sun remained; these lights in the sky wave rapidly to and fro. We were transfixed. Freddie nudged me, offering a cigarette, which I took; we lit up without taking our eyes off the sky. The sun had gone but it was still quite light and those lights were still flashing around in the sky. We look around, a couple nearby are busy snogging—more than snogging by the look of it—but we still sit there looking at the sky. We look at our watches, still clearly visible in the twilight, and decided that we had better be making our way as we will have to walk. The streets were empty as we cut through the Old Town to Fríkirkjuvegur and up the side of the lake. The bright white houses with their coloured roofs across the lake stood out in this pink twilight; some ducks on the lake were still swimming around and quacking. As we were on the last leg, just approaching the guard room, the sun was coming up again—it was about 1 a.m.

Another day, while we were walking around the Lutheran cathedral, which stood on a grass covered mound roughly between the Old Town and the Lake, an Icelander who spoke perfect English came to speak to us. This was unusual, so our first thoughts were, 'Who is he? What is he trying to find out?' He turned out to be quite harmless and was anxious to tell us about his town. He took us to see a statue of the first settler in Iceland, Ingólfr Arnarson, standing there in the middle of another grassy mount and holding a big long spear. We trundled around to another square, where he pointed out various government buildings and another statue; this one was to Jón Sigurðsson, regarded as Iceland's national hero as he led the long struggle for independence from Denmark. Our friend told us that Iceland became independent in 1918 but they still recognised the King of Denmark as head of state but moves were afoot for the country to be declared a Republic and he was sure that this would come about within a year or so. He told us that Ingólfr Arnarson was a Norseman. It was some time in the ninth century when he sighted this uninhabited volcanic island, so in keeping with Norse tradition, he threw overboard his sacred high-seat pillars, which were from his home in Norway, offering them to the natural spirits of this unknown land as it was considered unwise to land in an unknown place, without making some peace offering to the spirits thereof. If the peace offering was washed ashore, this would indicate that the gods had directed him there and that the natural spirits of the place would accept him. Eventually, after searching the coastline for three years (what he lived on during this time we forgot to ask), he found them washed up on the shore where Reykjavík now stands. He looked at the hot-springs, sending columns of steam up all round the bay, decided that the Gods had directed him here, and called the place 'Reykjavík' (Smoky Bay).

Whether or not the story of Ingólfr Arnarson is true, or an Icelandic saga, Reykjavík certainly seem to be the ideal spot to build the settlement, certainly from what we had seen of the rest of the Icelandic coastline. It was now such a smart, clean little place, those hot springs now all harnessed to supply everyone with free hot water and keep the pavements free of snow in the winter. Our friend told us that it was very nice around the country's second town (Akureyri) at the head of a fjord on the north coast, some places up there had more sunshine than Reykjavík, many different flowers grew, also some trees. It was unlikely we would ever get up there as there were no trains or buses in Iceland.

We asked him about hot springs. He told us there was an area of hot springs and 'geysers' not very far away, between Selfoss and the Langjökull, also some spectacular waterfalls or 'fosses', which you could get to along dirt roads and rough tracks. As we showed interest in these, he took us to a bookshop, where he helped us to buy a map, which, although a very sketchy affair compared to an ordinance map, showed the 'roads' and tracks. It seemed that the locals drove out to the geyser area and also to nearby ski slopes; the map showed a place, which our friend said he would call a 'ski bunkhouse' for people on holiday.

Another week went by, then we got another op—only the third this month—to meet ON190, which was fairly well south at 54 37N, 37 22W. Take-off was round about midnight; in the twilight, as we climbed, it would get light, then as we headed away to the south-west, it would get dark again so we would get two dawns in one day. We were given one of the new VLRs, taxiing out with 3,004 gallons of high octane fuel (except for the few gallons used in run-up), which was over nine tons of petrol. We had a nice breeze down the runway, everything was perfect. We lifted off easily, wheels up, and trimmed. Chalky started to bleed up the flaps when bloody bluish flames poured out of the inner starboard engine. Freddie, who was kneeling between Chalky and me, instantly said, 'Hydraulic oil. Keep her going. Full revs.' With that, he disappeared.

I kept her going, straight ahead, across the tongue of rough land at the other side of the inlet and turned gently to follow the coast, which I could clearly see in the twilight, thinking that if we had to come down, this was the best place to do it. Glancing to my right, I could see Chalky outlined against the light from those flames – the flaps had come right up so we had sunk a bit, otherwise she was okay and flying okay. It seemed an eternity but, it could only have been a few minutes before the flames suddenly went out and seconds later, Freddie, without his helmet and with blood running down his forehead from the top of his bald head, was pulling my helmet away from my right ear and shouting, 'okay now. Only hydraulic oil. I've cut the pipe. Everything is okay'.

I started to climb, called the Tower to tell them we were okay, that the fire was hydraulic oil, and that I would call them again after talking to the Flight Engineer. We climbed up into the daylight and I told Chalky to maintain a three-minute leg-holding pattern to the west of the airfield while Freddie and I had a conference. Freddie explained that there must have been a fracture, or a faulty joint, somewhere within the engine nacelle on the pressure side of the hydraulic pump, so hydraulic oil had leaked onto the hot exhaust. It could not happen again because he had cut through the pipe from the hydraulic reservoir to the pump on the engine with his pliers; we had only lost hydraulic oil from above the level of this pipe. Fortunately, I had studied all these systems with Freddie, so I knew there were outlets from the reservoir at three different levels: the engine driven pump drawing oil from the top outlet, the electric booster pump from the middle outlet, and the emergency hand-operated pump from the lower outlet.

The booster pump circuit and the hand pump circuit should be okay; they definitely would be. The pressure in the two hydraulic accumulators was okay, both showing 1,050 lb per square inch, so the brakes would be okay and we could always top those accumulators up by opening a cock and using the hand pump, so we were okay for using the auto-pilot and bomb-doors as these came off the starboard accumulator, the same accumulator as works the inboard brake shoes.

There was also an emergency hand winding system for getting the undercarriage down so, we decided that, apart from getting Chalky to pump the hand pump like billy-o when we came in, there would be no problem. However, we made sure that everything seemed okay with the engine, pressures, and temperatures. We then throttled back and cut each magneto in turn—nothing unusual—so we both agreed that there was no point in not going on as things would be no different in sixteen-hours' time than they were now. In any case, we were well over maximum permitted landing weight, which would mean dumping 2,000 gallons of petrol, which to me seemed a much dicier operation than carrying on.

I called the Tower to tell them that we had had a full investigation and discussion and had decided to proceed. The Squadron Engineering Officer wanted to speak to Freddie, after which they gave us permission to go. When we were all settled down and stuck into the coffee (flask coffee this time), I asked Freddie how he knew so quickly that it was hydraulic oil.

'By the colour,' he said, 'it was blue, engine oil would have been more yellow. But, hydraulic oil shouldn't burn that readily, its flashpoint is different from that of engine oil.' Freddie had certainly 'saved our bacon'; as I have said before, a good flight engineer was worth his weight in gold and what Freddie did not know about a Lib was not worth knowing. After a few hours, Freddie went back into the bomb bay, bent over the pipe he had cut off, and topped up the reservoir from the 5-gallon emergency supply of fluid that we always carried. It suddenly struck me that it was 29 June—things happen in our family on the 29th—so there were still some pebbles in my bucket. The rest of the trip was a boring anti-climax: no U-boats, the convoy serenely steaming on in good order, the escorts riding the swell at a reasonable speed, instead of dashing around like greyhounds, they even had time for a bit of banter with us with the signalling lamps. We had a little extra to do with transferring fuel as the auxiliary wing tanks as well as the bomb bay tanks had to be transferred via the transfer pump into the main tanks and Chalky did a bit of pumping now and again to keep up the pressure in the hydraulic accumulators.

On landing, we were met by the engineering officer, who was very keen to have the engine and hydraulic system examined while he was there. The fitters were obviously worried in case it revealed that someone had dropped a clanger. Although Freddie was bloody tired, he stayed with them and when he joined us in the Mess later, he said that they had been unable to find a leak but had taken the pump and piping off and the engineering officer had locked it away until the morning. It was next day when we learned that they had found a pinhole fault in the pipe, so under pressure, the oil would have come through as a fine jet, or more likely in the form of a mist, so everyone was relieved; it was not the fault of any of our fitters but a faulty bit of tubing.

The Wingco called us in, telling us that he was still in the Mess when we took off. They called him to Control when they saw we were on fire. He dashed over and just as he arrived, our message came through that the fire was out. He hung on with the engineering officer discussing what they should tell us to do if we could not carry on and how relieved they were when we eventually came back to explain what the trouble had been and everything was under control. He complemented Freddie and I told him that it was Freddie who saved the day; Freddie had told me to 'keep it going', which I did, before I had time to think of doing anything silly.

He smiled and said, 'Sometimes it pays, not to react too quickly. Anyway, its time you chaps had a bit of time off. Take a truck and buzz off for four or five days, as long as you are back in a week. Sort out what you want to do and let me know in the morning, I'll tell the MT to fix you up with a truck and some cans of fuel and speak to the Mess about rations.'

Back in the hut, we discussed our holiday. We wondered whether it would be possible to get to the north of the island but it did not look as if this would be feasible, so decided to make for the area of the hot springs and geysers, then, if we were making good progress, we would see if we could get as far as the big glacier, the Vatnajökull. We told the Wingco of our plans, he had laid on a two-ton truck plus jerry cans of petrol and boxes of rations were waiting at the Mess; he told us to take a Very pistol and some cartridges in case we got stuck and someone had to come to find us. Joe had also got together a box of goodies bought from the American PX, plus a few bottles of Canadian Club—should be plenty of drinking water in the streams. We gathered a Primus stove, a can of paraffin, a bottle of meths, matches, shovel, bucket, toilet paper, mugs, plates, irons, tin opener, compass, Freddie's tools, tin of engine oil, blankets, and the map and we were ready for off.

28

Icelandic Safari

We set off heading east-south-east, Freddie taking first stint at the wheel, on a dirt road across a pinky-brown lava field. The three of us in the front heard frantic banging on the back, stopping to see what the trouble was; the lads in the back shouted out, 'What the hell are you doing? We're choking with dust.' Looking back, we could see clouds of lava dust slowly drifting away from the road. We erected the canvas cover over the back, lowered the rear flaps, and proceeded on our way, rather more slowly.

It was a lovely day, broken cloud causing dark shadows to float across this dark pink lava. An hour or so later, we approached a settlement with lots of big greenhouses, we stopped to change places in the truck and Dave, referring to his map, told us that this must be Hveragerði. A chap who spoke English came over to talk to us, telling us that they grew lots of tomatoes and lettuce as well as flowers and plants, all of which they sent to Reykjavík. The greenhouses were heated by water from hot springs; we gathered that they could grow things all the year round. He pointed roughly to the north, telling us that there was a geyser a little way up there.

We had now left the lava field and, going south-east, appeared to be approaching a large, flat cultivated area, the first hint of green we had seen in Iceland. Very soon, we arrived at a bigger place, Selfoss, and a river. We realised that this was the river we bombed a bit lower down to get rid of the ice. Kaldadarnes, the Hudson airfield, must have been near here but we were on holiday, so we pressed on. We took a gravel track to the north and soon came to a river so decided this was the place to stop for a brew.

We were all covered with the pink lava dust, so shook ourselves off and washed in the river; Freddie was able to wash the top of his head but the rest of us had pink hair. We examined the rations; they looked okay but Joe sat on his box of goodies, telling us that these were for later. As we sat around drinking tea, we could see a small glacier rising, not all that far away to the north and the snow-capped summit of Mount Hekla (the volcano) to the east, but around us, there was short grass and a few sheep not far away.

We decided to press on a bit further. There was a fork in the gravel track. We took the right fork, and the grass got rather patchy and less green, almost brown and lumpy. The track was still okay but had rather more loose stones. Around us was as flat as a pancake, with high ground ahead and gradually closing in on both sides. Dave checked the milometer and told us that we were nearly at the geysers. The track was fizzling out, just a flat area, partly gravel and partly areas of scrubby brown grass. We proceeded slowly as we noticed a small circular patch of water, which was perfectly round ('could be a bottomless hole'). The water was dead flat with the surface of the ground, then, some way ahead, we saw a great column of water gush up into the air, maybe 150 feet.

We proceeded with extreme caution. There were some circular pools, some bubbling—'Better keep up-wind of them, in case they shoot up'. We left the truck and walked around. The area seemed to be riddled with these perfectly round pools but each one seemed different. Some looked to be perfectly flat, clear, cold water; others were a vivid blue, just like a copper sulphate solution; others were bubbling and steaming; others looked to be full of soap flakes; some looked really angry, bubbling and bubbling, spilling water over the brim, making us stand well back. Then, with a great whoosh, a column of water would shoot into the air. Everywhere there was a smell of sulphur. We must have carefully wandered around these fascinating pools for a couple of hours, during which there were two little 'blow offs' and one jolly big one.

We all felt that we ought to get away from this area before kipping down for the night because God knows what it must be like just under the Earth's crust around here and we did not want the two-ton truck to go crashing through with us in it. We started to make our way back, aiming for a little feature on which Dave had taken a compass bearing.

We got back in the truck and back on the track when, someone in the back banged on the cab, and looking back, we saw the biggest column of water in the air, one side as sharp as crystal and the other fuzzy where the wind would be blowing it away. It seemed to stay there for ages before gradually sinking back.

We soon came to a stream and decided that it would do for the night. Joe opened up his box and pulled out a bottle of Canadian Club, saying he had one for each day. We got the mugs, some water from the stream, and cracked the bottle. Joe and Eddie got cracking with the Primus and soon we were tucking into sausage, bacon, spam, and fried bread, with tinned pears and condensed milk out of Joe's box to follow. It was like being on another planet. We finished the bottle, sat looking at the crimson and purple sky as the shadows lengthened and finally disappeared. Then, we all piled into the back of the truck together, wearing our flying kit, blankets stretched across the lot of us.

We awoke to the pitter-patter of rain on the canvas cover. Fortunately, the only thing we had off-loaded and left outside were the cans of petrol, so we had breakfast undercover and discussed our plans. Dave reckoned that we could head almost due east until we came to a river and this would bring us roughly to the position of the waterfall, the Gullfoss. The rain soon stopped, the sky cleared, and we made good progress over flat short grass, keeping a sharp eye for any circular pools, but we seem to have left the geyser area.

The ground ahead turned into low hills, the grass seemed a bit lusher, and there were even some pink flowers. We climbed a slight hill and there it was: a big, wide, fast flowing river. We carried on a little way along the top of this ridge to a point where you could look right up this river, which was very wide, then cascaded down over several ledges into a pool. At the nearside of this pool, the water spilled out into waterfalls with a little island of rocks dividing the two, and into a deep gorge, to flow away at right angles to the waterfalls. We stopped the engine and could then hear the roar of the water. We walked around, went down to the lower level, towards the edge of the precipitous gorge, where it was impossible to talk due to the noise of the water and the air was noticeably chilled.

There is something magnetic about moving water. For ages, I watched it fall off the edge into the chasm, big lumps of it hurling down, and rainbows dancing about in the spray. What a noise, and what power—no wonder water can wear away rock. From another vantage point, you could see along into the bottom of the chasm, a heaving torment of foaming water and spray. Back at the truck, Chalky was bemoaning the fact that we had no camera with us. Freddie topped up the tank and we calculated how far we had come, how much petrol we had used, and how much we had left; we decided to move a bit further away from the noise and make coffee while we planned the next stage. Somehow, somewhere, we had to cross this river. We agreed with Dave that this would mean having to go back towards Selfoss and hope to find a bridge. The petrol was doing very well, so we decided to head south-east for the coast and Vik, as soon as we could find a crossing place.

We soon picked up a track. It seemed to be taking us away from the river but going towards Selfoss. We forded a couple of shallow rivers. The land seemed to be greener and cultivated around here, then nearly at Selfoss we came across a proper wooden bridge over the river so over we went, still following a track. We saw a much bigger river coming up and decided that this must be the one coming down from Gullfoss. This was bridged too. It was a bit rickety but it carried us okay. We made good progress along a flat coastal plain, fording some shallow rivers and streams without any trouble, passing a few sheep and cows near isolated homesteads, but no trees or hedges (nothing over a few inches tall). Ahead, we saw high ground and a glacier which appeared to be right across our track. Dave tells us that there is a narrow flat strip where we will squeeze between the high ground and the coast. We began to climb a little and got a sight of the coast with the Vestmannaeyjar islands not far off the coast. We carried on a little way, not far inland, parallel to the coast, well above the sea level, with towering high ground to our left rising to the Mýrdalsjökull. We stopped to take in the view and decided that this would do for the night. Joe and Dave said they would stay with the truck and start doing the meal in an hour or so while the rest of us went for a walk.

Towards the coast, we found taller, spiky grass, some clumps of things like miniature foxgloves, clumps that looked like dwarf daffodils just about to flower, and some unusual green things like a small football on top of a short stem, the ball part being made up of lots of smaller balls formed by short fat juicy petals. We spotted a colony of puffins, hundreds of them, nestling in a rocky outcrop.

Back at the truck, we found the meal nearly ready. Joe had the Canadian Club ready. It was great to see this change in Joe; he really seemed to enjoy doing things, and shortly he was to surprise us with a tin of ham—almost a whole leg of ham—which he had got from the PX and had hidden away in his box.

No sooner had we settled down to eat than we were besieged by hundreds (more like thousands) of seabirds. They were screeching, diving at us, wheeling around, and squawking. Chalky seemed to know a bit about birds. He pointed out kittiwakes and some real big ones with an enormous wing-span, sleek pointed bodies, white and black wing-tips and fawn heads, which he said were gannets. They were putting on a great show but the noise was terrible and when those big devils swooped low, I was not at all comfortable, so I took my food inside the truck and soon, the others followed. After our meal, with all the food put away, the birds gradually decided to push off, which was a relief as I did not fancy that racket going on all night.

After a check on the fuel situation and miles covered, we made our plans for the following day: an early start and we would see what it was like after Vik; if it was okay, we would try to get to the edge of the glacier. It would not take us so long to get back as we would not then be making the detour by the geyser and Gullfoss. If we made tomorrow night the extent of our journey, we would have two days in hand in case of trouble. We had a final stroll, looked at the colours in the night sky, had a final whiskey each to finish the bottle, and then went to bed.

Day three began as a lovely sunny morning. It was my turn to be in the back, with Freddie driving with Dave and Eddie in the front. I realised we were going downhill and soon we were in the little fishing village of Vik. We got out, intending to have a look around but noticed that the few people around either turned their backs on us or walked away, so decided it would be politic to move on. The high ground, capped by the Mýrdalsjökull, seemed to overshadow this little fishing village. The track out of Vik soon deteriorated and we were crossing a desert of black sand and grit; it looked bloody depressing. We had to turn inland to round an inlet, then ford a stony river and head off again north-east towards Vatnajökull. We seemed to be on a dead flat lava plain, covered here and there with very short grass. We picked up a track of sorts, taking us more to the north.

After fording more shallow streams, surprisingly, we came to a very small settlement. In a fenced off area of grass, there were some horses: short stocky ones with beautiful long tails, almost touching the ground; some were brown some black and some piebald but all had lovely long floppy manes that continued right over the top of their head, almost down to their eyes. While we were looking at these horses, a middle-aged man appeared. He seemed friendly so we waved and he came up to us. He spoke jolly good English. He was interested to hear where we had been. He asked about Reykjavík as he had not been there for a couple of years; he was also interested in our truck and proud to show us his 'Viking ponies'. We asked about getting to the Jökull; he said it would get wet but the ground was hard, and there would be some shallow streams to cross, but we should be okay. He went that way sometimes on his horses, which he bred and sold to people further along the coast. He told us that there was a spectacular area on the edge of the glacier at a place called Skaftfell, where there were green mountains and trees going up to the edge of the glacier but the nearest point to the edge of the ice itself—where the ice actually came right down to the flat was a tongue that he pointed out to us—about thirty miles away. Dave made a note of the compass bearing so that we could find our way back if the weather closed in, and off we set.

Soon, we were back on black sand and gravel, just like a beach after the tide had gone out, wet with little pools of water. Now, the whole area seemed to be covered with a thin layer of water; we had to go very slowly. Sometimes, we came across channels six inches or so deep. We were so near but would we make it to the ice? Most of us had donned our Wellies and in one area, two of us walked in front to check the depth of the water as we certainly did not want to get stuck in a place like this. We thought we had come to the end of the trip once or twice when the water seemed to be getting too deep and we had to paddle around to find a shallower bit. Just ahead, at the foot of the glacier, there was a peculiar band of cloud, only about ten feet high but sitting right on the ground. Another half hour of stopping, wading a bit, and then going on, we were at the very edge of the ice. It was weird. A long tongue of solid ice but a gap between the ground and the bottom of the ice—a gap of about eighteen inches out of which cold water was running; our feet were frozen. The ice seemed to finish in a rounded wall about six feet high and the surface of the ice was also running with water. Chalky and Eddie were determined to set foot on the glacier, so we bumped them up on our shoulders and with an ice-pick they tried to get a grip and work their way up but it was hopeless, they just slid off. It was about 3 p.m.—no worry about getting dark—but, we all decided that we would get to hell out of this place and back on to some dry ground for the night. The thirty miles back took us about six hours. We seemed to hit more bits of deep water than we did on the way out, had to make several detours and twice had to dry the ignition. Getting on for 10 p.m., we were off the gravel, back on some grass not far from where we had been talking to the chap with the horses. Our feet were cold, we were hungry. Someone soon had the soup on, a tin of stew with beans, two bottles of Canadian Club went that night and we were soon huddled together in the truck, feeling satisfaction at mission achieved but bloody glad to be away from Vatnajökull—no wonder they called it the 'Water Glacier'.

When we 'took stock' next morning, we were happy to find we had only used half the petrol and still had plenty of grub. It was still fine, so we decided a nice leisurely drive to somewhere just this side of Selfoss would do nicely for the night, with a break near the coast overlooking the Vestmann Islands. We found the fellow with the horses and told him how we got on, then headed back to Vik where we thought it wisest not to stop, spent a couple of hours near the coast, and found a nice grassy spot by a stream around 6 p.m. where we decided to spend the night. We had a real slap-up meal and went a bit mad on the remaining rations and two more bottles of Canada Club. Dave led the sing-song, Eddie and Rob told the stories, and we all went to bed in very good mood—what a really grand bunch of lads.

There was no bother with lava dust as we covered the last leg back to Reykjavík. It was raining all the way, but we did not mind as it had been a grand trip. On our return, Freddie and Eddie took the truck back to MT and gave it a wash. I phoned the Wingco at the Mess to tell him we were back and to thank him for the use of the truck. Then I had a nice hot shower, meal in the Mess, a few drinks while we told the other lads of our trip but, by Jove, it was nice to get into a proper bed and know we could have a lay in in the morning, as we were only halfway up the Mayfly list.

29

Quiet Time

For the next four weeks, everything seemed to have 'gone dead': no U-boat sightings. The only alarm was when one of the skippers—a Canadian flying officer—was hit by appendicitis while out on a trip. It took them five hours to get back, for the last couple of hours he was unconscious on the floor of the flight deck, his second pilot was not checked out on Libs, which caused a bit of a panic all round, but he put her down in one piece and Hank was rushed off to the RAF hospital in Reykjavík with peritonitis. This made those skippers who never let their second pilot practise a few landings have second thoughts. Hank recovered okay. We visited him in hospital several times but it had been a very close call.

Nearly a week into August, at last, we were off into the Atlantic again to meet a fast west bound convoy, ON195 at 56 54N, 25 57W. We had a Mark I and an extra navigator flight lieutenant, who normally worked in the ops room but the Wingco thought he ought to 'keep in touch'. It seemed that winter was back with us as we had three hours of lousy weather soon after take-off. We left the bad weather before reaching the convoy, which seemed to be in immaculate order maintaining radio silence and all very peaceful. We chatted by Aldis lamp, went off on 'sweeps' in various areas, returning for fresh instructions each time, then, about an hour and a half to go before we would have to leave, Freddie spotted a U-boat on the surface a long way off. Full power and we were off after it, but with no cloud cover, it obviously saw us. I pushed the throttles to see if they would go any further. Chalky called the escort on R/T; she was not heading for the convoy (which was out of sight) but she was diving; she would be down before we get there. The bomb doors opened but—damn it—she was gone and it was too late for D. C.s.

'I'll drop the Oscar, Freddie—get ready with a smoke float,' I tried to identify the swirl where she went down and dropped the Oscar. We circled around the smoke float, looking all round to see if we could see any sign of an underwater explosion. We climbed, thinking we would see better, but there was no sign of anything. It either got it bloody deep or missed it—so much for this American device. We remained near the smoke float and kept dropping another when we thought it was going to run out, dropping some dye and transmitting so an escort could home in on us. It was about an hour before a Destroyer followed by a Corvette arrived; we stayed with them for half an hour or so. It was now quite dark. I suppose they were still dashing about with their ASDICs but there was no more we could do. In any case, we could not stop any longer. We thought it was an odd U-boat, perhaps making her way home on her own, and she probably had no idea that there was a convoy nearby.

It was a lovely ride home. We did not catch up with the bad weather, which by now had probably passed to the east of Iceland. The moon soon appeared, casting a shaft of shimmering silver light on the sea some 2,000 feet below. Here and there, just outside this silver shaft, the moonlight would catch little whitecaps, which seemed to be giving off a cold white light of their own. It was so smooth and in spite of the bright moonlight, the bright stars were twinkling at us in their thousands. We always felt we had company when we could see the stars, but I never ceased to marvel at the fact that they were not there anymore as we were looking back in time, in some cases hundreds of years; when Rigel was where we now think it is, the Normans had not yet conquered England and the bloody Germans were not going to do it now. There must be some sort of folk somewhere up there; they would not have made all those stars just for us to look at, or to help us navigate across the oceans.

Chalky was on duty now so I tried to have a doze; the moonlight lit us up almost like day but it was a very white light, not the yellow light of day time. The instruments glowed green under the resin lights; outside our big wing looked so white and I dreamed that we had 4,800 big white stallions with their manes and tails flying in the wind, taking us home at a steady canter. At 137 knots, we only needed 1,600 revs now as we were light, so they were drinking only 122 gallons an hour. By the time we got home, they would have drunk 2,500 gallons and between them taken 1,728,000 steps.

What would Peggy be doing? I wonder if she was fire watching? I wished she was here beside me; she would have loved this. A little change of noise brought me out of my doze—one team of stallions was getting out of step.

I opened my eyes to see Chalky adjusting the pitch to bring them into line and we carried on cantering into the night. Smiling Joe was soon putting a mug of coffee in my hand and some biscuits on a tin plate. I took over from Chalky. Nearing Iceland, some broken cumulus clouds appeared, like big white heaps of candy floss. Now, a cloud would pass in front of the moon, its dark centre fringed with a wavy pattern of gold. As the cloud obscured the moon, the green phosphorescent instruments appeared to brighten till the moon burst forth again, bathing us in stark white light. The sky was brightening, the stars were getting harder to see, and we were getting near Iceland where it would be getting light again. Almost before we realised it, it had become light and the sun was there, very low in the sky, almost dead ahead—a huge, weak sun. The coast of Iceland was discernible but not as well-lit as we were up here. Shortly after, we were landing, in daylight, at 2 a.m. 'Hope our flight lieutenant friend does not think all trips are as pleasant as that'.

Suddenly, it seemed to be 'all go' again. Two days after our nice moonlight trip, we were away again on another fifteen-hour 'Moorings' patrol where they were certainly getting some bad weather at the Faeroes end. After a day's rest, then it was some more BABBS and dropping practice. Norman was due to leave the Squadron shortly, having completed his twelve months on ops. He invited Freddie, Joe, and me to join him for a meal in Reykjavík for 'old times' sake'. We had a really good night. There were not many of the original crews left now. Little 'Titch' was with us; he seemed to have 'opened up' a lot since he arrived to take over from me as Norman's second pilot.

Then, the next day, after spending the morning on air tests and practice dropping, we were rushed off to search for a suspicious vessel north of Iceland. This was to be my third Arctic op. The Wingco thought it would be a good idea if the Flt Lt navigator came with us again to get a bit of first-hand experience of Arctic navigation. All we knew was that some radio signals had been picked up, which appeared to come from roughly 71 degrees N, 14 degrees W, some 100 miles or so west of Jan Mayern Island. It may be a German weather-reporting ship, as it seemed they did have trawlers reporting from those areas during the early years of the war, or it may be a tanker U-boat meeting U-boats in transit on the long route between Germany and the Atlantic. We were to see what we could find. If it should be a surface vessel, we were not to try to sink it but report its position and shadow it until someone came to relieve us as it would be more important for the Navy to capture it than to sink it. It was thought that U-boats may well be trying to get through the Denmark Strait, but we had already set up standing patrols between Iceland and Greenland to try to shut this off.

We were away early evening but the time of day did not matter as it would be light all the time where we were going. There was some cloud building up to the west as we swung to port, across the peninsula, and port again to follow the south coast eastwards, leaving the clouds well behind us. We were interested to pick out the things we recognised from our trip in the truck: the plain round Selfoss, the Vestmann Islands, Vik with the glacier behind, and the black flat stretch to the Vatnajökull; it looked bloody inhospitable from the air, although the big white mass of the glacier itself was most spectacular. We followed the coast north-east to the most easterly point and then due north. Dave asked for several dog-legs as the coast of Iceland gradually receded on the port side. He wanted to calculate some good winds as he knew there would be no Astro on this trip. We had a pretty strong following wind and plenty of whitecaps on the water to give us an indication of any change in drift. It was not long before the compass became sluggish; after doing a dog-leg, turning on the directional gyro, the compass was likely to be pointing anywhere when we resumed the original course. By tapping it, it would move a bit and stop. Another tap and it moved a bit more; our Flt Lt friend had not encountered this before and was getting quite worried. Then, the ruddy static started; whether or not the Aurora was performing we did not know, with it being daylight, but it certainly sounded like it. Anyhow, there was no cloud and a very low sun almost dead ahead, which seemed to get bigger and bigger. The wind continued to freshen and our drift to port increase; I doodled with my chinagraph pencil on the Perspex over my little map, roughing in some isobars that would indicate a low-pressure area on our port. I guessed that the cloud we saw from Reykjavík was a warm front and sketched this in too.

When Dave reckoned we were at the point given, we commenced an expanding square search. The sun had now dipped to its lowest point and was now starting to slowly climb up again. Doing this square search, the compass was useless as it never got settled down before it was time to change course again. We had to rely on the directional gyro and reset it every half hour to allow for precession, hoping that the precession table was accurate. The sun was too low and big to be of any reliable use for steering purposes.

As we flogged around on our square search, which was getting bigger and bigger, we found that the wind at the western end of the area was stronger and almost from the east, the visibility was not so good either.

In another hour, we were getting into icing cloud at the western end. Our extra navigator began to look very dejected as we had to come lower and close the distance between legs due to the much-reduced visibility. The ice building up on the wings and bits coming off the props did not seem to help his confidence and he asked me whether we were going to carry on in this. Cheery Joe heard this over the intercom and chipped in to tell him that we had not had the St Elmo's fire yet, to which Chalky remarked that it was a pity we would not see it in daylight. It was like two different days as we carried on round our ever-increasing patch; bad in the south-west but fine and clear in the north and east.

For seven hours, we had been going around and around our area, which we had now altered to a rectangular instead of a square. We had another hour to go before we set off for home. The nasty weather had moved eastwards and was now almost in the middle of our patch; at the west end, the wind was almost from due north and the air as clear as a bell. I doodled on my Perspex and decided the centre of the low would have passed to the east coast of Iceland, almost certainly east of Reykjavík.

'If we go back the normal way we will, as likely as not, be flogging down the length of this front for four hours or more, but, if we set off from the south-west corner of our area and come around the west side of Iceland, in all probability we will be behind the front and in good weather. Also, we should have a following wind, the normal way, we could well have a head-wind.' I roughed out the distances and then told Dave we would come the other way around Iceland, work out a course for the north-west tip of Iceland, and build in a deliberate error to port to put us to the east by thirty miles as we did not want to miss the landfall; we may be able to get a little help from the RAF radio beacon at Hrisey Island, near Akureyri if we needed it as it was only 'on request' but we would not bother to request it yet.

We settled down for the return trip. The weather was quite good and soon, as bright and clear as a bell. The sun was now fairly high in the sky and almost in the south—it was funny how at this latitude, it just went around and around, dipping almost to the horizon at midnight in the north and then climbing up again for another circuit. Another trip with nothing to report, I wondered what that signal was. I considered it must have been a U-boat as we were sure that if it had been anything else, we would have seen it, unless it could do about 50 knots and had got out of the area. We realised we were tired and cold, with no hot food in the VLR Lib and the coffee barely lukewarm. We knew we could be miles off track; an accumulation of small errors in the precession of the gyro, in steering the course, in airspeed, in wind calculations could all add up to a hell of a lot. On the other hand, with luck, they could cancel each other out. A bit of darkness for a few stars shots would be a blessing but there was no chance of that. Anyway, the weather was perfect: blue sky, blue sea speckled with white caps. and a stiff following wind. I felt sure we were coming the better way. I decided to give it three and a half hours before thinking about asking for the Hrisey beacon.

Just as I was thinking of asking Joe to request the beacon, Chalky pointed out on his bow, saying, 'There's something there, Skip, that bump on the horizon. Looks like a glacier with a bit of dark to the right of it'.

I thought, 'Glacier? There aren't any glaciers in northern Iceland, surely we haven't found Greenland.' I told Chalky to head towards it and referred to my map of Iceland; there was a little glacier, Drangajökull, about 30 miles from the extreme north-western tip of Iceland. It was getting much clearer now, with rugged dark land stretching both sides of the little white glacier. I told Chalky to turn starboard and head for the end of the land, then called Dave to tell him that we knew where we were, so he and his friend could pack up now as we would map-read our way from here on in. First, however, I asked him to give me an ETA. I congratulated Dave on his work but purposely did not overdo it as I did not want the Flt Lt to think we ever had any doubts about it. Joe bashed out a signal to Reykjavík, giving our ETA, and I told him to add that we were approaching from Snæfellsjökull direction, then we settled down to enjoy a sightseeing tour down the west coast of Iceland.

Rounding the northerly tip, we saw the entrance to a big wide fjord with steep rugged sides, and caught a glimpse of a tiny settlement nestling in the south side of the fjord. Then, there were more rugged cliffs and fjords till suddenly, the land turned abruptly away and we were heading across a big bay. We turned to port to head for the tip of the peninsular some 45 miles across the bay, the Snæfellsjökull giving us a good spot to aim for. Approaching the peninsular, we saw a couple of little fishing villages on the coast, and passed over the tip of the land, looking up at Snæfellsjökull and heading across Faxa Bay, 70 miles to Reykjavík. We learned that the bad weather passed through while we were away, starting within an hour of us leaving. The Met man wanted to know where it was now; we told him we did not know as we did a circular tour to avoid it. The signals from the Arctic remained a mystery.

One day, the Wingco called me, asking me to find Freddie; we met him to go for practice drops and cannon firing in the Mark I. When we met him, he was accompanied by another wing commander and a group captain from Headquarters plus, of course, his dog. He told me we were going to show the others 'how it is done'. Just to be on the safe side and make sure there was no misunderstanding between us, I confirmed with him that he was to be 'skipper' on this trip as I did not want to find him waiting for me to do something and then get a ticking off for not doing it.

For two and a half hours, he threw that Lib about over Faxa Bay—poor old Freddie was knackered with hanging practice smoke bombs on the racks and pulling out the safety pins and changing cannon magazines. A hook came off one bomb after the pin had been removed and it went off when it hit the closed bomb door; the Wingco opened the bomb doors to let the smoke out, leaving Freddie marooned on the catwalk, hanging on, blinded by smoke and with the wind whistling around his feet. What with smoke and cordite fumes hanging around from the cannons, we were all coughing and spluttering with Les hanging on to the dog to make sure he did not leap out of the open bomb doors. I thought the other Wingco and the Groupie were suitably impressed, especially when the Wingco gave a blast on the hunting horn over the R/T to let them know we were coming back. As we left the aircraft, he remarked that he noticed I was down for an op the next day and he would be coming with me as it was Friday.

We felt by now that the Wingco was part of the crew. He was certainly leading his squadron, and he was flying about twice a week with someone. Also, we easily fitted into the routine: either he or me in the left-hand seat with me or Chalky in the other, so we all got a break every three hours. We were on a 'moorings' patrol. The weather was okay at the northern end but pretty mucky towards the south. During the darkness, we must have scared the living daylights out of a poor Icelandic fishing boat. Eddie picked something up on the ASV, at about 2,000 feet, so we flew directly over it; in ten seconds, we turned at right angles and dropped four parachute flares, then put the nose down, with the bomb doors open as we turned another 90 degrees for thirty seconds, another 90 degrees, then another 90 degrees. Landing lights ready, we saw an outline silhouetted against the light of the hanging flares, which were nearly down to the sea, headed for it, landing lights on. There was an innocent little fishing boat, probably out of Vik. Thank goodness, we identified it in time and I did not press the tit, otherwise the good folk of Vik would certainly not welcome RAF chaps passing through their village. Yet, by Jove, I did not envy those Leigh Light chaps their job; it was bloody scary diving down to the sea in the dark.

Daylight arrived so we took up our normal positions, each searching our allotted sectors to cover the whole 360 degrees, with the 'off duty' pilot covering an overlapping sector ahead so that Dave could concentrate more on his navigation and Freddie, who normally stood between the two pilots, could keep a regular check on the engines, fuel, and the like. Everyone was looking out except the WOP looking after the radio and ASV. The weather in the south of the area seemed to get progressively worse; it hardly got light, just a dull grey, the cloud base was down to about 600 feet with rain showers, the visibility was down to less than a mile, and the sea below was a dull grey but not particularly rough (at least not by Atlantic standards). We did not want to keep the ASV on the whole time as we were pretty sure that U-boats could detect this old Mark I ASV, so we only used it in short bursts. I tried to keep Joe on the ASV because he had now become very good at spotting little blips, almost as good as Ginger used to be. The day wore on as we peered out into the great murk above a miserable-looking cold sea with lazy rollers, sometimes shedding their crests like a ribbon of dirty foam. Our binoculars were not much help as they could not increase the visibility; if only we had the new Mark III ASV, which could see forty miles all the way around and we could leave it on all the time, instead of our old stuff, which could only see 12 miles ahead and 20 miles on the beam and we knew could be picked up by the U-boats.

Just after we had some swapped around for what would be our last hour before setting course for home and all beginning to feel a bit bored, Joe piped up to report a blip nine miles ahead, slightly starboard. Although I was in the second pilot's seat, with the Wingco in the left-hand seat, I immediately knocked out 'George', began a slow turn to starboard, and told Joe to tell me when it was dead ahead. At the same time as the Wingco sounded his hunting horn, Freddie opened the bomb doors. I pushed the mixture forward into Rich, increased the revs and boost, Joe reported 'Dead ahead' so I straightened out.

In a second or two, I asked Joe if 'Still dead ahead?'

He came back, 'Yes, seven and a half miles'.

'Right, switch off the ASV. Dave, get on the front gun'. I nudged the Turbos open a bit more, put the nose down a bit more then realise that the Wingco would have to do the rest as the only release tit was on his control wheel so said, 'She's all yours, sir'. We should have seen something in sixty seconds—maybe only a fishing boat out from the Faeroes—but no, there was nothing. So, on with the ASV again. Joe confirmed the blip had vanished. We strained our eyes in the hope of seeing at least a swirl in the water; if we had done, I was sure the Wingco would have dropped our Oscar. However, in this sort of sea, the swirl would very soon have dissipated and the visibility was shocking. As we counted the seconds off we dropped a flame float when we arrived at the spot where we reckon the blip disappeared but there was nothing to be seen, just dirty grey sea with streaks of light grey where the water ran off the tops of lazy rollers. Joe was quite certain that he picked up a distinct blip and as he had had a short rest only a few minutes earlier, it was unlikely that tired eyes had been playing a trick on him. We decided to do an expanding square search around this point in case the U-boats decided to surface but the legs had to be under a mile apart as the visibility was so poor so it was possible that the U-boats could surface and still get through. We knocked out the W/T signal reporting a possible U-boat based on the ASV 'sighting', giving our position and holding the key down a while so that someone may be able to get bearings on us.

We only had another hour to do, but as we were in a VLR Lib, we could, according to Freddie's calculations, stay another three hours and still be okay for possible diversion. I discussed with the Wingco being able to stay for even longer than three hours in view of our position, roughly halfway between Iceland and the Hebrides as long as either Reykjavík or Benbecula could guarantee us favourable landing conditions. So, we flogged round and round in this ever-increasing square, using the ASV in short bursts as we went around each corner and again in the middle of each leg as the legs got longer.

After a while, we changed to a rectangular search, the longer leg being in the direction in which we thought the U-boat was most likely to be travelling. We wanted to find him and get him on the surface but we mused to ourselves that, even if we could not find him, if he was able to pick up our ASV, he might have thought he was surrounded by several aircraft, which might have driven him down into the mines. The area between Iceland and the Faeroes had been 'deep-mined' in an effort to force U-boats to make this stretch on the surface. More and more U-boats were using this route as their bases in the Bay of Biscay were becoming more hazardous to use, the bay area having been 'flooded' with aircraft using Leigh Lights allowing them to attack U-boats on the surface at night as they attempted to cross the bay.

After two hours searching and with one hour to go, I suggested to the Wingco that it may be a good idea to close in back towards the position where we reckoned he dived, as he may have 'stayed put' for a while after he dived, rather than risk making way submerged, so he may now be on the surface again. We did a search, tightening up onto the position where we lost him. It seemed to be getting darker with more frequent rain showers.

In some places, visibility was nil so we had to keep using the ASV more frequently; our eyes were getting sore. The dog was the best off, curled up asleep on the flight deck floor with a rug over him. Just as we were coming to the end of the third hour and I was about to tell Eddie to get a landing forecast for home and for Benbecula, we received the signal telling us to return to Reykjavík as another aircraft had arrived in our area.

It was only when we set course for home that we realised how tired we were. It was lucky we had three pilots as by cutting the 'watches' down to half-hourly stints, we were each able to get a rest fairly soon but the trouble with the VLR was that there was nowhere to go for a rest. Even poor Freddie did not have a seat, so it was a matter of either standing up, or curling up on the floor with the dog but at least the dog was warm and it was far too cold and draughty in the tail end (of the aircraft). With a sleeping dog, a resting pilot, and a resting WOP on the flight deck, poor old Freddie could hardly find anywhere to put his feet when he wanted to check on something upfront. All the drinks in the flasks were stone cold, the sandwiches all eaten; there were just a packet of dry biscuits and some cheese left, but things looked up as we got further north. We came out of the clouds, the sun shone in, and we all perked up.

As we closed with the coast of Iceland at Grindavík, the sea and the coast were a picture in the clear sunshine. The blue sea with lazy waves breaking on the coast was such a contrast to the muck and rubbish we had been in for the best part of eight or nine hours. The Wingco suggested that he did the take-off this time and with that he moves into Chalky's seat. Sure enough, as we rounded Sangerdi, he blasted 'Tally-ho' on the horn straight into the mike. The dog leapt up, knowing we were nearly home, and our comprehensive landing clearance was instantly received. I made doubly sure that everyone was on the flight deck before starting the pre-landing check as I did not want a fiasco like we had at Benbecula when Fred was trapped in the nose-wheel door.

At debriefing, we had a good moan about us not being able to get the new 10-cm Mark III ASV. We knew the Wingco was doing his best to get some but thought if we had a good moan at debriefing, it would not do any harm. I was perfectly convinced that Joe had picked up a U-boat but it had clearly detected us. If only we had had the Mark III, I was sure we would have got it, instead of us having to muck around in lousy weather for three hours and still not find it. For good measure, we also had a bind about us not being able to get any of the radio altimeters, which we had heard about. The attitude seemed to be that as the Squadron were finding U-boats and getting in attacks, several of which had already been confirmed as 'kills', we were quite capable of carrying on with what we had but we tried to point out how much better we could perform if only we had the latest equipment.

Then, just to add insult to injury, a junior officer at the debriefing chipped in to tell us that we should have reported the position of the sighting as a bearing and distance from the nearest known Naval vessel as our position in latitude and longitude would be inaccurate after so many hours. When we asked him how the devil you could do that when we had not seen a Naval vessel and nobody told us where one was, he did not seem to have an answer. He admitted that they had obtained a bearing on us and although this tied up with our stated position, it was not sufficient to give a fix. I suggested that we should plot our courses backwards from our landfall and I would be surprised if it did not tie up within five miles. The Wingco did not say a lot at debriefing; he seemed happy to sit there drinking tea while Dave, Joe, and I got on with it. When we parted, it was the first time that the Wingco called me by my Christian name, so he could not have taken offence at a flight sergeant telling an officer not to talk rubbish about not knowing our position and telling him that I had been up here for ten months and had never failed to find a convoy, even if this did often mean using one's loaf to estimate when they may have been delayed, or altered course, due to heavy weather.

When we were eventually in bed and having a chat before putting out the lights, I asked Dave how he managed so well with the navigation and we had made such a good landfall after we had been flying so many short legs, especially at the south end of the area, where we had been for so long. He said, 'It was luv-lee,' and explained that at the north end, he could get a few bearings on the civil radio beacon on the Westman Islands, which was on for ten minutes every hour, VVV then nineteen dashes repeated ten times. At the south end, 'MYG' at Myggenæs on the Faeroes seemed to be on all the time, although it was rather faint. I remarked that there was nothing about them in his log. He laughed and replied, 'I know. If I had logged them, some silly bugger would have asked me what I was playing at as one bearing at a time would not have been any use where we were but I kept a record on a separate piece of paper and noted how they changed. I then did a bit of fiddling to keep us right'.

'You crafty devil,' I replied.

To this, he came back, 'Anyway, for once, you three drivers must have flown my courses correctly!'

'Good night, lads. And Joe, don't wake up dreaming of blips!'

30

Wolfpacks Return

With the arrival of September, daylight hours were almost 'normal'. Long days were rapidly shortening, with daylight from between 5 a.m. to 7 p.m. and getting less every day until; in another couple of months, it would be hardly light at all. The frosty mornings were back. Defrosting the aircraft was once again a regular routine.

From the ops room, we learned that shipping losses had fallen drastically since the peak period between March 1942 and March 1943, and it was suggested that if ever a date was given to the Battle of the Atlantic, it would probably be those days in May 1943 when ships and aircraft were really able to hammer the U-boats, it being estimated that at least ninety U-boats were sunk in the Atlantic, but we all knew that this was not the end of them. They would be back. We knew they now had acoustic torpedoes, they had more AA guns, and intelligence believed that they had been working on a device to enable them to run on the diesel engines while submerged, thus being able to travel more quickly while submerged and cut out the necessity to surface to recharge their batteries. However, we were better organised now, more specialist anti-U-boat escorts with better equipment, more aircraft and more Naval and air crews experienced in U-boat warfare. In a way, we wished they would come back as now we felt that we were on the offensive but the acoustic torpedo was a real menace.

Reporting to the ops room for our next briefing, the Wingco remarked, 'This is right up your street: a search for possibly two vessels in areas 66 30N, 24 00W; 67 30N, 19 00W; 69 00N, 22 00W; and 68 00N, 26 00W, not far from the north coast of Iceland and the coast of Greenland, followed by an "ice recce" down the coast of Greenland from 72 00N, southwards.' We were to chart the extent of the ice, note any icebergs, and investigate and report any signs of a vessel having passed through the ice. We were to have a VRL Lib so, we may be instructed to do a block in the Fox patrol for the endurance we had left. We were quite excited to have the chance of having a good look at the east coast of Greenland and timed take-off to arrive at the search area at first light.

The flaming Aurora put paid to any radio communication right from the start. The flashing shafts of coloured light blotted out the stars but as we flew northwards, across the two big bays of Western Iceland, the light from the Aurora enabled us to clearly pick out the coastline, so we had a good accurate position on the coast from which to set course. Dawn soon broke to reveal the Arctic at its fascinating best: a cloudless blue sky met a calm blue sea at a knife edge horizon, just the odd lazy, snow whitecap on the blue water. Visibility was unlimited.

We started our methodical search at 1,500 feet with 7 miles between legs, which we reckoned would not allow anything to get through unnoticed in this visibility. Not a damn thing to be seen, just bloody cold, so we made sure the pigeons had plenty of bedding. Search completed, we set course for the coast of Greenland. The radio was okay now so we told base what we were up to and confidently reported nothing on the surface in the search area. These signals they kept picking up must, it would seem, be U-boats making their way to, or from, the Atlantic, but there was nothing we could do when they were submerged.

Approaching Greenland, we first saw the top of the huge glacier, which covered almost the whole of Greenland but as we got nearer, we could see that the land for maybe 10 miles inland was ice-free—just a dirty black, like the black of a coal-mine. Drift ice covered the sea so we turned south to chart the extent of the ice. There were lots of rugged inlets. It would seem that rivers must be running out of some inlets as the ice was swept away in a snake-like pattern. We went close in to have a look at one inlet, which looked as if it may be a suitable place for a vessel but saw nothing so continued along the ice edge. Ahead, the glacier seemed to come almost down to the coast but before we got there, we came across the entrance to a huge fjord, which must have been at least thirty miles across; it was wider than the English Channel and it seemed to go a hell of a way inland, almost like an inland sea. I decided we would have a look in there. Maybe a bit melodramatic, I told Joe to send a signal telling base we were investigating a fjord at 70 45 N and told the lads to stand by their guns as I thought this could be an ideal place for a U-boat refuelling base.

We flew in close to the north shore and immediately spotted a small settlement; I circled over the water while we looked through the glasses and decided it was a harmless Eskimo settlement. They looked up at us but there was no sign of anything sinister or any wireless aerials. There was a long narrow inlet, which we looked up but did not venture into. For over half an hour, we flew up these enormous fjords, scanning the shoreline with our glasses. The fjord was even wider now; we could hardly see the other side, only a huge glacier in the distance. we now seem to be heading almost north and still no sign of the end. I decided this was far enough, so commenced a big slow turn to port to pick up the land on the other side. Gosh, it was like a big inland sea. We picked up land on the other side, now going roughly south, the big towering glacier ahead of us but 50 or 60 miles away as far as you could judge in these funny conditions, but as long as I had plenty of water under and around me, I was quite happy.

Suddenly, the land turned abruptly away. This must have been a branch off the fjord going inland. I was not going down there, even though it was wide enough, so maintaining course, we spotted land ahead, perhaps 20 miles away, and headed for that, with the glacier behind it but fading away to port so that must have been the south shore of the main fjord. We followed this south shoreline out to the sea giving it a good once over with the glasses but nothing to see but colonies of sea-birds.

We resumed following the edge of the ice, south-westwards down the coast, and sent another position report back to Iceland. Here, the glacier came down much nearer the jagged, indented, black coastline and, in places, came right down to the sea in long tongues. Dave's chart did not show heights, only the coastline, but that glacier seemed to rise very steeply to a hell of a height. It was difficult to try and estimate the height of a big, smooth, featureless, glinting white mass rising into a clear blue sky, especially when you were not sure how far it is away. Between us, we estimated anything from 8,000 feet to 15,000 feet. The true height was probably somewhere in between; it was certainly a hell of a lot higher than we were.

Nearby, where it came right down to the sea, we spotted icebergs of all shapes and sizes, surrounded by slabs of drift ice and being carried away to the south by the polar current. We logged the positions and continued to do so as we continued south-south-west. The dark ice-free areas varied in width. We passed another four or five places where the glacier slipped right down to the sea. Following more icebergs, we spotted the lazy motion of the water just outside the drift ice, which, on investigation, was caused by a 'growler'—the type of iceberg dreaded by sailors as it was floating so low in the water that there was not enough above the water to be spotted but enough underneath to cause a disaster.

Passing 65 57N, we decided to give the American staging post at Bluie East a call on the R/T, 116.1 M/cs VHF. They came back to us as clear as a bell: 'Snowgoose this is Snowshoe. Reading you a-okay. Are you landing at Optimist'?

We replied, 'Snowshoe from Snowgoose. Negative, just calling to see if you're okay'.

'Sure appreciate it, Snowgoose, we all just fine—good luck'. 'Optimist' was the codename for Bluie East, used by the Americans for ferrying some of their short-range aircraft, with a 4,800-foot runway, available to us in emergencies only. Very soon, we saw the inlet leading to this airstrip but did not go near; the Americans would know what was going on in there.

Continuing south, the glacier came right to the sea again, with little black islands dotted along the coast. We noticed that the horizon ahead was no longer clear and sharp but lost in a haze. Then, we spotted a ship—a funny-looking ship, not a cruiser, destroyer, frigate, or Corvette, but a single funnel, tall mast, and a boxy shape superstructure all dead amidships; the dead vertical bow, a yacht shaped stern, high in the water with a perfectly flat deck; and some guns fore and aft. While we held off at a distance, viewing her through the glasses and thumbing through our sketches of ships, we came to the conclusion it was a US Coastguard cutter. I thought it unwise to use R/T as she may not be very pleased if we gave her position away, so asked her to identify herself by using the lamp. Having identified ourselves, we closed with her and, over the lamp, gave her the position of the nearest icebergs, as well as warning her about the 'growler'.

It was getting quite misty—must be somewhat warmer air coming up from the Atlantic meeting the cold air and turning to thin fog. Actually, this was quite a relief as the bright sun on the white ice had made up our eyes rather tired in spite of the sunglasses. The fog continued to thicken so we tried to follow the edge of the ice and use the ASV to tell us how far we were away from the land but this was not very accurate due to the floating ice. We did not do this for long, however, as base called, instructing us to proceed to a particular block in the Fox Patrol and we set course for the nearest corner of our block at 64 00N, 28 00W.

On arrival at the point to begin our Fox patrol, we reckoned we had just over three hours of daylight left. There seemed little doubt that we would be able to get into Reykjavík okay; in any case, we had the BABBS operating there now, so only strong crosswinds would keep us out and there did not seem to be any danger of that, so we settled down to another four hours patrolling and searching. After a couple or so hours, we were sent off to keep patrol between 66 00N, 28 00W and 64 00N, 28 00W, up and down the 120-mile line due north-south. Somebody must be picking something up from round here. We flogged up and down this line four times, using the ASV in short bursts until well after dark.

The Aurora started off again so the radio was 'zig' and we were all finding it difficult to keep awake. The last we heard from Reykjavík, the weather was okay and we were not far away at 64 00N, 28 00W but I remembered O. P.'s sound advice and decided it was time to go home, so we set off, almost due east. It was murder trying to stay awake; I felt my head nodding and would wake up with a start but I did not dare let myself go because Chalky was the same. I got Freddie to kneel between us to give as a shake if he saw us nodding. We ran into some cloud, which shut out the Aurora (except on the radio).

I woke with a start to see the props glowing with St Elmo's fire and little lights on the points of the ASV nose aerial but was so sleepy that I could not care less. Fortunately, we seemed to run through the cloud. I tried to pick up the Keflavík range through the crackles and soon, we saw the red flashing 'KF' of Keflavík beacon, not much off dead ahead. I took out 'George' to hand-fly her, hoping that this would wake me up. The red light passing below and the site of the lights of Reykjavík ahead brought me to; we could just manage to talk to Control through all the static. The pre-landing check was done in a sort of automatic daze and a few moments later, the welcome squeal as the wheels kissed the deck and the runway flares were coming to a halt. It lasted only just over seventeen hours but I think we were all so tired because we had been peering for so long into bright sunshine and part of the time at glaring white ice as well; also, we were cold and only had cold food. In the warmth of the debriefing room, I went fast asleep while waiting for Dave to finish his debriefing. We learned that the large fjord into which we flew was Scoresby Sund.

Our next trip, eight days later, was a very different sort of affair—a melodramatic fiasco. Another second pilot was added to the crew. All I was told at briefing was that we were to be on hand to support a 'secret force' if called. I was told to set off for a certain position; when we got there, I was to open a large sealed envelope, which would tell me where to proceed, and would also contain further instruction: a special code card, which we should use from that point on and several smaller sealed envelopes. I would be told which of these other envelopes to open by W/T, the whole lot to be returned personally to the briefing officer on return, with seals unbroken on the envelopes we had not been told to open, but if diverted elsewhere, I was to personally see that the whole lot were burned—what a carry on. I remarked that this seemed to infer that we could not be trusted not to talk, or that the safety of ordinary convoys did not matter, if they went to lengths like this but the Naval briefing officer's 'sealed orders' were quite usual in the Navy.

A bit before arrival at point 'A', I opened the big envelope that told us to proceed to point 'B', which was another three hours flying time away, making five hours altogether. There was also a card of frequencies and call-signs to be used from here on, which I passed to Joe. At point 'B', we would be told which of the other envelopes to open. We were to pass an ETA for point 'B' half an hour beforehand, after which we were not to transmit unless instructed but to listen out on two frequencies.

The weather gradually deteriorated as we approached point 'B' until the sea was great troughs between peaks of driving spume. We were forced down to under 1,000 feet by continuous cloud base and it was getting bumpy as hell. I had spent a good while with Dave in the nose but decided it was time I took over the left-hand seat in this rough weather. Sure enough, before point 'B', we received the signal that, when decoded, told me to open envelope five. This told us to go to a position some fifty miles to the east and then remain in a given area until further instructions received. The area was a rectangle about 90 miles long and 10 miles wide, running practically due east-west.

The weather in this area got even worse. Before long, we were trapped in a 300-foot sandwich between sea and cloud, not daring to get into the cloud as it would be too hazardous to let down out of it again in case it came right down to the sea. If only we had those radio altimeters we had heard about; we supposed it was the same tale as to why we could not have the Mark III ASV—Bomber Command wanted them to use as H2S sets so that they could bomb civilians while we were trying to protect convoys against U-boats and get their fuel through to them. It was raining in torrents now; the wipers made no impression, just a white seething mass of foam beneath us—thank God, I was not in the Navy. I did not know whether it was rain or spray on the windscreen. Chalky had to help me haul the wheel back sometime as we were hit by a gust and then seemed to drop helplessly as the engine revs increased, the props flailing around to get a bite on the air. We choked and were sick as we dropped and seemed certain to hit the sea. It was even worse than that earlier trip with Norman.

Chalky and I were tightly strapped in and the others holding on like grim death. I did not know how a boat could live in this sea.

As we reached the east end of the area, things improved a little bit, so I told Chalky that we were not going back west into all that shit, but we would stay in the east end of the area doing ten-mile legs. This gave us a bit of a respite to wipe the sick off our jackets and trousers but I knew that, if the weather followed its usual course, it too would be moving eastwards and would catch us up. After buggering about doing ten-mile legs in a square, which meant changing course every three or four minutes, which was liable to put our dead reckoning navigation miles out, we picked up another signal. Decoded, it told us to move to another area a little further east—thank goodness. It was still filthy weather but not so rough, so I left Chalky and the other pilot for a while and popped down to see Dave. His chart showed us to be almost slap bang in the middle of the Atlantic, further south than the usual convoy routes and a bloody long way from any land.

We tried to figure out the weather pattern; it seemed that we were running right along a damned active front. We were getting really pissed off after flying short legs for two hours or more and now it was getting really rough weather again. It had been hand-flying for hours and hours, now it was getting really rough again, I made sure I had Chalky in the front with me as I didn't know much about this other chap. I found myself talking to the aircraft: 'Come on baby, you can take it. I'll try to make it easy for you. For Christ's sake keep your tail on, that's a good girl, nice and easy. That was a nasty thump, right under your tummy. Who's a good girl? I got you into this, just hang together a bit longer and keep those engines turning and I'll get you out of it. Just stay in one piece. There we are, getting a bit better now. Nobody will ever call you a pregnant duck, you're a beautiful big white angel. That's my girl, we're getting out of it now, at least the worst of it'. I thought: 'Better get them to check the airframe, engine mountings, especially the tail, when we get back.'

As we had been flying above the speed for maximum endurance due to the rough conditions, I asked Freddie to let me know the fuel situation. Poor old Freddie looked ghastly, but soon had it all worked out. I was thinking what a complete waste of time this trip was because if we got called to this 'secret force', there was bugger all we could do if it was in all this shit, when Joe handed me another signal. I decoded it and was delighted to tell the lads we were off back home due to weather, but the signal did not say whether it was because of the weather here or the weather back in Iceland. It was a five-hour trip back home but sod the weather now, I opened up and climbed right up through it—a bit of icing to deal with as we climbed—and emerged at about 9,000 feet for a nice ride back with plenty of stars after dark for Dave to get some good fixes.

Two days later, all available skippers were called to the ops room to be told that at least one wolfpack of about twenty U-boats had been located at about 25 degrees west, almost due south of us. Two westbound convoys had recently left the UK; slow convoy ONS18 of twenty-six ships plus a merchant aircraft carrier and eight escorts, on 12 September and a fast convoy, ON202, of forty ships plus six escorts on 15 September. One of the convoys, ONS18, had been re-routed to the north-west following the interception of signals from U-boats and an escort support group had been sent to join this convoy. A Liberator from the UK had, at dawn that morning, attacked a U-boat ahead of the convoy and had confidently reported the U-boat as sunk. These convoys would both be entering our patch at dawn tomorrow; we would be giving maximum effort as they passed through our area, at least two aircraft with them throughout the hours of daylight. We were fifth on the Mayfly list.

The following morning, operations informed us that during the night, ONS18 had been attacked several times but all the attacks had been frustrated by the escorts. Radio silence was not being maintained so the air was full of signals from escorts, aircraft, and also the U-boats, on which the escorts were now able to obtain bearings using their HS/DF. The fast convoy, ON202, had now almost caught up with the slow one with and the intention was for them to join forces for the rest of the voyage. One of our Libs had reported seeing ONS18 at dawn that morning and another should be joining him imminently.

That evening, we returned for our briefing and were elated to hear that our first Lib had dropped an Oscar and this was followed by an explosion so, even if it did not sink him, at least the U-boat would be extensively damaged, so that looked like two U-boats to Libs already. We were told that the U-boats now appear to be fitted with quadruple 20-mm AA guns (two of them, one mounted forward and one aft, which was eight 20-mms altogether). Then came news that two ships had been sunk and an escort, the frigate *Lagan*, had been hit and was returning to base. The *Lagan* had reported that acoustic torpedoes were being used. So, the score seemed to be two U-boats for two ships and a damaged Frigate.

We were the first away on the second day, take-off about 4 a.m. On calling at ops for final last-minute briefing, there was more bad news: the Ninth Support Group had arrived okay but one of their numbers, the destroyer *St Croix* had already been sunk, and an acoustic torpedo had detonated against the noise-making device being towed by one of the other escorts. Then, just as we were about to leave the ops room, another signal came through; 'Corvette *Polyanthus* sunk'; then, another signal from the NSO: 'Entering fog.'

Well, we got away, thinking, 'Just our bloody luck. All that trade about and when we get there we probably won't see a damn thing for flaming fog, although it may save the convoy but the main thing now is to catch U-boats, not just protect the convoy'. Sure enough, as we approached the convoy, there was bags of chatter on the R/T, but the visibility was shocking and I was jolly glad to be able to get an altimeter setting (QFE) from the SNO so we could at least have the altimeter reading correctly because the surface of the sea was fairly flat and difficult to judge in these foggy conditions. The SNO also gave us a homing to bring us over his ship. I asked him how high the tallest ships' masts would be. He asked us to fly a particular sector and report the extent of these conditions; he reported his visibility as 600 yards and cloud base 'nil'. For an hour, we flew away in the given sector, some 130 miles and conditions were still the same. The short-range R/T had faded by now. As we returned to report we began picking up lots of inter ship chatter, he then homed us right over his Destroyer and asked us to see if we could locate ships as the two convoys were now supposed to be combined into one but they were only just managing to get together at dusk last night, then with the fog this morning he did not know where they all were.

For a couple of hours, we did a methodically increasing square around the moving track of the SNO's ship, using the ASV to plot the position of the 'blips'. Altogether, we plotted over sixty blips spread over miles and miles of ocean, then tried to summarise them and pass the SNO a précis of their positions. Next, he told us to do a creeping line ahead along the proposed track of the convoy as DF indicated that the U-boats were racing ahead of the convoy, presumably to lay in wait for it when it came out of this fog. We used the ASV and soon got a big blip, homing onto it we emerged over a Destroyer, going like the clappers in the same direction as we were. We only saw it for two or three seconds with great white clouds of spray showering over its foredeck, briefly glimpsed chaps on the open bridge then it was lost in the fog. He spoke to us on the R/T. We asked him if there were any other ships nearby; he replied, 'Affirmative three,' so, they must be on the same errand as we are. Another blip, this time we flashed over a Corvette and decided to ignore any more big blip, just look for little ones; it was too scary coming out on top of these ships.

Now some 120 miles ahead of the main part of the convoy, we were out of touch with the SNO on the short range R/T, but heard our fourth Lib saying, 'I go', which meant he was returning to base and the sixth Lib acknowledging his instructions from the SNO. We were still in foggy conditions and I was getting a bit worried that our altimeter setting could, by now, be inaccurate, when Joe came up with, 'Looks like something, about fifteen miles on starboard, hold it, don't turn yet as out of range of forward aerials'. The trouble was that with our ASV all we knew was that it was somewhere on the starboard side, but not exactly where. Joe reported that the blip was coming a bit nearer, 14 miles, then he said it looked like two blips, very close together. If this meant two U-boats, I knew this meant that, in all probability, they would stay on the surface and shoot it out.

Joe then reported that they were beginning to move further away; I reckoned that this must mean that they were now slightly aft of directly abeam, so turned through 120 degrees to starboard, hoping to pick them up on the forward aerials. I asked Dave to assume that they were fifteen miles ahead of us on this course and convert that to a bearing and distance from that destroyer we had passed over. Minutes passed by but no blip appeared, so I altered course to port and then to starboard, trying to 'sweep' the sea in front of us but absolutely nothing; the bastards must have picked up our ASV transmissions. I cursed about only having this obsolete Mark II ASV; if only we had the new Mark III, not only would they not have picked us up, as far as we knew, but it would have given us a complete plot forty miles all around us and we would not have lost them with having to change from beam to shorter range forward aerials. What was more, the destroyer and Corvette would probably have just come within the forty miles as well, so we could have read off an accurate bearing and distance from these vessels to the blip. Instead of that, all we could do was pass them the estimated bearing and distance of a 'contact' now lost and the Navy would probably think we were a real useless bunch of 'nanas'. If they went at full speed without having the correct position, the noise they made would make them very vulnerable to an acoustic torpedo. I comforted myself by thinking that we could probably not have been able to get ourselves into a position to attack in this visibility whereas the Navy, with its Radar and ASDIC may be able to find them. We hung around the area for some time but made no further contact and it was now time to make a return sweep to the convoy.

As we neared the convoy, conditions changed. The fog on the sea was now only about 10 to 15 feet thick. I always got quite a kick out of meeting a convoy and seeing all those ships but this was really uncanny. There was no sign of any sea but ships all around poked up through the fog; some ships did not seem to have any decks, just a bridge, funnel, and masts floating on top of the fog. Some of those low in the water were probably unable to see the other ships around them. The SNO asked how much longer we could stay; we had another three hours. He could not be aware of the position of all the ships or how far they extended, in this visibility, especially as they were now two convoys merged and some ships, originally with slow convoy, could well be straggling. Our final job was to help to round up the convoy before dusk, telling those out of contact the bearing and distance of the main group and reporting back to him on those ships which seemed to have lost contact. After three hours of shepherding, it was time for us to leave and we set course from 56 00N, 29 30W for a trip of nearly 600 miles back to Reykjavík. Just before we departed, an aircraft from the MAC (merchant aircraft carrier) took off on a patrol, we did not see it but it was probably the old faithful Swordfish but it would not be able to remain for long as it was nearly dusk. Our other Lib would be there for another three or four hours.

Tucked up in our nice warm beds in our cosy Nissen hut, we were having a quiet natter before going to sleep. We mused that it was a wicked shame that although we had all the gen on the Mark III ASV, we had not got a single set on the Squadron. I also thought about the potential plight of those men out in those treacherous seas. Those chaps are the real heroes of the Battle of the Atlantic—the Navy chaps and the Merchant Seamen.

When we awoke, there was a message that the Wingco wanted to see me and Freddie. He told us that he had received instructions from group that we were both to be posted back to the UK as we had completed our tour and that the other lads were being put on other crews. This came as a bit of a shock. I had never thought about leaving the Squadron; I just took each day as it came.

We spoke about what I wanted to do for a 'rest'. I immediately suggested a return to Ferry Command, saying that, Tug, my old navigator should also be due for a rest, and it would be nice if he and Freddie could go with me. The Wingco suggested that I had had enough of the Atlantic weather for a while, but I quickly pointed out that on the Ferry job, we would be above the worst of the weather but really, in the back of my mind, I had thoughts of the good living in Montreal and getting on to southern routes, which should now be open to exotic places like Africa and India. The Wingco thought it unlikely that they would let me out of Coastal Command but promised to see what he could do.

Back in the hut, we all felt a terrific melancholy. Freddie and I had been together for over a year, Joe had been with us for nearly as long, and the other lads for about six months. We had lived in the same hut, done each other's laundry, gone to town together, made each other tea in the mornings, and flown together. They were a grand team of lads and Joe, after his initial trouble, was now one of the best lads you would ever wish to meet. So, we had done our last op together; it seemed that the chaps remaining were to be split up between two crews.

31
The Hunting Horn is Silent

The Wingco informed me that the group would not agree to me going back to Ferry Command. There was, however, now a Liberator Operational Training Unit at Nassau now in the Bahamas and he would recommend that I be posted there if I wanted, but he did not know what I would do when I got there. I told him that the idea of six months or so in the Bahamas was inviting but I did not want to find myself off flying and doing some ground job. In that case, he asked what I thought about Beaufighters (Torpedo Beaufighters) as Coastal certainly wanted Tor-Beau pilots. It would be six months or thereabouts before I went back to ops, so during that time, I would fit in a conversion to Beaus at an OTU followed by a Torpedo course. He suggested that I should think about it and let him know in the morning. I got the feeling that he would rather like to be on Tor-Beaus himself.

I mulled over what I should ask for. The Bahamas sounded attractive but I could not see myself as an instructor and did not fancy a ground job. I had always had a sneaking desire to throw a Beau around, something with a bit of speed, shorter trips, and not such a long-winded business to get away each time as there was on a Lib. Before going to sleep, I had made up my mind—I would ask for Tor-beaus. The Wingco confirmed that he would recommend me for Tor Beaus, telling me that he would also be making some other recommendations but would not tell me about them till just before I left. He would arrange for Freddie and me to have a lift back to Northern Ireland instead of having to go back by boat but it would be a week or more before an aircraft would be going down for a 'major', so, he said, 'Just hang around till I let you know.'

Freddie and I went into town for some part of every day for the next ten days. We both felt rather 'lost' with having nothing to do. We took what money we wanted from the whiskey proceeds, had meals in town with coffee and cream cakes in the afternoons. I bought a silver fox fur for Peggy, some nylons and other presents hoping that we would land at a non-customs airfield. We went to the cinema and one night, it started to snow quite heavily on the way back. We felt as though we had seen the seasons around. It did not seem a year since Freddie and I made our first excursion into Reykjavík and it had started to snow then. We had really grown to like the place and we did not want to leave such a grand Squadron.

In the Mess, we heard, 'The Wingco is out and ops are getting worried. Haven't heard from him for a very long time. He is not acknowledging any signals'.

Every time the phone rang, someone dashed up to answer it. We really could not believe that anything could happen to our Wingco. We kidded ourselves that he should have enough fuel for a couple more hours, but we knew it was more likely to be only one, and that would be taking into account the fuel that he would be keeping for possible diversion, so it looked pretty bad. It could not just be that he had lost all his transmitters because he should be back by now. Who had he got with him? Two warrant officers and the flight sergeant from our Mess; Les with whom I flew when I was with Norman and was now back as a Flt Lt section leader; 'Little Titch' who joined Norman when I left; another Flt Lt section leader; and a flying officer.

As the minutes ticked by, I strolled over to the Control Tower with Freddie. We found a lot of the other chaps there; it was a queer sort of silence, most of us looking at the R/T speaker, willing it to blast out the sound of that hunting horn and its familiar 'Tallyho'. The dog had not gone on this trip. An officer had brought him to the Tower; the dog knew something was wrong as he too was looking at the speaker with those sad Spaniel's eyes and the least crackle grabbed our attention. In low tones, one of the flight commanders remarked, 'He must be out of fuel by now, even if he cuts two engines'.

Someone else remarked, 'We have been on to all possible diversion: Benbecula, Aldergrove, Nutts, 'Kelly, even Gander, Goose, and Bluie —nothing'.

The R/T remained silent. In twos and threes, we drifted away. There were no survivors or prisoners on this job. We would not forget 5 October or our grand Wingco. I do not know what eventually happened to the dog, but during the next two days before we left, several times, he escaped from the officer who was looking after him and was found sitting on the runway, looking at the sky.

Without the Wingco, the adjutant seemed to have too much on his plate to bother about fixing Freddie and me with a lift to Northern Ireland. A boat was due to sail for the UK so we came back by sea—what a flipping boat, the *Leinster*. In peacetime, she was on the Liverpool to Ireland run. She tossed and rolled, the loos were blocked up, water sloshed to and fro across the wash-room floor, and it was smelly and damp, but the food was not too bad—if you could keep it down. All the time, I was thinking about U-boats; it would be just our luck if one got us on the way home after twelve months hunting the sods. The one Destroyer with us was not a complete reassurance as we knew you needed two working together to be effective. A brief stop at the Faeroes to pick up some Army chaps then we were bloody glad to be sailing up the Clyde, past Ailsa Craig, and be permitted to take off those uncomfortable bulky cork life jackets.

I now had two weeks leave before reporting to East Fortune near Edinburgh. I felt sorry to be leaving Freddie, the world's best flight engineer, who kept me out of trouble. By Jove, he looked green after that boat trip.

Some weeks later, the *Daily Telegraph* commented:

Inherited Airmanship
Widely deplored in the RAF is the loss of Wing Commander Richard Longmore who failed to return from the brilliant Coastal Command battle against a pack of U-boats in which he led a squadron of Liberators. He had inherited the qualities which brought his father Air Vice-Marshall Sir Arthur Longmore, at one time Air C-in-C Middle East, to the top of his profession.

An RAF Officer described Dick Longmore to me yesterday as a fine airman with the gift of leadership. It seems from the available evidence of his last operation that he is more than likely to have got his U-boat first and then to have either been hit by return AA fire or to have been the victim of his own depth charges.

32

Away From It All With Peggy

It was dark when the dirty train pulled into York station, in spite of 'summertime' being on all the year. I could not tell how the repairs to the station had progressed; only a few dim lights glowed to help you find your way. I looked in the station canteen in case Mother was on duty, then set off over the Scarborough Bridge footpath and St Olaves Road to Bootham Crescent, finding my way by memory and saying 'Good night' to invisible footsteps so that we did not bump into each other. The weak shielded light from a passing vehicle would, now and again, give a clue as to my progress.

It was great to be with Peggy again. 'I've finished in Iceland and have nearly two weeks leave, then I'll be in the UK for a while'. Peggy seemed to have been keeping herself very busy, helping at the Forces Canteen at St Sampson's church, along with the other girls from her office, she had been away for a week potato picking, and fire watching came up once or twice a week. In the summer, she had played tennis at Acomb but now the nights were drawing in. To me, everything seemed dimly lit and dull; I was not used to the blackout, or the odd air-raid warning, which people now just seemed to accept as routine. Also, you seemed to queue for everything to get the grocer to take your coupons, to get a bit of meat, and to get on a bus. I had heard that, as a member of the Forces on leave from overseas, you could get a small allocation of petrol coupons; it took me half a day queuing, then filling in forms, then being referred to somebody else before I eventually, begrudgingly, was given coupons for 6 gallons of petrol. I thought of the 3,000 gallons we carried in the Lib. Next, I had to queue again at the Tax Office and show them lots of papers to get a temporary Tax Disc.

That night, we met some of Peggy's friends in the Olde Starr: Walter and Irene, the Landlord and his wife, who were good fun. We were invited into their private room after closing time where Walter said he reckoned that Peggy could drink me 'under the table' but we did not take her up on it. I was glad she was having a good time while I was away, as long as she did not find another fella.

The next day was spent getting the car going: getting it off its blocks and the wheels on, cleaning the plugs and points and hey-presto, she was running. We spent that evening with Peg's Uncle and Auntie main topics of discussion being the surrender of Italy, the Allied landings near Naples, and the German seizure of Rome, as Heather's boyfriend, Ron, was out there as an observer in the RAF, flying in Bostons. I think they felt that I had been keeping away from all the action with having been in Iceland but I would not talk about that. Peg's Uncle agreed that she could have the next week off, so on the way home, we decided to push off in the car to the Pateley Bridge area and have a few days on our own.

I learned that Cousin Mary, now an officer in the WAAF, was at a Bomber Group Headquarters in the ops room and that her brother Henry, who I saw in Toronto, had volunteered for the Canadian Air Force and was starting pilot training. The Canadians had now moved into Linton, flying Lancasters. They appeared to have made Betty's Bar their No. 1 haunt. We called in there one evening and I was horrified to hear girls, who seemed to me at the ripe old age of twenty-four, to be no more than schoolgirls, shouting out to each other, 'so-and-so, will not be in tonight, they're going to Frankfurt'. Whether this was all talk and they were just trying to show off, or whether some stupid chap had phoned to tell his girlfriend where they were going, I did not know, but we had been brought up not to tell anybody who need not know what we were doing and it made me bloody glad I was not flying with that lot and hope to goodness that sort of thing does not go on elsewhere in the UK. If it did, let us get overseas again as soon as possible.

So, Peg and I boarded the Vauxhall 10 and set off for Nidderdale, where we booked in at the 'George' at Ramsgill for five days of beautiful peace and quiet. We should have come here for our honeymoon instead of going to London. We used the car a little but had to keep enough petrol to get home. We walked by the river and by the reservoir; took tea with the elderly folk in the lounge; ate trout, lamb, and ham in plenty—you would not have known there was a war on. Even the blackout did not bother us here and some nights, we could gaze at the stars—those same faithful stars that would be guiding lads like me over the Atlantic. It all came to an end far too quickly and I was going away to East Fortune but, 'don't worry, love, I'm only going on a rest and you can come up some weekends'.

Epilogue

Jack's tales of the rest of his war, flying Beaufighters and Mosquitos over the North Sea, in the Middle East, India, and over the steaming jungles of Burma are for another book. After the war, Jack flew until 1953 as a commercial pilot for British European Airways, which he loved. During that time, he was lucky enough, by chance, to bump into O. P. again, to swap tales and thank him again for all his good advice. However, an oversupply of pilots meant that Jack eventually returned to the Yorkshire Insurance Company, for whom he worked until his retirement in 1984 although by then, the company had become part of General Accident and now Aviva.

After retiring to Huby (9 miles north of York), he and Peggy lived a quiet life. He joined the local Aircrew Association and attended meetings often held in the local pub. He proudly attended and wore his service medals at Remembrance Day Services every year in York. Through the Association, he reconnected with Freddie Thorpe, a fellow crew member (navigator) when he was second pilot to Norman, and with Freddie Payne who had been his most respected flight engineer. He reconnected with 120 Squadron, then based at Kinloss in Scotland, to whom he presented a much-appreciated unabridged version of his diary of memories. He and Peggy attended occasional reunion dinners where he met, after many years, his best man Peter Stembridge, who had been the Station Commander for a period of time in the 1960s.

Jack was particularly thrilled and honoured in June 1994 to be asked, along with three other 120 Squadron veterans, to celebrate the winning of the Battle of the Atlantic, which coincided with the fiftieth anniversary celebrations of the independence (from Denmark) of Iceland. They were flown to Iceland in a Nimrod—'appreciating spending a generous amount of time in one of the front seats'—for a few days of celebrations with contingencies from the U.S., Canada, Norway, Denmark, France, the Netherlands, and Germany taking part in a fly-past and a wreath laying ceremony in the bay off Reykjavík. His letter of gratitude to the Squadron's Wingco is copied:

> Dear Bob
>
> Until I receive my films back from processing, I find it hard to believe that I did actually return to Iceland after 50 years and that the whole experience was not just a wonderful dream.
>
> I thank you, and Jeremy, for making the trip possible for me.
>
> It would be unfair to refer to individuals as without exception, every member of the party was most friendly and helpful, making me feel that once again, I was part of a splendid crew. Thank you all most sincerely.
>
> Being with you all was testimony to there being virtually no 'age gap' between aviators. When I served with 120, none of today's crew would have been born in some cases, maybe their parents would not have been born either, yet we seemed to knit perfectly. Perhaps even harder to appreciate is that, if we were to look back fifty years from 1944 instead of forwards, no practical heavier-than-air machine had yet flown.
>
> I hope that some of you will be invited to Iceland for the Centenary Celebrations. Regretfully at the age of 125, I will have to send my apologies.
>
> Thank you all again,
> Sincerely,
> Jack Colman

Barely a few months later, Jack developed lung cancer and died in December 1994. In the foreword of his story and throughout, there are numerous references to his admiration of the bravery and the hardships suffered by Navy and merchant seamen in the North Atlantic when delivering and protecting the convoys. His final wish was that his ashes be scattered over the Atlantic, in recognition of and with enduring respect for them, an honour that 120 Squadron was only too willing to undertake, as described by myself and added as the final chapter of his diary.

On Thursday, 22 June 1995, Jack Colman began his last journey accompanied by Peggy, Richard (one of their two sons), and Freddie Thorpe, an old comrade and crew-member. That evening, Jack's ashes were transferred into a canister ready for his last flight. At approximately

7 a.m., after a slight delay for malfunctioning bomb doors, on the glorious sunny morning of 23 June, Nimrod XV240 left Kinloss, on a 'routine' training flight. Accompanied by Freddie and Richard, the squadron's *padre*, and Sqn Ldrs Jeremy Nash and Tim Newman, they headed east to practice bomb drops before turning north to Wick, the Orkneys, and then west on route for Rockall.

At 9.03 a.m., flying at about 300 feet, with the sea shrouded in mist, in keeping with his wishes, Jack's ashes were committed to the Atlantic at 57 30.2 N, 13 44.7 W. The flight back to 120's base was in clear skies over the Western Isles with a majestic sweep at 2,000 feet above Loch Ness to Kinloss. The exercise continued with circuits and bumps before a final fly-past for Peggy on the ground.

Jack would have been glad to know that in his committal, he was part of a regular exercise and in the company of some of the crew that had taken him to Iceland almost a year previously. He would have been deeply honoured by the courtesy, kindness, and respect shown to him and his family.

JACK COLMAN 15/9/19–5/12/94

APPENDIX

List of Significant Events

1929

September   Pleasure flight aged ten

1935

September   Begins work aged sixteen for the Yorkshire Insurance Company

1939

August   Meets Peggy at Scarborough

1940

July   Attends Aircrew Selection Centre; accepted for pilot/navigator training
15 September Twenty-first birthday
5 October   Called up. Begins five-month 'Signals' course at Blackpool by mistake

1941

15 March   Attends Aircrew Reception Centre Babbacombe
April–May   Initial Training Wing, Torquay, for eight weeks. Gets engaged to Peggy
June   To Canada
23 June   Begins Elementary Flying School, Oshawa
5 July   Flies solo after ten hours
10 August   First solo 'cross-country' Oshawa to Kitchener
20 August   Graduation (sixty-five hours flying time clocked up)
1 September Begins 'Service' Flying Training School, Brantford
1 October   First night solo
21 November Wings Parade
13 December Begins 'General Reconnaissance Course', Charlottetown

1942

February–May	'Operational' Training Hudsons, Debert for three months
May	To Ferry Command Dorval (Montreal)
3–4 June	First ferry to Prestwick
June	Seven days leave; captain/navigator competency card, Hudsons
August	Competency card Liberators
September	To Costal Command: Ballykelly Northern Ireland
30 September	Married while on fourteen days leave
6 October	To Reykjavík, Iceland. second pilot to Norman. Liberators
16–23 December	Seven days leave

1943

February	Promoted to flight sergeant
April	Becomes a 'skipper' first pilot
April	Seven days leave. Spring days in Scarborough
19 May	Covering SC130. Seven U-boats attacked, one possible kill
5 October	Wing Commander Richard Longmore fails to return.
October\	Leaves 120 Squadron and Iceland